MILTON'S DRAMATIC POEMS

TO OUR PREDECESSORS

Milton's Dramatic Poems

edited by

GEOFFREY & MARGARET BULLOUGH

UNIVERSITY OF LONDON
THE ATHLONE PRESS
1958

Published by
THE ATHLONE PRESS
UNIVERSITY OF LONDON
at 2 *Gower Street, London* WC1
Distributed by Constable & Co. Ltd
12 *Orange Street, London* WC2

Canada
University of Toronto Press

U.S.A.
Essential Books Inc
Fair Lawn, New Jersey

© *Geoffrey and Margaret Bullough,* 1958

Printed in Great Britain by
WESTERN PRINTING SERVICES LTD
BRISTOL

CONTENTS

ILLUSTRATIONS

INTRODUCTION

The three dramatic pieces presented in this volume are not only valuable in themselves and indicative that the poet of *Paradise Lost* was as interested in drama as in epic, but they also illustrate the changes which came over Milton's views of life and art during more than thirty years of self-dedication and struggle. *Arcades* and *Comus* were both written in the poet's twenties, when he was full of hope; *Samson Agonistes* was published in 1671 when he was sixty-three, blind and failing in health. The first two are the work of a gentle and gracious poet trained in the chivalric courtesy and Platonism of the Renaissance; the third is a product of defeat and dis-illusionment, of hard-won resignation. A reading of these poems should convince anybody that Milton cannot have been the harsh, contemptuous extremist in religion and morals that some have made him out; and this be-comes clearer if we look into his upbringing and the circumstances and substance of the first two pieces.

Milton's paternal grandfather was an Oxfordshire Catholic who disinherited his son John for turning to the Church of England. This John came to London and flourished as a scrivener, i.e. a lawyer and law-stationer. His marriage brought six children of whom the poet John was the third. The father was a noted musician who wrote songs in praise of Elizabeth for *The Triumphs of Oriana* (1601) and psalm tunes which are still known. He took a keen interest in John's education, and the poet later described how, 'I had for my first years by the ceaseless diligence and care of my father (whom God recompense!) been exercised to the tongues, and some sciences, as my age would suffer, by sundry masters and teachers, both at home and at the schools' (*Church Government*). The tongues he learned were Latin, Greek, French, Italian and Hebrew, and he took a lasting pleasure in natural history, geography, history, and literature ancient and modern. For a time he had a tutor, Thomas Young; then he attended St. Paul's School, and (as he stated in explaining his blindness) 'from the twelfth year of my age I scarce ever left my lessons and went to bed before midnight'. At Cambridge (in 1625), he entered, not the extreme Puritan college, Emmanuel, but the more liberal Christ's.

At college Milton proved rebellious and was rusticated for a time in 1626 after trouble with his tutor, William Chappell. At first he was unpopular with some of his fellow-students, and his dislike of his nickname suggests that he was called 'the Lady of Christ's' not only for his beauty but also because his sensitive taste was offended by the coarser undergraduate pranks. Intending at first to become an Anglican priest, he was shocked at the behaviour of some other aspirants to Holy Orders, and disgusted with their precocious dogmatising. 'I find here hardly any congenial fellow-students', he complained to his friend Alexander Gill, son of the headmaster of St. Paul's School.[1]

Obviously he was sadly out of step, but things improved after a time. He obtained his B.A. in 1629, the M.A. in 1632, and when he left the college he knew that he could have stayed on and become a don.

Milton got more from Cambridge than perhaps he expected. Though he despised the lack of scholarship of his fellow-students and the methods of his teachers, he read much, and the Academic Exercises in which he had to defend one or other side of a question, like a lawyer or

[1] *Milton: Private Correspondence and Academic Exercises*, P.B. and E. M. W. Tillyard, Cambridge, 1952, p. 8.

Introduction

philosopher, gave him a habit of verbal debate which affected all his work, from *L'Allegro* and *Comus* to *Samson Agonistes*. He became a good Latin and Italian poet, and he followed in occasional poems the literary fashions of the day.

While at Cambridge Milton gave no sign of religious heresy. He was an Anglican of the Puritan centre, no predestinarian Calvinist but no follower of Laud. But before he left Cambridge or soon afterwards he gave up the idea of taking Orders because he disliked the authority of the bishops and the necessity of accepting the Thirty-Nine Articles.

Perhaps his retirement to Horton in Buckinghamshire where his father now lived was originally suggested so that he could decide quietly on his future career. If his father was disappointed he never tried to force his son into another profession, but let him spend six years in study, though he disliked the idea of his becoming a professional poet.

Milton had been writing poetry since he was a boy, and the English part of his Vacation Exercise of July, 1628, shows that when only nineteen he already aspired to be the poet of religion, science, history and legend. He experimented in several contemporary manners. He owed something to Spenser whose *Faerie Queene* he admired for its combination of romantic story with lofty Platonic moralising; something also to John Donne and the Metaphysical manner; more to Ben Jonson the 'classicist' whose rugged nature schooled itself into grace and ease.

Such influences prove that Milton was no literary Puritan, hostile to the elegance and polish of the age. The gaiety of *L'Allegro* is not far removed from Herrick's manner, and *Il Penseroso* is anything but Puritan in its meditative mood, which became habitual at Horton. There he wrote *Comus*, and probably *Arcades* as well.

9

Introduction

When Milton was sent down from Cambridge he enjoyed his stay at home in London and could 'feel no great desire to return to the sedgy Cam'. He loved his books, 'which are my life', but

> when fatigued, the magnificence of the arched theatre diverts me, and the garrulous stage invites my applause, whether it be the cautious old man who is heard, or the prodigal heir . . . Often the wily servant is abetting the lover-son, and at every turn leading the rigid father by the nose . . . Or again, furious Tragedy shakes her bloody sceptre and rolls her eyes, with dishevelled locks, and it is pain to look, yet there is pleasure in having watched and been pained; for sometimes there is a sweet bitterness in tears. Or the unhappy boy leaves his un-tasted joys, and falls off, a pitiful object, from his broken love; or the fierce avenger of crime comes back over the Styx from the shades, perturbing guilty souls with his funeral torch. Or the house of Pelops or that of noble Ilium is in grief, or the palace of Creon expiates its incestuous ancestry.[1]

The comedies here described are of the classical kind written in Rome by Plautus and Terence. The tragedies are of the Senecan kind in which ghosts, revenge and woe are treated in rhetorical speeches. The account reads like a description of academic drama as presented in the universities and the Inns of Court rather than of plays in the popular theatre, though classical comedies were written by Jonson and Middleton. Later, in 1642, Milton wrote a scathing account of the unseemly behaviour of Divinity students who acted in university plays and were 'seen so often upon the stage, writhing and unboning their clergy limbs to all the antic and dishonest gestures of Trinculoes, buffoons and bawds; prostituting the shame of that ministry which either they had or were nigh having, to the eyes of courtiers and court-ladies, with

[1] To Charles Diodati. Latin *Elegy* i (1626). Cf. *The Life Records of John Milton*, ed. J. M. French, vol. i, 1949, pp. 110–11.

Introduction

their grooms and mademoiselles'.[1] The attack is on the amateur actors because of their intended profession, not on the plays themselves, though he did not approve of the low moral tone of much contemporary drama. But he certainly approved of Shakespeare, for in 1630 he wrote an Epitaph ('What needs my Shakespeare for his honour'd Bones') which was printed in the second Folio of the Works (1632). In *L'Allegro*, after describing the pleasures of country evenings in terms reminiscent of the 'fairy' poetry of *A Midsummer Night's Dream* and *Romeo and Juliet* he turns to the pleasures of 'tower'd cities', the court festivities of 'wit or arms' and the marriage masques:

> There let Hymen oft appear
> In saffron Robe, with Taper clear,
> And pomp and feast and revelry,
> With mask and antique Pageantry.
> Such nights as youthful Poets dream
> On summer eves by haunted stream.[2]   (125–30)

From court he moved to the popular theatre:

> Then to the well-trod stage anon,
> If Jonson's learned Sock be on,
> Or sweetest Shakespeare fancy's child
> Warble his native Wood-notes wild.   (131–34)

In *Il Penseroso* there are parallel pleasures, lyric poetry, Chaucer's romantic tales, the Anglican church choir 'in service high and anthem clear', the enjoyment of Tragedy:

> Sometime let Gorgeous Tragedy
> In Sceptred Pall come sweeping by

[1] *An Apology for Smectymnuus* (1642).

[2] Had Milton, by his 'Aonian stream' at Horton, been reading Jonson's *Hymenaei*, a wedding masque first performed at court in 1606 and printed in that year? In it Hymen appeared 'in a saffron-coloured robe, his under-vestures white, his socks yellow, a yellow veil of silk on his left arm, his head crowned with Roses, and Marjoram, in his right hand a torch of pine tree'.

> Presenting Thebes', or Pelops' line
> Or the tale of Troy divine
> Or what (though rare) of later age
> Ennobled hath the Buskin'd stage.   (97–102)

Milton did not despise either the court masque or the best popular comedy and tragedy; he did not agree with William Prynne's ferocious onslaught on the stage, *Histriomastix* (1632). But he preferred the ancients to most of the moderns; he bought the works of Euripides in 1634, a Terence in 1635.

Sometime between 1630 and 1633 Milton was invited by Henry Lawes to provide words for an Entertainment in honour of the Countess Dowager of Derby at her mansion at Harefield, Middlesex. Lawes (1595–1662) was already a well-known musician, an official of the Chapel-Royal, and one of the King's Musicians. He was also music-tutor to the large family of the Earl of Bridgewater at Ashridge, and maybe his commission to write for the Countess Dowager came because she was the Earl's mother-in-law and the two houses were not far apart.[1] Milton would have got to know Lawes through his father. The Countess was seventy in 1630, and this would be an appropriate time for a family tribute to her. Milton's poetry in *Arcades* however is so much closer to *Comus* (1634) than to the *Nativity Ode* (1629) that, with most editors, we attribute it to 1633. Family gatherings may have been frequent at Harefield and there were hosts of grandchildren to take part in a 'play'.

THE MASQUE

Actually *Arcades* is an elementary form of Masque, an entertainment which for over a hundred years had been popular at formal gatherings in noble houses and at court.

---

[1] See Commentary for further information.

Introduction

Originally the masque was a 'disguising' in which members of the party entered wearing masks or vizards and engaged in dumbshow acting and dancing. Henry VII and Henry VIII enlivened their court-balls by interludes when courtiers in fancy dress were led in by torchbearers to music. If there were women masquers they danced first and then stood aside while the men danced; after this sometimes professional morris dancers performed in their very different style; lastly the gentlemen paired off with the ladies and danced courtly dances together, first slow ones, then quicker ones. A popular innovation occurred when the gentlemen masquers began to choose partners from the spectators, thus bringing them into the entertainment. Something of the sort happens in *Romeo and Juliet* (I. v) where the hero and his friends enter the Capulets' house in disguise with torches, dance formal dances, then join the ladies of the house—and this is when Romeo speaks to Juliet for the first time.

Gradually the masque developed by the addition of song, speeches, settings and properties until it formed a striking union of all the arts in which music, dancing and spectacle were all-important. But under the influence of the Morality play and the Renaissance love of mythology and allegory the dancers became characters in a pageant of contrasted gods and goddesses, Virtues and Vices, who expressed their natures in dumbshow and speeches; and at times this produced a little drama with a situation affording some conflict or plot.[1] The masque was usually introduced by a formal Prologue who explained the 'device' or situation and often did most of the talking. The writers of late Elizabethan and Stuart masques who were often dramatists, like Ben Jonson, Samuel Daniel and James Shirley, gave increased importance to poetry

[1] For the history of masques see E. Welsford, *The Court Masque*, 1927, and E. K. Chambers, *The Elizabethan Stage*, 1923, vol. i. For specimens, see *English Masques*, ed. H. A. Evans, 1900.

and drama by enduing their allegorical figures with vitality of speech and action. This often led to conflict with the producer, who was chiefly interested in spectacle, and Jonson's career as a court masque-writer involved a long struggle with Inigo Jones the brilliant designer of settings and costumes, in which the poet was finally worsted. The spectacular masque triumphed at the extravagant courts of James I and Charles I, culminating in such amazing displays as James Shirley's *The Triumph of Peace*, which, played on 3 February 1634 before King Charles and his Queen in the Banqueting House at Whitehall, cost the Inns of Court (who put it on) over £21,000.

An important feature was the Antimasque which developed out of the contrast afforded between the courtly dances and costumes of the gentlemen masquers and the morris dancers in their traditional garb. The idealised moral atmosphere of the allegory was relieved and set off by the intrusion of professionals in bizarre costumes as satyrs, witches, Indians, gipsies or plebeian types dancing grotesquely and cutting acrobatic capers. To introduce these figures into the 'device', the plot was based on antithesis, between good and evil, beauty and ugliness, elegance and oddity. *The Triumph of Peace* has a long series of Antimasques showing aspects of contemporary life—tricksters, scientific projectors, highwaymen, etc., while other characters included Opinion, Confidence, Fancy, Jollity, Laughter, Novelty, as well as Irene (Peace), Eunomia (Law), and Diche (Justice). A 'Genius or angelical person' presents the masquers ('sons of Peace, Law and Justice') to the King and Queen as 'The children of your reign, not blood'. The masque contains many changes of scene—a noble street, a tavern, 'a woody landscape with low grounds proper for hunting', a hill with the masquers sitting on steps cut into it.

Introduction

With such elaboration neither *Arcades* nor *Comus* has much in common. *Arcades* however *is* a masque, or *part* of one, as Milton's title shows, for he preserved only his poems, without any description of the complete 'device', which probably included an Antimasque of dumbshow and dancing. It belongs to the same species as Jonson's *Entertainment at Althrope*, given at Lord Spencer's on 25 June 1603 when a Satyr presented Lord Spencer's eldest son, dressed as a huntsman, to the new Queen Anne, who with Prince Henry was travelling from Scotland to London. *Arcades* is mainly a fanciful way of presenting some young members of the family to the Countess Dowager. Its 'device' is simple: some shepherds and shepherdesses come from Arcadia in Greece seeking the Countess, lured by her fame. It is a secular Epiphany, as the visitors from the east move towards the 'seat of State', perhaps set outdoors in the early evening, and brilliantly lit with torches or lamps. There is no preparation in the text as we have it. The visitors burst into song on seeing the Countess, and the Genius's speech, which would normally have been the Prologue, is in part unnecessary. But Lawes, as we shall see again in *Comus*, liked to begin with song. The Genius informs the audience who the Shepherds are, describes his own functions beautifully, and turns all to compliment before he leads the masquers (in the second Song) to dance towards the Countess to pay her homage. There would be set dances between the second and third Songs. Besides writing the music Lawes probably played the Genius and sang the second Song to the lute. In the third Song (probably a part-song) other Arcadians are advised to leave their barren land for the rich soil of Middlesex. The poet has woven charming fancies round the simple domestic occasion.

Introduction

Comus was written for a formal, public occasion, as part of the celebrations at Ludlow Castle, Shropshire, marking the inauguration of the Earl of Bridgewater as President of the Council of Wales and Lord Lieutenant of the Counties on the Welsh Border. Appointed in 1631, he did not go to Wales till 1633 and he took up residence in September, 1634. For the festivities on Michaelmas Night (September 29) Henry Lawes was asked to prepare a masque in which three of the older children could perform: Lady Alice (who was about fifteen years old), Lord Brackley (the eldest boy), and Thomas Egerton. The two boys had taken part at court in Carew's splendid *Coelum Britannicum* on February 18 of that year. The new masque could not hope to vie with that, but it would have to be more spectacular than *Arcades*. Lawes had good taste, and when he asked Milton to write the piece he did not insist on emphasising song, dance and costume, but allowed him to compose something which in number of verses (1023) and poetic unity transcends any previous masque. Doubtless Lawes loved acting and verse-speaking, for Milton gave him a fat part as the Attendant Spirit who sings five songs, speaks some three hundred lines, and is the pivot of the action.

The basic scheme is similar to that of *Arcades*, and may have been suggested by fact. We do not mean that the Earl's children were actually lost in a wood, as a later tradition held, but that the parents probably went to Ludlow well before the celebrations and the children arrived later. In the masque the young people come seeking their parents (like the Arcadians seeking the Countess Dowager) and to attend the inauguration (l. 35); but whereas in *Arcades* they arrive, see, are presented, and that is all, in *Comus* obstacles are invented out of which Milton makes a highly poetical complex.

Milton's originality (like Shakespeare's) did not consist

16

in the invention of ideas and situations never previously
thought of. So although the Attendant Spirit says:

> I will tell you now
> What never yet was heard in Tale or Song,
> From old or modern Bard, in Hall or Bow'r.   (43–5)

the poet was not claiming absolute novelty but a fresh
combination of, and new light upon, existing material.
Milton was a 'classical' writer, drawing inspiration and
strength from tradition. He was one in whom 'we shall
often find that not only the best, but also the most indi-
vidual parts of his work may be those in which the dead
poets, his ancestors, assert their immortality most vigor-
ously'.[1] Although it is possible to enjoy *Comus* (as no
doubt most of its first audience did) as a passing enter-
tainment, a proper critical study of the piece involves
consideration of Milton's sources and how they were
worked into a new pattern by the urgency of his indi-
vidual approach to life.

There are four main elements in the story: (i) the
enchantment and release of the lost girl; (ii) the method
of the enchantment; (iii) the nature of the enchanter and
the Lady and his temptation of her; (iv) the method of
her release, with the intervention of the goddess.

(i) *The Lady's enchantment*

In making his plot out of the obstacles preventing
reunion of the children with their parents Milton intro-
duced a theme suitable for young people. The Lady gets
lost and is found by a wicked enchanter who takes her to
his palace and casts a spell on her. Her brothers search
for her and are helped by a good spirit who tells them
how to overcome him. This is done in fine fairytale style;

[1] T. S. Eliot, 'Tradition and the Individual Talent' in *Selected
Essays*, 1932. An important essay for students of Milton and of
literature in general.

but Milton lengthens his piece and introduces another supernatural helper (Sabrina) who frees the Lady, after which the essential Masque takes over.

Now Milton had loved such stories since boyhood, when

I betook me among those lofty fables and romances which recount in solemn cantos the deeds of knighthood founded by our victorious kings, and from hence had in renown over all Christendom. There I read it in the oath of every knight, that he should defend to the expense of his best blood, or of his life, if it so befell him, the honour and chastity of virgin or matron; from whence even then I learned what a noble virtue chastity sure must be, to the defence of which so many worthies, by such a dear adventure of themselves had sworn.

(Apology for Smectymnuus)

Chivalric adventure and the praise of feminine virtue; these went together in Milton's mind with memories of old romance.

He remembered Spenser's *Faerie Queene*, where the Red Cross Knight and Una, lost in the forest, meet the wicked magician Archimago (I. i. 29) disguised as 'An aged sire, in long black weeds yclad', who separates them and works them ill; where the false Duessa sprinkles poison from her golden cup on to the Squire so that he is seized by the Blatant Beast (I. viii. 14); where Sir Guyon, seeking the virtue of Temperance, has many dire adventures before he overcomes the enchantress Excess in the Bowre of Blisse (II. xii). He knew the adventures of the knights of Charlemagne in Ariosto's *Orlando Furioso* (1516), which he read both in the Italian and in Sir John Harington's translation (1591). Tasso's *Jerusalem Delivered* (1581) he came to admire most maybe, because it was more like a true epic and religious in tone. He was well acquainted with romantic drama too, and had a special fondness for Shakespeare's supernatural plays. He drew on that astonishing farrago of fantasy and burlesque, George

18

Peele's *Old Wives' Tale* (1595) in which two brothers seek their sister Delia who has been enslaved by the magician Sacrapant (the name from Ariosto) and been made by his potions to forget her identity. An old man gives them riddling advice. They call out for their sister and an echo answers. The sorcerer, whose power is contained in a light in a glass buried underground, is overcome by a ghost who takes his wreath from his head and his sword from his hand.

Peele's plot is fragmentary in the extreme, but Milton seems to have taken hints from it which he used to better advantage.

(ii) *The Method of Enchantment*

In *The Old Wives' Tale* Sacrapant declares:

> In Thessaly was I born and brought up;
> My mother Meroe hight, a famous witch,
> And by her cunning I of her did learn
> To change and alter shapes of mortal men.

No doubt this hint recalled to Milton Homer's *Odyssey* (bk. x) where the companions of Odysseus are bewitched by Circe: 'They had pigs' heads and bristles, and they grunted like pigs; but their minds were as human as they had been before the change. Indeed, they shed tears in their sties.'[1] They are freed when Odysseus, having been given a protecting herb, Moly, drinks the enchantress's poisoned cup without ill effects, and overawes her with his sword. The story, retold by Ovid in his *Metamorphoses* (bk. xiv), appeared in divers forms, in Ariosto's episode of Alcina (*Orlando Furioso*, bk. vi), Tasso's of Armida (*Jerusalem Delivered*, bk. xiv), in Spenser's episode of Acrasia (*Faerie Queene*, ii. xii) and the story of Amoret and Busyrane in which the damsel is freed from a male

[1] Students of *Comus* should read books x and xii of the *Odyssey*. Citations here are from the translation by E. V. Rieu (Penguin edn.).

enchanter by Britomart (*Faerie Queene,* III. 12). On all
these Milton drew without *imitating* any, but Ariosto and
Spenser coloured his treatment most for they came near-
est to his blend of romance and idealism. The story of
Amoret, tempted by Busyrane's cruel lust and tortured
while bound to a pillar till Britomart invades the hall and
reverses his spells, was dear to Milton as a tale of Chastity
in difficulties; and Harington's *Allegorie* to his translation
of Ariosto gave a satisfactory moral interpretation of the
Circe legend, when he wrote of the swine:

what other meaning can be gathered than this: that idleness
and sloth, and the not betaking one's self to some honest
travail causeth men to prove drunkards, gluttons, etc.

The victims of Comus's magic, unlike Homer's swine, are
unconscious of their degradation, 'But boast themselves
more comely than before' (75).

(iii) *The Nature of the Lady and the Enchanter*

The obvious moral appealed to Milton's refined nature
and his determination to reduce his own often rebellious
passions to temperance. To write a masque of Chastity
would be to suit his theme to his chief actress, and be a
compliment to the Lady Alice, a girl of fifteen. Here
again Milton worked in a tradition, for pastoral dramas
usually made much of the opposition between true and
false love, chastity and lust. Milton knew Tasso's *Aminta*
(1581) and Guarini's *Pastor Fido* (1585), and was parti-
cularly attracted to *The Faithful Shepherdess* (*c.* 1610) of
John Fletcher, which had been revived and played at
Somerset House before the court on Twelfth Night, 1633.
This lengthy and complicated pastoral drama presented
the adventures of several ladies and their lovers in a
wood. There are enchantments, a magic well and a
benevolent River-God, and Milton seems to have remem-
bered especially the first scene, in which the maiden

Clorin, who (mourning for her dead lover) dwells in the forest and collects simples, explains that she has no fear because she was told by her mother that

> if I keep
> My virgin-flower uncropt, pure, chaste, and fair,
> No goblin, wood-god, fairy, elf or fiend,
> Satyr or other power that haunts the groves,
> Shall hurt my body, or by vain illusion
> Draw me to wander after idle fires . . .　　(i. i.)

A Satyr comes and serves her, and she comments:

> Sure there is a power
> In that great name of virgin, that binds fast
> All rude uncivil bloods, all appetites
> That break their confines: then, strong chastity,
> Be thou my strongest guard . . .　　(i. i.)

Encouraged by this Milton confronts his virtuous Lady with more than a Satyr or a Sullen Shepherd. Instead of Sacrapant the son of Meroe he gives us Comus the son of Circe, and makes his masque no trivial show but a conflict between Chastity and Sensual Excess.

That such antitheses were common in the masque some titles by Ben Jonson show, e.g. 'Love freed from Ignorance and Folly' and 'Mercury Vindicated from the Alchemists at Court'; while the conflict of virtue against false pleasure had been one motif in Thomas Carew's *Coelum Britannicum* (1633) in which Lord Brackley and Thomas Egerton had played. There Hedone (Pleasure) a young woman with a smiling face, dressed in 'a light lascivious habit', defends herself in philosophical terms to prove

> that since I am
> The general desire of all mankind,
> Civil felicity must reside in me.

Her Antimasque is of the Five Senses. She is banished by Mercury who admits that 'thy Circean charms transform

.the world'. Milton certainly knew this masque, for which Lawes composed the music. He may also have known Ben Jonson's *Pleasure Reconcil'd to Virtue* (1619) although it was not published till 1640. In this Hercules, fresh from his conquest of Antaeus, the Giant of Inhumanity, banishes false Pleasure in the person of 'the voluptuous *Comus*, god of cheer'.[1] The opening scene shows Mount Atlas, 'out of which, to a wild Music of Cymbals, Flutes and Tabors, is brought forth Comus, the God of Cheere, or the belly, riding in triumph, his head crowned with roses and other flowers; his hair curled.' The song his attendants sing praising Comus as the inventor of cooking and lord of gluttony must have been too crude for Milton. But with the final lesson of Jonson's masque he was in harmony; that our mission is

> To walk with Pleasure, not to dwell.
> These, these are hours by Virtue spar'd
> Herself, she being her own reward,
> But she will have you know,
> That though
> Her sports be soft, her life is hard.

Milton's Comus is not just the 'belly-god', the glutton, but a more insidious tempter; and the moral of the piece is not so much 'spare Temperance' as an almost ecstatic ideal of Chastity.

The tradition of Comus seems to have been a purely literary one. Not one of the classical gods, he arose by personification of the word κῶμος, 'revel', or 'band of revellers'. He was first described in the *Eikons* or *Descriptions of Pictures* by Philostratus (third century A.D.), and this description was passed on in the Renaissance by writers such as Vincenzio Cartari, whose descriptions of the gods were much used by painters and stage-designers:

[1] *The Works of Ben Jonson*, ed. Herford and Simpson, vol. vii, 1941, pp. 475–91.

Introduction

Comus, who according to the Ancients was the god of feasting, is very like Bacchus, for his picture too was of a young man with the first down appearing on his cheeks. Philostratus describes him thus in a picture made specially for him. The god stands at the door of a chamber where a splendid and joyful wedding has been celebrated and the bride and bridegroom are now consummating their love. Comus was delicate and soft, ruddy-faced because he had drunk too much, and so intoxicated that he could not keep his eyes open, but slept there as he stood, letting his rosy face bend towards his chest. . . . Everything round was strewn with flowers. . . . As I was saying, Comus was young, happy and genial, since when men drink in moderation their vital spirits are roused . . . [1]

This is more like Milton's *Comus*, who is presumably attractive to look on, since he is 'Much like his Father, but his Mother more' (l. 57). But there is no 'moderation' or temperance about his incitements, and his geniality is sinister.

Milton seems to have drawn on another source in which Comus was less obscene than in Jonson and more evil than in Cartari; this was the Latin *Comus* of Hendrik van der Putten (known as Puteanus, 1574–1646), Dutch Professor of Rhetoric and Classics at Louvain. This work was first published in 1608 and reprinted at Oxford in 1634.[2] It is an extravaganza in prose with some verse passages, describing a dream of festivities in honour of the god, with moral comments. Comus, god of Love and Pleasure, appears to the author and expounds his philosophy (somewhat as Milton's does to the Lady). The shocked author wishes to escape, but cannot; he is carried in clouds to the land of Cimmerian Night, where he sees the wonderful Palace of Comus (cf. *Com.* s.d. 659). With

[1] V. Cartari, *Le Imagini dei Dei degli Antichi*, 1556, and A. H. Gilbert, *The Symbolic Persons in the Masques of Ben Jonson*, 1948, pp. 69–71.
[2] *Eryci Puteani Comus, sive Phagesiposia Cimmeria. Somnium. Lovanii. Typis Gerardi Rivii.*

his friend Aderba he enters and finds a throng of revellers. Night and Darkness, Sleep, Fear and Horror, cannot penetrate the Rabelaisian paradise, where Comus's crew, Love, Pleasure, Joy, Rapture, Delight, Wit and Laughter revel at ease. At the feast which follows the visitors learn that the masked guests are really wolves and other animals of prey in disguise. The visitors enter a sanctuary after taking wine from a youth at the door. They discover that the deities worshipped within are gods of sexual lust. Comus is there at a banquet-table in the greatest luxury. A drunken orgy follows. The moral meaning of the vision is explained at length by old Tabutius. Comus is a deceiver; he deludes young people and destroys their souls with his seductive pleasures, replacing Sincerity with Deceit, and using Lust and Luxury to enslave and degrade them.

From this phantasmagoria Milton has taken a few general hints as well as particular allusions illustrated in our Commentary; Comus becomes the god of all sensual delights; but he is more subtle than his namesakes in Jonson and Puteanus. He explains his philosophy with a plausibility which shows how Milton's practice in presenting a lawyer-like case in his *Prolusions* led on to real, if limited, dramatic power.

(iv) *The Release of the Lady by Sabrina*

The Brothers are told that in order fully to overthrow the Enchanter they must not only break his glass but seize his wand. Since they fail to do the latter the Lady is not freed, but the resourceful Attendant Spirit remembers the power of Sabrina the Goddess of the River Severn. She is invoked, rises, releases the Lady, and descends again into her realm followed by grateful thanks.

It was a fine compliment to the local gentry and to the Lord Lieutenant of the Marches, to introduce a goddess

of Severn as *dea ex machina*. But Milton did not invent
Sabrina. Her story appeared first in Geoffrey of Mon-
mouth's Latin *History of British Kings* (twelfth century)[1]
and then in William Warner's *Albion's England* (1586).
Spenser rewrote it in *The Faerie Queene* (II. x) before
Michael Drayton retold the story in *Polyolbion*, Song 6.
Milton handles the well-known story with grace and
charm. Maybe the idea of a feminine 'disenchanter' arose
from some desire of Lawes for a female song to contrast
with the Spirit's invocation; or from the Amazon Brito-
mart's intervention in Book III of *The Faerie Queene*.
Something may have been due also to Fletcher's *Faithful
Shepherdess* where the God of the River revives Amoret
who has been erroneously accused of lust, and wounded
by Perigot.

THE GOVERNING IDEAS IN COMUS
This long exposition of possible sources does not signify
that *Comus* was simply a patchwork of other men's
notions. It has a remarkable unity arising not from the
events themselves but from the ideas and sentiments
which govern their presentation.

In the *Apology for Smectymnuus*, after describing how
through reading romances he came to have a high respect
for Chastity, Milton declares that from reading Plato and
Xenophon he learned much more

of chastity and love, I mean that which is truly so, whose
charming cup is only virtue, which she bears in her hand to
those who are worthy (the rest are cheated with a thick intoxi-
cating potion, which a certain sorceress, the abuser of love's
name, carries about); and how the first and chiefest office of
love begins and ends in the soul, producing those happy twins
of her divine generation, knowledge and virtue.

The reference to Circe's cup recalls Comus and his
potion, and the passage throws light on the spirit in

[1] See Commentary, 824–41.

which the masque was written. For Milton, as for
Spenser, Romance and Platonic idealism went hand in
hand. If the two Brothers are two knights, their sister
must be an embodiment of Chastity. But she must be
tempted; for Milton already could not 'praise a fugitive
and cloistered virtue' but believed, as he wrote in his
Commonplace Book, that God permits evil 'so that virtue
may be justified by it, be illuminated and trained by con-
flict with it'.[1] Moreover the Lady must be tempted
insidiously, not blatantly, by arguments which cunningly
mix good and evil, since 'the Devil flavours his lethal
potion with the most pleasing gifts of God'.[2]

She must not fall, however; indeed, at the time of
writing, when Milton had little experience of life and
great faith in the easy supremacy of goodness, she could
not fall; for like St. Ambrose and other early Christian
writers he made something of a *mystique* of Virginity and
Chastity, believing them absolutes, proof against assault.

His doctrines in *Comus* were a mixture of Platonism and
Christian asceticism. From Platonic dialogues such as the
Phaedo and the *Phaedrus*, as from Spenser's works, he
came to apprehend the aspiring soul as moulding body
and mind to ever-increasing spirituality, and the yearn-
ing for the serene air of philosophic detachment revealed
in the first words of his masque recurs whenever he
speaks of a life above the material though at times he
writes of it in mythological terms. The heavenly vision in
the Epilogue of the suffering Venus watching over the
healing of her beloved Adonis and of Cupid's marriage
to Psyche (the Soul), producing Youth and Joy as off-
spring, is to be thus interpreted, as a spiritual contrast
with the animalism of Comus. The virtuous soul aspires
to divine union.

[1] Cf. *The Works of John Milton*, Columbia edn., vol. xviii, 1938,
p. 128.
[2] *Ibid.*, p. 128.

Introduction

On the other hand Milton is inclined to worship Temperance, as if the act of self-denial were an end in itself and its result the Platonic vision of absolute joy; here repeating the confusion into which Spenser falls in *The Faerie Queene*, where the virtues are sometimes a Platonic aspiration to heavenly Beauty, Love and Goodness; sometimes Aristotelian, an earthly and temperate mean between moral extremes.

When Temperance is equated with Chastity and Chastity is identified with Virginity most modern readers find it hard to sympathise fully, because they regard Virginity as a physical or negative state rather than as a dynamic passion for purity; and Milton could hardly go deeply into 'the sage and serious doctrine of Virginity' without making his Lady seem more like a nun than a brave young girl lost in a forest. (And the lines in which he broached it (779–99) are apparently an afterthought, composed possibly when he realised where his ideas were leading him.)

So there is some discrepancy in the ideas as expressed. But the glow and ardour generated in the attempted union of Christian renunciation and Platonic sublimation suffuse the poem with a warmth and light and joy which Milton never recaptured.

THE DRAMATIC STRUCTURE OF COMUS

A brief summary of the contents of the masque as Milton printed it will help to show its diversity and ingenuity. The special features linking it to the masque tradition, picturesque setting, song, action, are italicised.

The first Scene discovers a wild Wood—'discovers' suggests a curtain drawn across the stage. *The Attendant Spirit descends or enters*—this suggests that Milton did not know whether the Hall of Ludlow Castle (60 by 30 feet) would allow the Spirit to descend from the 'heavens', or whether the machinery could be provided.

Introduction

The Spirit's Prologue, explaining himself, describing the time, place and personages, complimenting the Earl, and relating the ancestry etc. of Comus (1–92).

The first Antimasque appears: Comus and his rout. He explains his philosophy of indulgence (93–144).

They dance their wild Measure. Comus sets his snare (145–69).

The Lady enters, explains her plight and her faith in Chastity (170–229).

The first Song (by the Lady) (230–43).

Comus appears as a villager and offers her shelter (244–330).

The Brothers enter, the younger afraid for his Sister; the elder, sure of her virtue, teaches his Brother the strength of Chastity and a Platonic view of the soul (331–489).

The Attendant Spirit, in Shepherd's garb, describes the Lady's mishap. This excites the Younger Brother's fears but the Elder remains confident and like a true knight will rescue her. The Spirit gives them the magic herb and advice (490–658).

The second Scene is revealed—Comus's palace and banquet, with the Lady in the enchanted Chair. Comus tempts the Lady. They debate. Pleasure and Lust are opposed by Temperance and Chastity (659–813).

The Brothers expel Comus. The Spirit explains that they must invoke the Goddess of Severn (814–58).

The second Song (by the Spirit) (859–89).

Sabrina rises with her Nymphs [this probably involved machinery]. *The third Song (by Sabrina)* (890–901).

Sabrina frees the Lady (902–21).

Sabrina descends and the Lady rises from her seat [machinery]. The Spirit thanks Sabrina and takes the Children away (922–57).

The third Scene is revealed—Ludlow Town and Castle [backcloth].

Introduction

The second Antimasque (Country Dances).
The Spirit enters with the Children.
The fourth Song (by the Spirit) (958–65).
The fifth Song (of presentation, by the Spirit) (966–75).
The Masquers dance their Dances.
The Spirit's Epilogue (976–1011).
The sixth Song (1012–23).

In performance Lawes made some alterations inclu-
ding 'cuts' in long speeches (which are noted in the Com-
mentary). In order to start with a song for the Attendant
Spirit he shifted the description of the Hesperides from
the Epilogue (976–99) and by changing the first line to
'From the ocean now I fly' and the last to 'Where many
a Cherub soft reposes'[1] he made it a suitable opening
number; though its tone is not quite in keeping with
his speech. He cut 1000–11 and set the remainder of
the Epilogue as a song: 'Now my task . . .' He provided
small singing parts for the two Brothers by dividing the
latter part of his invocation to Sabrina between them
(871–89). The manuscript of his music does not in-
clude a setting for Sabrina's song: 'By the rushy-fringed
bank'.

The outline makes it clear that although the poetic
story and dialogue are expanded far beyond what is usual
in a masque, they do not destroy its masque-qualities;
rather they give them meaning and a humanity rare in
such entertainments. It is the more necessary to insist on
this because Dr. Johnson criticised *Comus* as a drama
rather than as a masque and as such declared it 'defi-
cient'. 'The action is not probable', he declared; the
Brothers' behaviour was not reasonable in letting them-
selves get lost 'when their sister sinks with fatigue in a
pathless wilderness'. He disliked the long speeches which
'have not the spriteliness of a dialogue animated by
reciprocal contention, but seem rather declamations

[1] This line was in the Cambridge MS. draft.

deliberately composed, and formally repeated, on a moral question'. 'The Brothers enter with too much tranquillity; and when they have feared lest their sister should be in danger, and hoped that she is not in danger, the Elder makes a speech in favour of Chastity, and the Younger finds how fine it is to be a philosopher.' And so on.

Johnson rightly demands action of a drama; but *Comus* is not an ordinary romantic play. Johnson admitted that a masque, 'in those parts where supernatural intervention is admitted, must indeed be given up to all the freaks of imagination'. He should have extended this charity to all the piece, not because of 'supernatural intervention' but because the whole conception of a masque was fanciful and artificial and could not be judged by the standards applied to drama. But Johnson, who knew little of masques, judged the moral debates in *Comus* by false standards. Yet something approaching moral debate of the kind found in *Comus* is not alien to Masque, with its allegorical antitheses and measured statements of opposed ethical principles.

Thus in Carew's *Coelum Britannicum* there are over four hundred lines of moral disquisition in the speeches of Mercury and his conflicts with Plutus, Poverty, Fortune and Pleasure. What Milton did was to organise such discussion round a central theme, and give it some dramatic point. Thus, without giving up the Masque's inheritance of song, dance, music, spectacle, he reached out towards a philosophical drama of a kind occasionally written in the modern world, where the situation and individual conflict set in motion a play of ideas, of general principles.[1] Such an intermediate form has some of the limitations of the Masque—lack of individual characterisation and urgency of plot. But Milton wrote for an

[1] As in some early plays of Shaw and Yeats and the more propagandist plays of J. B. Priestley.

audience accustomed to formal speeches, and even today
Comus acts well.

The style of Milton's masques suits the form as he used
it and the themes he treated. Both *Arcades* and *Comus*
were courtly entertainments meant for great houses, and
the climax of each was an act of fealty. A dignified style
was needed therefore, although the setting might be
pastoral.

Dignity of style was usual in masques, where deities or
moral qualities described themselves. Milton seems to
have pored over Ben Jonson's 1616 Folio before writing
Arcades, and the language and heroic couplets of that
piece resemble those in Jonson's *Marriage mask at Lord
Haddington's* (1608), *The Masque of Beauty* (1608), and the
Masque of Queenes (1609). Like Vulturnus in the second of
these the Genius of the Wood moves smoothly through
a sinuous succession of couplets without straying far from
the basic five-stress beat or ignoring the rhymes that
justify the form:

> Hither, as to their new Elysium,
> The spirits of the antique Greeks are come,
> Poets and Singers, Linus, Orpheus, all
> That have excell'd in knowledge musicall;
> Where, set in arbours made of myrtle and gold,
> They live again, these beauties to behold,
> And thence in flow'ry mazes walking forth,
> Sing hymns in celebration of their worth . . .
>
> > (*Masque of Beauty*, 137–44)

Milton however owed something to Drayton and
Fletcher, which may explain his freer movement, the
repetitions and lack of economy apparent in the Genius's
description of his labours (*Arc.* 44–60) where almost
everything is said charmingly, and twice. A favourite

image of Drayton's—describing groves as 'curl'd' or having 'curl'd heads', is transformed into a sustained conceit with excessive alliteration:

> To nurse the saplings tall, and curl the grove
> With ringlets quaint and wanton windings wove
>
> (46–7)

Other images come from Shakespeare, but the effects are always different and Milton studiously avoids plagiarism. The Songs, so musical in themselves and so apt for setting to music with their varied line-lengths and preponderance of vowels and soft consonants, reflect a liking for Fletcher and Campion, and above all, Jonson, whose formality, grace, and imagery blent of classical allusions, abstract ideas and light, appear in the first Song.

In *Comus* these qualities and influences recur, but the greater length and scope afford opportunities of stylistic experiment. Dr. Johnson recognised that in this masque Milton 'formed very early that system of diction and mode of verse which his maturer judgement approved'. The technicalities of Milton's blank verse have been frequently discussed.[1] Masson declared that Milton's special aim in verse was to perfect not the single line or couplet but 'the free musical paragraph' 'in which the verse-system is elastic or determined from moment to moment by the swell and shrinking of the meaning or feeling'.[2] Such freedom however, though obtainable in the choruses of *Samson Agonistes*, was unattainable in the five-stressed blank verse of *Comus* or *Paradise Lost*; and though these poems show him perfecting the verse paragraph, they show him working willingly within the limits of the five-stressed line.

---

[1] Cf. D. Masson, *Milton's Poetical Works*, vol. ii; R. Bridges, *Milton's Prosody*; O. Elton's edn. of *Comus*; F. T. Prince, *The Italian Element in Milton's Verse*.

[2] Masson, 'Essay on Milton's versification'.

Introduction

The stiffness of Milton's later blank verse has been ascribed to an attempt to make English epic style more formal and lofty than it had been in other writers. Dr. B. Rajan asserts: 'the essence of that [style] is that it cannot be dramatic'; but he rejoices occasionally to find in it 'the variety controlled by the steady persistent momentum of the paragraph, the nuances of sound and the refinements of tempo, above all that sense of fidelity to an immediate experience which occasionally springs to action in a simile'.[1]

This describes excellently the nature of the blank verse in *Comus*, where in fact Milton learned how to write the form, and if it does not show great dramatic variety, it is more flexible than some critics have thought.

Well-known features include:

(i) Considerable freedom in the placing of stresses and in the number of unstressed syllables, e.g.

At last betakes him to this ominous Wood   (61)

Th' earth cumber'd, and the wing'd air dark with
    plumes.   (730)

Lingering and sitting by a new-made grave   (472)

Bacchus, that first from out the purple Grape   (46)

Who, piteous of her woes, rear'd her lank head   (836)

Root-bound, that fled Apollo. Fool, do not boast   (662)

(ii) A fair proportion (about 1 in 12) of lines have feminine endings. This practice comes from Shakespeare and Fletcher, and helps to give speed and variety.

(iii) To build up the verse-paragraph run-on lines are frequent, especially in dramatic speeches such as 580–609, where there are ten.

(iv) The pause is very variable. Most clauses and sentences finish at the end of a line, but there are frequent

[1] B. Rajan. *Paradise Lost and the Seventeenth Century Reader*, 1947, p. 111.

medial periods, e.g. seven in lines 580–609. Minor pauses
may occur anywhere, but usually after the third, second,
or fourth foot. An examination of lines 46–58 will show
how flexible the cesura is, and how effective.

In dramatic speeches Milton rarely tries to catch the
give and take of conversation with its irregularities of
rhythm. Lines 580–90 have some of this movement, but
the lines which follow are more typical in their sustained
flight of rhetorical argument. On one occasion the rapid
exchange of question and answer is attempted, at 276–90,
where Milton uses the stichomythia common in Greek
tragedy, the balance of line against line; a device any-
thing but naturalistic.

When the Attendant Spirit disguised as a shepherd
comes to the Brothers the dialogue slips into heroic
couplets, presumably because they were the usual form
for pastoral writing; but as soon as the Spirit begins his
long narration he reverts to blank verse. Speaking to
Sabrina and afterwards, he assumes the typical four-
stressed couplet of most masques, and uses it with great
suppleness.

In *Comus* Milton wrote with a flexibility and clarity
which few in his age could rival, and his combination of
flowing ease with substantial sound is due in part to his
use of Latinate forms, which often give sonority to the
line. He is fond of using words in their Latin senses:
office (89); habits (157); infamous (424); crude (480);
horrid (429); fabulous (513). Latin constructions are
found, though less commonly than in *Samson Agonistes*
and there is little of the contorted syntax used in the
later drama.

Milton has been accused of seeing Nature through the
spectacles of books, and it is true (though not a short-
coming) that what he saw he liked to describe in terms
sufficiently close to those of earlier writers to hand on a
shared experience. So when he writes about the

> drear Wood
> The nodding horror of whose shady brows
> Threats the forlorn and wandering Passenger
>
> (37–9)

he fills his imaginary wood near Ludlow with all the
fears faced by Petrarch as he passed through the Ardennes
towards Avignon (Sonnet 176), and adds an allusion to
Tasso's Christian knights moving through their en-
chanted forest. Many examples could be given of this
habit, which Mr. Eliot has praised, of letting us see the
dead poets and their experience ranged behind the living
one, enriching his mind and ours. When Comus tempts
the Lady to use her beauty in a natural earthly way,
praising fertility (682–6), Milton recalls Shakespeare's
counsel in Sonnet IV to his friend to marry and have
children. The reader is expected to perceive the contrast
between Shakespeare's virtuous aim and Comus's wicked
one. Here is deliberate irony, which reappears when
Comus quotes the Bible at least twice (720–2, 727). God,
he says, would be unthank'd if all men in 'a pet of tem-
perance' should 'feed on pulse'. Now in the Book of
Daniel, when Nebuchadnezzar wanted to fatten Daniel
and his friends to make them courtiers, Daniel, to avoid
eating 'unclean food', asked to be fed on pulse for ten
days; and proved to be fatter and healthier than the rich-
living Babylonians! So Comus's allusion turns against
himself. Similarly at 727 he says that abstinence means
living 'like Nature's bastards, not her sons'. This is an
allusion to Hebrews xii where the writer says 'whom the
Lord loveth he chasteneth', and 'if ye be without chas-
tisement . . . then are ye bastards, and not sons'. So
Comus has got it wrong. The self-indulgent are not the
true sons who shall inherit the earth.

Milton is of course at home in the Bible, and in
classical mythology, history, geography. But he is also
skilled in the generalised depiction of Nature. Perhaps he

is at his best at moments when he combines an airman's view of the earth with one more intimate, passing from one to the other like a ciné camera, as in the allusion to

> all the sea-girt isles
> That like to rich and various gems, inlay
> The unadorned bosom of the Deep   (21–3)

where what is seen from a great height becomes, seen nearer, the dress of a goddess. Similarly in 111–21 he moves from the 'starry quire', by way of the ordered seasons, to the dance of the tides and the dance of fairies and nymphs. It is the poetry of science uniting with the poetry of literature and folk-lore.

MILTON'S LATER VIEWS ON DRAMA

Before Milton wrote his only other dramatic work, *Samson Agonistes*, many years passed and he experienced many joys and sorrows. He left England in April 1638 for a Mediterranean tour which would have included Greece had not events at home limited his stay abroad to Italy. In Florence, Rome and Naples he probably saw some of the classical Italian tragedies which he was later to praise in his preface to *Samson*, works in which the Italians imitated the Greeks, using Choruses and varied metres. Nearly a century later Voltaire asserted that Milton had written an act and a half of a tragedy on the theme of Adam after seeing the *Adamo* of the actor Andreini.

He got to know many literary men, but the imminence of war brought him home, where he set up as a schoolmaster and in 1641 entered the field of religious and political controversy in support of his old tutor Thomas Young and other Puritans against Bishop Joseph Hall and episcopacy. From then on till 1660 his pen was never idle on the side of reform in Church and State. After his marriage in 1642 to a dowerless Cavalier girl of half his

36

Introduction

age and her desertion of him two months later he began to write his *Tractates on Divorce* which turned the Presbyterians against him. In *Areopagitica* he defended the liberty of the press. He wrote a short treatise on Education which showed how to rear the élite of the country so as to ensure good, strong government. He defended the Regicides after the trial of Charles I, and he became a firm supporter of Cromwell ('our chief of men') and Latin Secretary to the Council for Foreign Affairs, but had to resign in 1655, for he went blind in 1652 after eight years of failing eyesight.

When he first came home from his travels he had great hopes of fulfilling his vocation in poetry, being encouraged by the praise of Joannes Baptista Manso (an old Italian nobleman who had been an intimate friend of Tasso) to think that he might write an epic following the example of Homer, Virgil, Tasso, and the Book of Job ('a brief model'). An alternative scheme was to write a tragedy after the manner of Sophocles and Euripides; or he might turn to the Bible, which

affords us a divine pastoral drama in the Song of Solomon, consisting of two persons and a double chorus, as Origen rightly judges. And the Apocalypse of St. John is the majestic image of a high and stately tragedy, shutting up and intermingling her solemn scenes and acts with a sevenfold chorus of hallelujahs and harping symphonies. (*Church Government.*)

His aim would be mainly doctrinal and exemplary, that is, to teach morals and religion and illustrate them through the lives of his heroes. Such writings had, he believed, the pervasive power to foster good citizenship,

to allay the perturbations of the mind, and set the affections in right tune; . . . to sing victorious agonies of martyrs and saints, the deeds and triumphs of just and pious nations, doing valiantly through faith against the enemies of Christ; to deplore the general relapses of kingdoms and states from justice and God's true worship. (*Church Government.*)

37

Introduction

To these aims he held fast, and *Samson Agonistes* mingles patriotism, religion, educational purpose and artistic effect. With such lofty ideals, Milton had small patience with the decadent tragedy of the Caroline stage, the lewd comedies, the amorous shadow-boxing of pseudo-Platonic courtier dramatists. He turned against what he called 'the writings and interludes of libidinous and ignorant poetasters'. Yet he wanted, not the closing of the theatres (a thunderbolt which fell in 1642) but their reform, by the

procurement of wise and artful recitations, sweetened with eloquent and graceful enticements to the love and practice of justice, temperance, and fortitude . . . not only in pulpits, but . . . at set and solemn panegyries, in theatres, porches, or what other place or way may win most upon the people to receive at once both recreation and instruction . . . (*Church Government*.)

He regretted bitterly that he was forced to give up his preparation for such writing by the need to defend truth against her enemies; but about this time he began to enter in his Notebook (the Cambridge MS.) the titles and outlines of suitable works on which he might embark.

There, after *Lycidas* we find two lists of persons for a drama on the Fall of Adam, each with a Chorus of Angels, Adam and Eve, Lucifer, Michael, and numerous allegorical figures. Then comes a list of thirty-three subjects for tragedies from Old Testament and British History. The Biblical subjects include several from the Books of Judges and Kings. Among the former are

Samson pursophorus [the Fire-bearer] or *Samson marrying* [the woman of Timnath]; or in *Ramath-Lechi* [the Battle of the Jawbone] Judges xv. *Dagonalia*. Judges xvi [the Feast of Dagon, i.e. the theme of *Samson Agonistes*].

Later Milton entered a full synopsis of *Adam Unparadized—Adam's Banishment*, followed by Scottish themes including Macbeth; and finally *Christus Patiens* (Christ in the Garden).

With the exception of *Samson* none of these projects ever materialised, though it may be true that Milton wrote part of his *Adam* tragedy, for his nephew Edward Phillips asserted that Satan's speech to the sun in *Paradise Lost*, book iv ('O thou that with surpassing Glory crown'd'), comes from it.

When in blindness and enforced retirement from office he returned to major verse it was to epic. *Paradise Lost* has no more dramatic quality than is proper to the epic, but *Paradise Regained* approaches drama more nearly, and in its presentation of conflict through debate it recalls *Comus*. When *Samson Agonistes* was begun is uncertain, but it was probably mainly written soon after *Paradise Regained*, and the two poems were published together in 1671.[1]

In *Paradise Regained* Christ rejects almost the whole of Greek thought and culture, praising their 'predecessors' the Hebrews instead. But it is noteworthy that He does not specifically answer the Devil's praise of

> . . . what the lofty grave Tragedians taught
> In *Chorus* or *Iambic*, teachers best
> Of moral prudence, with delight receiv'd
> In brief sententious precepts, while they treat
> Of fate, and chance, and change in human life. (iv. 261–5)

Milton could not bring himself to recant the views he had expressed in *The Reason of Church Government*; so *Samson Agonistes* is a compromise between the two principles at odds in *Paradise Regained*; it is a Biblical drama in the form of a Greek tragedy; it is the *Dagonalia* of his notebook.

SAMSON AGONISTES—THE PERSONAL BACKGROUND

In returning to the Samson theme after more than twenty-five years Milton was doubtless impelled by many

[1] Cf. M. Y. Hughes on theories of an earlier date, in *Complete Poems and Major Prose*, 1957, pp. 531–40.

motives. It is dangerous to seek autobiographical allusions in epic and drama, but Milton's interest in Samson must have been increased by parallels between himself and the Jewish hero, and this may explain the unusual emotional force of many passages in the tragedy.

Milton was blind and failing in health; he had introduced in *Paradise Lost* the pathetic reference to the sun and

> these eyes, that roll in vain
> To find thy piercing ray, and find no dawn   (iii. 23–4)

Through the agonised lament of Samson (67–100) we hear the poet recalling his own despair in the early days of his blindness.

Like Samson he was defeated and subject to the will of his enemies. As a notorious defender of the Regicides he was in some danger at the Restoration; but owing to the help of friends he was allowed to live in retirement. Samson's captivity and the jeers and insults of his enemies, are an element in the tragedy (106–14; 366–7; 645–6; 1156–63, etc.).

Moreover Milton was disillusioned by the failure of the political and religious propaganda to which he had devoted the twenty middle years of his life. He had seen Church and Parliament rejecting freedom and godly discipline and walking the ways of tyranny, dissension, and return to episcopacy and monarchy. Such an experience speaks in Samson's complaint:

> But what more oft in Nations grown corrupt,
> And by their Vices brought to servitude,
> Than to love Bondage more than Liberty.   (268–76)

his allusion to their desertion of their Deliverer, and the Chorus's pointed reference to the treatment of the dead Cromwell's men (687–702. Cf. Commentary).

Like Samson Milton had lived a temperate life, though he did not abstain altogether from wine (cf. 541–57). He had always felt himself in some way 'Select, and Sacred' (363), and had been 'great in hopes . . . of high exploits' (523–5). Like Samson too he had experience of unfortunate marriage (373–433, etc.).[1]

Lastly Milton, like Samson (1377–90), recovered from defeat and despair, and if he could not slay the Philistines he could at last fulfil his early ambitions in poetry, thus justifying the ways of God to man and achieving for himself 'calm of mind, all passion spent'.

THE BIBLICAL SAMSON

In choosing Samson as a subject Milton knew that those for whom he wrote would be well acquainted with the Bible story in Judges xiii-xvi. The Book of Judges was popular among seventeenth-century Puritans for many reasons. It contained several exciting stories suitable for sermons and moral lessons: Jael and Sisera (iv–v); Gideon and the Midianites (vi–viii); Abimelech the usurper (ix); Jephthah and his daughter (xi–xii); Samson (xiii–xvi); the lustful Benjaminites (xix–xxi). It described a period when the Israelites were struggling to free themselves from the domination of the Philistines— another Semitic tribe who had taken possession of Canaan from the sea: this situation was attractive to the patriots who opposed Stuart tyranny. Moreover it told of a period before the coming of monarchy, when Israel was ruled by chosen leaders, when life was simple and

[1] We should not make too much here of his experiences with Mary Powell. Certainly she was a 'Philistine', coming from a Royalist family heavily in debt, but she was no Dalila, except maybe that as a girl of seventeen she ensnared the Puritan of thirty-four with her youthful charm. Her desertion of him was more like the behaviour of the woman of Timnath; but she returned and bore him three daughters and a son before she died in 1652. She is more likely to have been the 'mute and spiritless mate' he complained of in his Divorce pamphlets than a wily intriguer; and Milton's two later marriages were happy.

heaven and earth were still so close that angels frequently came down to bring God's word to men. On the one hand it was an age of fierce passions and racial back-slidings; on the other of heroic deeds celebrated in folk-tale manner. The story of Samson combines such themes in a tale of human error and Divine inspiration very attractive to an English Puritan.

Samson was probably in origin a sun-god, like Gilgamesh of Babylon and the Greek Hercules; and Milton used this latter parallel in *Paradise Lost*, ix. 1060 ('Herculean Samson'). For the Jews he was the son of Manoa whose wife was barren till an angel told her that she would have a son who would be dedicated to God, a Nazarite whose hair must not be cut. He would free the Israelites from the Philistine yoke (Judges xiii). The boy grew up and married an unnamed woman of Timnath though his parents did not wish him to marry a foreigner. On the way with them to make the match, Samson slew a lion. On a later visit he found honey in the carcass, and when he was given a retinue of thirty Philistine youths for the wedding he wagered clothing for them all on a riddle he made up about that discovery (xiv. 14). They learned the answer to this by getting the bride to worm it out of him. Furious at the betrayal he went to Ashkelon, killed thirty Philistines and gave their clothes to the young men, then went home (xiv). The father of the bride he had deserted married her off to one of the groomsmen, whereupon Samson took revenge by catching 300 foxes, tying them in pairs with torches between their tails, and loosing them to burn the Philistine corn and vineyards. When the Philistines tried to catch him he retreated to a fastness in a rock until he was persuaded by his fellow-countrymen to give himself up, since they feared reprisals. They bound him and handed him over but he burst his bonds and slew many Philistines in Ramath-Lechi with the jaw-bone of an ass; and afterwards God made a spring gush miraculously to quench his thirst. He then 'judged' Israel for twenty years (xv).

Samson had another adventure when he visited a harlot at Gaza in enemy territory. The Philistines got to know of this and lay in wait by the walls till the city-gates would be opened in the morning. But Samson got wind of their ambush, went out early and carried off both of the barred gates on his shoulders and placed them on top of a hill some distance away.

The downfall of this wild and grimly humorous adventurer came through another Philistine woman, for he fell in love with Delilah, who acted treacherously. Being offered large sums of money to find out the secret of his strength she tempted him continually, but for a long time he was wary. First he told her that he could be overcome if he were bound with seven green withes; so she bound him thus while his enemies lay hidden in the chamber. Then as if to warn him she cried, 'The Philistines be upon thee, Samson!' At once he burst his bonds and she knew she had failed. A second time he told her that new ropes would hold him. Again she tried and failed. The third time he told her to weave the seven locks of his hair into the loom. Once more she failed. Then she wearied him out with questions until finally he told her that his strength would be lost if his hair were shorn. She got a barber, lulled Samson to sleep, had his hair shorn, and called once more, 'The Philistines be upon thee, Samson!' This time when he woke he knew his strength had departed. The waiting Philistines took him prisoner, blinded him, and put him into the prison at Gaza where he was made to grind flour in the mill Judges xvi).

This summarises the saga up to the beginning of Milton's tragedy, which must be studied in conjunction with Judges xiii–xvi. To us today the Biblical Samson seems a barbaric but truly national hero, who combines

the strength of Hercules, with the rustic slyness of a Till
Eulenspiegel. He is resourceful, cunning and amorous;
enjoys putting himself into dangerous situations; and he
is betrayed at least twice by women. He is vengeful, and
when at last, his hair having grown again, he is taken to
the feast of Dagon, he gets a boy to lead him between the
supporting pillars of the house and prays for strength
'Only this once, O God, that I may be avenged of the
Philistines for my two eyes' (xvi. 28). His death is a
patriotic triumph.

Like most religious men of his time Milton was a student
not only of the Bible but also of the vast store of
Scriptural interpretation accumulated by scholars and
preachers for sixteen hundred years. From the early days
of Christianity when the Epistle to the Hebrews ranked
him as a great hero with Gideon, Jephthah, David and
Samuel (xii. 32–4), Samson was regarded as a holy man,
but his weakness was reproved because, though a Nazar-
ite consecrated to God, he let himself be ruined by a
woman. Some Christians agreed with the Jewish his-
torian Josephus (first century A.D.) that Samson also
sinned by pride, for 'he was more elate than he should
have been', and thought that his triumphs were due to
his own virtue, 'confessing not that they were done by
the help of God'. Gregory the Great declared that Sam-
son was thus 'blind in mind' before he was made blind
in body. Milton took over these ideas and his Samson
falls partly through pride and spiritual blindness.

The Church supplemented the literal study of the
Bible with other methods of interpretation which en-
riched the surface meaning of Scriptural story; and the
student of Milton should be aware of these. Thus the
moral or *tropological* interpretation drew lessons of general
application from Samson's life, e.g. the value of courage,

44

Introduction

the need of chastity. St. Ambrose (fourth century) used
it to show the evils of marriage between a believer and
an infidel—and this idea may have influenced Milton's
treatment of Dalila. The *allegorical* interpretation saw
Samson as an ante-type, a foreshadowing, of Christ's
work on earth. Rabanus Maurus, a ninth-century Arch-
bishop of Mainz, thus summarised Samson's resem-
blances to Christ:

> First, because his birth was announced by an angel. Then
> because he is called a Nazarite and frees Israel from its enemies.
> Lastly, because he overthrew their temple and slew many
> thousands of men who mocked him. Also Samson means 'Sun',
> and our Redeemer is also called 'Sun' . . .[1]

The third chief method of interpretation, the *anagogic*,
was prophetic or mystical. 'Samson', wrote Hugo of St.
Victor, 'signifies the mind illuminated with divine know-
ledge. Samson's head is the principle of mind, and the
hairs of his head are the rays of contemplation.'

By such means every detail of a Biblical story could be
given very many interpretations. In the sixteenth century
the Reformers continued the tradition, and Martin
Luther used it energetically in his Commentaries on
Judges and the Psalms. For him the Philistines were the
slaves of the five senses; that was why they had five pro-
vinces and five satraps in their land. Their name meant
'falling with drink' and their god Dagon's name meant
'wheat'; so he was a god of gluttony and the Philistine
equivalent of the Greek Bacchus or Ceres. Luther also
gave a topical turn to allegorical interpretation, regard-
ing Dalida (as he called Delilah) as a 'type' of the false
monks and bishops who lord it with great wealth instead

[1] B. Rabanus Maurus, Commentary on the Book of Judges, in
Opera Omnia (Migne, *Patrologia Latina*, 109). For a full treatment of
this subject see F. M. Krouse, *Milton's Samson and the Christian
Tradition*, Princeton, 1949.

of doing their duty. Samson is the true Church which falls asleep, is betrayed, deprived of its strength and made blind to the truth.

Milton enjoyed finding allegories in Scripture. 'The whole book' (he wrote of Revelation) 'soars to a prophetic pitch in types and allegories'; and in the Conclusion to *The Reason of Church Government* he adapted Luther's topical interpretation of Samson, making him a parallel to Charles I under the evil influence of the bishops. We see no trace of this particular allegory in *Samson Agonistes*, but the traditional conception of Samson as a type of Christ probably helped Milton to choose this story to follow *Paradise Lost* and *Paradise Regained*. In the first great poem Adam lost Paradise by an act of self-will; in the second Christ by resisting temptation regained what Adam had lost. But Milton believed that what Christ had done all men might do, in their measure; so he would write a third poem showing how by God's Grace fallen human nature could be raised from almost total defeat to victory. Such a theme was provided by Christ's ante-type, Samson, whose story, besides carrying on the heroic idea, could be used to vindicate true tragedy in the modern world.

Milton is influenced by topical allegory in those passages in which any Puritan would see parallels between Samson and the 'Saints' who had tried (and failed) to free England from tyranny; between the Israelites and the English people who had been ungrateful to Cromwell; between the Philistines, 'Drunk with Idolatry, drunk with Wine', and the libertine Cavaliers.

Milton makes great use of moral or tropological interpretation; for one of the main functions of his Chorus is to draw moral generalisations from Samson's condition and its causes. But his drama is not allegorical in the same way as *Comus*. The Lady and Comus are little more than personifications of virtue and vice; but Samson

46

is a real personality as well as an illustration or 'exemplum' of moral principles. So it is on the literal tradition which regarded Samson as a historical figure that Milton mainly draws, and his characteristics, and the questions about them asked during the tragedy, are those which had been long discussed.

Milton depicts him as a hero who has devoted himself to God's will despite the uncertain support and the ingratitude of his fellow-Israelites (242–6). As Luther declared, he was predestined to do God's work (23–4; 634), no private adventurer, but his country's servant (1211–13). He failed in his mission through his own fault (44–6; 197–205), for he trusted in his 'mortal strength' (348–9) and became 'swollen with pride' (529–32). Great in physical prowess he was 'of wisdom nothing more than mean' (207). Hence he fell an easy prey to Dalila's wiles.[1]

In discussing Samson's relations with Dalila and with the 'woman of Timnath', as elsewhere in his poem, Milton gives his views on old controversies caused by scholars who occasionally questioned Samson's sainthood. Was he not a murderer, since he slew so many men? A suicide, since his last words were 'Let me die with the Philistines!'? And his relations with women were not above reproach; his wives were unbelieving foreigners whom the Hebrews were forbidden to marry. St. Augustine of Hippo had defended Samson against such charges because he obeyed God's will, and 'If God commands . . . who dare call this obedience in question?' (*City of God*, I, xxv). Luther had followed this lead, insisting that 'Samson was born by divine predestination and received commands from God which he carried out.' Whatever he did in pursuance of God's will was therefore justified, even though it might seem to go against one of the

---

[1] Most editors take the 'fallacious Bride' (320) to be Dalila. We believe that his first wife is meant here. See Commentary.

Commandments. This is the background against which we should read Samson's defence of his first marriage (219–26), and the Chorus's slighting reference to the 'wandering thought' of those who 'would confine the Interminable . . . Who made our Laws to bind us, not himself' (300–21).

The Book of Judges says nothing of visitors to Samson in prison; but they were necessary to make dramatic dialogue possible; and Milton saw some resemblance between the situations of Samson and Job, for though Job is essentially the good man suffering undeservedly whereas Samson rightly blames himself, Job likewise endures extreme anguish, physical and mental. Now Job has three friends, Eliphaz, Bildad and Zophar, who come to condole, and discuss the reasons for his suffering. Doubtless the Book of Job influenced Milton here, as well as Greek tragedy. But most like Job are the Choruses in which the inscrutable mystery of God's ways is discussed (e.g. 652–704).

As will be shown later each of Samson's visitors plays an important part in the drama by recalling the past and affecting his mind. It was a bold stroke to introduce Dalila; but some commentators had surmised that the Philistines intended her to live with Samson in his captivity! (cf. Commentary, 807–8). Harapha is made the father of Goliath (1249) whom David slew later. His encounter with Samson allows Milton to oppose the suggestion of the medieval critic Rupert of St. Héribert that Samson did his great deeds by magic not by the power of holiness (cf. 1131–44).

In exploring Samson's mind and motives Milton followed, not the simple Bible tale, but the Christian writers who had analysed his inner failure, his blindness of spirit. For the poet Samson's repentance is all-important, since that makes possible the return of hope when he slays his own pride and admits his fault to his visitors, each of

48

the subject of the play is the spiritual regeneration of Samson.
how what each episode of S.A. contributes to this process of
regeneration".

Introduction

whom tempts him to new error. The central theme of the drama is the regeneration of the hero by withstanding temptation. Consideration of this can best be included in discussion of the way in which Milton adapted his subject to the form of a Greek tragedy.

SAMSON AGONISTES AS A CLASSICAL TRAGEDY

Many poets before Milton had used the Samson story. Chaucer in *The Monk's Tale* (following Boccaccio) told his tale briefly as an example of a man who revealed his secret to his wives, 'through which he slew himself for wretchedness'. There were French and German plays in the late fifteenth century, and in the next hundred and fifty years many tragedies appeared in Latin (five), French and Dutch. A Dutch play by Joost van den Vondel is claimed (inconclusively) by some critics to have influenced Milton. In England there were plays in the popular theatre in 1567 and 1602; both have vanished. Francis Quarles presented *The History of Samson* (1631) in twenty-four episodes in prosaic heroic couplets, each episode being followed by a 'Meditation' sermonising over his narrative.

Milton owed little to these literary predecessors, though he probably knew some of them, including Vondel and Quarles. In his preface to *Samson Agonistes*, 'Of that Sort of Dramatic Poem which is call'd Tragedy', he both defends Tragedy against its detractors and shows that he has gone directly to the ancient Greeks for his form.

He begins by referring to Aristotle's justification of Tragedy because it produces a moral 'katharsis' or purgation of the dangerous emotions Pity and Fear (or Terror) which are excited and 'worked off' in drama by means of an imitative fiction. He supports Aristotle from the homoeopathic practice of physicians since Galen who use 'sour against sour', 'salt to remove salt humours'. Philosophers and theologians alike agree that Tragedy is

D   49

a worthy form of art; and great men have written tragedies. This proves how wrong the extreme Puritans and others have been to despise Tragedy; though they might rightly object to abuses of Tragedy such as the introduction of comic scenes and vulgar persons. Here Milton agrees with Sir Philip Sidney's celebrated *Apology for Poetry*.

Turning to his own work Milton declares that he has modelled his poem after the Greek and modern Italian manner, using a Chorus. Since *Samson Agonistes* is not intended for performance he has not divided it into Acts and Scenes but it is not more than five Acts long. He does not analyse his plot but points to Aeschylus, Sophocles and Euripides as the models he has imitated; he has kept the Unities.

All this tells us much about Milton's self-restrictive aim and method. Some details may be added. His title combines Greek and Christian ideas. Classical tragedies often linked the chief character's name with some indication of the part of his life to be portrayed, e.g. *Oedipus Tyrannos* (Oedipus the King), *Hercules Furens* (Hercules Mad). 'Agonistes' however has distinct Christian meanings, not only Wrestler or Athlete but also Champion or Advocate. Samson is both Athlete and God's Champion.

The tragedies of the three great authors he admired were not divided into Acts and Scenes, so Milton followed good practice. He also followed them in the organisation of the smaller sections of the work. Aristotle defined tragic structure thus:

Structure of Greek Tragedy.

The Prologos is that entire part of a tragedy which precedes the Parode of the Chorus. An Episode is that entire part of a tragedy which comes between complete Choric songs. The Exode is that entire part which has no Choric song after it. Of the Choric part the Parode is the first undivided utterance of the Chorus; the Stasimon is a Choric ode without anapaests or trochaic tetrameters; the Kommos is a final lamentation of Chorus and actors. (*Poetics*, xii. 2–3. Butcher's trans.)

Introduction

Milton's Prologos consists of the hero's opening Soliloquy
(1–114). Then the Chorus enters and speaks its Parode
(115–75). Five Episodes and five Choruses follow. Each
Episode consists of dialogue between Samson and a visitor
—the Chorus, Manoa, Dalila, Harapha, and the Officer,
in succession. After Samson's departure and the (fifth)
Chorus's benediction (1427–40) the Exode begins with
Manoa's return, and includes his dialogue with the
Chorus, and the coming of the Messenger with his Narra-
tive. The Kommos (1660–758) does not agree with
Aristotle's definition since the Chorus takes part in the
Exode and ends it, but this is often found in Greek tragedy.
The lament begins with a brief apostrophe by the full
Chorus, which then divides into Semichoruses; Manoa
gives his view of the sad triumph, and the full Chorus
brings the play to a close. It is all very simply and beauti-
fully organised.

The Unities

The action of most Greek tragedies took place within
twenty-four hours, 'a single revolution of the sun'; but
there was no invariable rule, although Renaissance critics
made a rigid law of it and not until Dr. Johnson blasted
it with his common sense in his *Preface to Shakespeare* was
the ghost of the Unity of Time laid. Milton's action is as
strict as the most rigorous could demand; its duration is
only the time taken to play it, and Samson is on the stage
until he goes to the temple, where he is killed almost at
once. This certainly helps to preserve the intensity and
concentration beloved of classical tragedians.

Unity of Action, on which Aristotle insisted, Milton
does not mention; but he keeps it, allowing no sub-plot
and no break or digression from first to last. Nor does he
permit any 'intermixing of comic stuff' as did Shake-
speare in *Romeo and Juliet* and *Hamlet*, no 'intruding vul-
gar and trivial persons' like the Porter in *Macbeth* and the

51

Players and gravediggers in *Hamlet*. The characters are few and all bear directly on the action, so there is no distraction or lowering of the tone. Harapha is not a 'trivial or vulgar person' but a Philistine champion.

As his Notebook shows, Milton may have planned a trilogy of classical dramas on the lines of the Oedipus plays of Sophocles and the *Oresteia* of Aeschylus. In *Samson Agonistes* he gives us the third play of such a trilogy, focusing on the last day of the hero's life and using that as a mirror to reflect back on previous happenings so as to explain both his misery and his recovery. Nothing irrelevant to the central issue is allowed to intrude, and a reading of Judges xiii–xv will show how much is omitted: many details of the 'miraculous' birth, of the adventure with the lion; the nature of the riddle. The episode of the foxes is omitted entirely (though he had once thought of writing a play on it), perhaps because it was both broadly comic and personally vengeful. The taking of the gates of Gaza is mentioned, but not the woman he visited —the hero must not be demeaned. The union with Dalila becomes a marriage (agreeing with some commentators) though Samson himself calls her a 'Concubine'. Details of her first three attempts at his secret are omitted. Whereas in Judges xvi 'all the people' in the temple are slain, Milton makes a class-distinction, saving all the common folk in the open air on the 'popular' side.

Like the Greek tragedians Milton took his story from the great religious tradition of his race and could rely on his readers' knowing its outlines so well that he need only allude to many of the incidents in Samson's life. He might embroider them but he must not change them fundamentally. He could however invent new incidents provided that he kept decorum. Hence Samson's stream of visitors, probably suggested by the Book of Job, and by Aeschylus who in *Prometheus Bound* had filled in the story of Prometheus by showing him being bound to the

Introduction

rock by Zeus's 'officer' Hephaestus, and visited by Oceanus (a friend and relative), Io (a woman), and Hermes (an enemy), as Milton's shackled hero is visited by his father Manoa, a woman (Dalila), an enemy (Harapha), and an Officer of the Philistines. The dialogues with these throw light on Samson's whole career, but there can be little surprise. The pleasure we receive is due partly to expectation fulfilled, as details of the Samson saga come in, and partly to Dramatic Irony, since the reader often knows more than the dramatic character about what is going to happen. Indeed the whole play until the Catastrophe is ironical in this sense, for throughout the despair and erroneous consolations of Samson's friends, the allurements of Dalila, the threats of Harapha, we know that Samson must die (but a heroic death) and that the doubts of God's justice will be proved wrong.

Dr. Johnson, who was surprised that Milton followed classical example rather than the 'exhibitions of the French and English stages', disliked the form of *Samson Agonistes* which, he declared 'has a Beginning and an End, which Aristotle himself could not have disapproved, but it must be allowed to want a Middle, since nothing passes between the first Act and the last, that either hastens or delays the Death of *Samson*. The whole Drama, if its superfluities be cut off, would scarcely fill a single Act'.[1] The modern student will of course read the piece more carefully than Johnson and realise that the drama is not only about the death of Samson but about his state of mind beforehand, and that each of his visitors has a positive, even violent effect upon him so that they illustrate and assist what Professor D. C. Allen has called 'the regeneration of a desperate man'.[2]

[1] Samuel Johnson, *Lives of the English Poets*, ed. G. Birkbeck Hill, 1905, i, pp. 188–9.
[2] D. C. Allen, *The Harmonious Vision*, Baltimore, 1954.

At first Samson is without hope, incapable of rest, disgusted with himself and longing for death (1–109), though he will not let himself question God's goodness (43–5). The Chorus bids him 'Deject not then so overmuch thyself' (210–14) and he rouses himself sufficiently to defend himself when they blame his choice of wife and his failure to free Israel (215–76). The Chorus expresses a state of mind already reached by Samson when it warns against rationalist doubts of God's justice.

When Manoa comes lamenting Samson tells *him* not to blame God, since he fell through his own sin (373–80). He also suggests that ere long Dagon will be discomfited, but not by him (460–71). He has a hope, though not for himself, and Manoa accepts it (472–8). But the proposal to ransom him casts him down. He prefers to stay and bear God's punishment at Philistine hands (481–598) rather than 'sit idle on the household hearth' (a fate which no doubt Milton dreaded). Manoa rightly accuses him of a passivity which would let him remain a slave useful to the enemy. This conversation shows that although Samson is filled with remorse he is sunk in spiritual torpor, self-contempt and despair of God's gifts. He is suffering from an 'inverted Hubris' for he is as self-centred in his nullity as he was in his pride (606–51). As the Chorus declares, he has not yet learned true patience for he has no 'source of consolation from above' (664). But the Chorus, like Job, cries out in wonder and fear at the seeming harshness of God (667–704). In a sense this is Samson's lowest ebb. He has resisted his father's well-meant temptation to ease and family-affection; but it has brought him no relief.

Dalila rouses him from sloth, and in his resistance to 'the bait of honeyed words' he overcomes a temptation to uxoriousness which has been his bane. He treats her as he should have done long ago, and she reveals that her sensual love for him is accompanied by a hatred for God's people. The Chorus discovers that the last vestige of Samson's infatuation has vanished (1003–9).

Harapha supplies another temptation, to fear of violence and insult by a triumphant enemy. He excites in Samson a desire for positive action, to challenge Dagon in the person of 'his Champion bold' (1151–2). Samson's physical (and moral) strength is returning now; he regards himself once more as the representative of God and his country, and though he still longs for death he hopes to take some enemies with him (1262–7). The beginning of the next Chorus is coloured by the revival of Samson's spirits, and it contrasts two possibilities, the divinely inspired activity of the Deliverer, and the patient endurance of the majority of Saints (1268–307).

Dramatically the end is still doubtful, but spiritually Samson has made great progress. So when the Officer orders him to the 'unclean' feast, he goes on conditions, admitting that he may be offending God and that he is afraid, but accepting the responsibility for his act, and feeling that there may be 'some important cause' for the summons (1369–426). When the decisive moment comes, we are told, he does not (as in the Bible) cry for vengeance and pray aloud for death. He does all quietly and gravely (1636–8); and thus

> With inward eyes illuminated,
> His fiery virtue rous'd
> From under ashes into sudden flame   (1689–91)

he makes of his death, not a suicidal act, but a sacrifice to God and country. We have seen him move from the depth of despair to the height of religious self-immolation, and each episode has contributed something to the change, though the movement is wavering and Samson is uncertain of God's will until the climax. Out of punishment comes opportunity, out of humiliation victory; the moment of victory is the moment of death; and death is a relief long-sought. Moreover so many unanswerable questions have been asked by both hero and Chorus that the ending cannot but be subdued.

THE GREEK SPIRIT IN MILTON

Much controversy has raged round this topic. On the one hand Goethe, himself a Hellenist, declared that *Samson* 'has more of the antique spirit than any production of any other modern poet'; on the other the great Greek scholar Professor R. C. Jebb argued that 'neither as a poem nor as drama is it Hellenic', and others have agreed with him. Much depends on how one defines the 'Greek Spirit' as shown in tragedy. Broadly we would suggest that a Greek tragedy was essentially grave and lofty in tone, concentrated and intense in development, essentially religious. The fate of the hero (not always death, and at the end of some trilogies alleviated by reconciliation) is made inevitable either by some flaw in his character or some concatenation of circumstances which he cannot escape. Many heroes suffer because of pride, or presumption against the gods. The gods themselves, though in the main on the side of goodness, are incalculable and punish the innocent with the guilty. Above them is an inexorable Fate which works through cause and effect, and sometimes what seems to men Chance. The ways of the Universe are thus unpredictable, and a man must accept and endure them. To live a good life and to achieve a serenity which could face disaster unbroken was the Greek aim; hence the austere calm at the close of many Greek tragedies.

Jebb said that the tragic pleasure in Greek tragedy arises from 'the sense on the one hand of the heroic in man; on the other hand of a superhuman controlling power', and he thought *Samson Agonistes* defective in both. Yet both are fundamental to Milton's drama. All Samson's life has been heroic, and his initial distress is

56

paralleled in the *Oedipus at Colonus* of Sophocles (which closes a trilogy) where we see a blind and broken hero remembering the past and finally brought to peace. The end of Samson is more heroic than that of Oedipus. Moreover *Samson* is filled with a sense of mystery. The hero has tragic flaws of pride and uxoriousness, yet there are suggestions that he is punished beyond his deserts; and Samson, Manoa and the Chorus all insist that the Deity is both moral and inscrutable. Clearly the drama has much in common with the Greek.

Yet differences in the tone and conduct of the drama make it un-Greek in spirit. E. E. Stoll wrote that its 'central situation . . . is that of temptation. What could be more Puritan? What less Greek?' With this we must agree, adding that the theme is not only Temptation but Salvation. Consequently the drama is much more introspective than any Greek play, as Samson and the Chorus search their own hearts and those of men in general. This is Hebraic and Christian, but the Platonic Christianity of *Comus* is absent. So the torments of soul suffered by the hero have a quality not found in Greek art. Purgation is achieved, but the quality and the objects of the tragic pity and fear are different.

Nevertheless the serene dismissal at the close is comparable to that sought by the Greeks, however different the theology. It is not the business of a dramatist to answer all the doubts excited in his characters' minds during the progress of an action. Men may still suffer apparently unjustly, but this hero's suffering was justified by the event. He erred, repented, and with God's aid fulfilled the heroic mission which he had temporarily neglected.

> Nothing is here for tears, nothing to wail
> Or knock the breast; no weakness, no contempt,
> Dispraise or blame; nothing but well and fair,
> And what may quiet us in a death so noble.

Homer's Greeks at least would have appreciated that.

Introduction

As a recent editor has written: 'The more closely we look at *Samson*, the more clearly we can see it as a wonderful dramatic machine, in which every part contributes to the whole, and no part can be judged . . . in isolation.'[1] The style is as functional as the rest. Compared with *Comus* the later drama is lacking in opulent imagery. Some readers find the result bald and dry. Certainly Milton (like others in his day) turned against floridity and the embroidered manner. In *Paradise Regained* Christ, disparaging Greek literature, speaks of 'their swelling Epithets, thick laid As varnish on a Harlot's cheek' (iv. 344) and praises the simpler Songs of the Hebrews. This might suggest that in *Samson* Milton aims at a Biblical style. There are Biblical phrases, but the style in general is un-Biblical in its dryness and intricacy. No doubt Milton sought to capture the starkness and severity of some Greek tragedies; and Milton was affected by setting his drama in a period (about the twelfth century B.C.) which barred out many historical and mythological references. Examination of the poem however proves that the style is both subtle and rich in certain kinds of imagery.

There are few classical allusions; but there is a cautious reference to Mount Atlas (150) and another to Tantalus (500); and there are references to ancient geography and sciences, besides many words with Latin or Greek connotations. Allusions to Hebrew history are confined to the early books of the Bible before Samson's birth, e.g. the several examples of ingratitude taken from Judges (277–89) where the story of Jephthah's battle with the Ephraimites provides a rare example of unnecessary length.

Of other images War provides a great many, aptly since Samson has long waged a one-man war against the Philistines. As Professor G. Wilson Knight has shown,

---

[1] *Milton, Samson Agonistes*, ed. F. T. Prince, 1957, p. 141.

Introduction

Milton thinks of him as a potential Cromwell;[1] but he is also described like an Archangel in the War in Heaven (*Paradise Lost*, bk. vi). Harapha is like a false medieval knight whom he challenges (1116–28). Dalila is also described in warlike terms. She is an enemy planting spies in a city, seeking traitors within, and besieging him with her nagging 'peals' of words (like gunnery). The image of war comes again when the Chorus thinks of revival at 1268–86; again *Paradise Lost*, bk. vi, springs to mind.

Throughout images of strenuous activity are opposed to those of passivity and servitude. Samson's dejection and blindness bring images drawn from diseases and the physical organs (606–28); but these are often used also of the mind, for 'Milton continually feels light and sight as spiritual energies, and certainly at his greatest moments makes less distinction between spiritual and physical action than any (other) of our poets' (Knight, op. cit., p. 93). Darkness and light, death and life are continually opposed (e.g. 80–105).

Mr. T. S. Eliot has pointed to the influence of Milton's bad eyesight on his imagery. Certainly there is little precise form and colour here, merely light and dark, translucency and opaqueness. The description of Dalila as a 'ship of Tarsus' may be a blind man's memory based on the rustling of a woman's dress (like the wind in rigging and streamers) and the scent of her passing.

There are many images of ambiguity or doubleness, sometimes expressed through puns, e.g. 'peal' (235); two kinds of 'baseness' (414–16); two kinds of 'conception' (390). Good things turn to bad (388–91), and the idea of the sting in the tail is used twice, of God's graces (360) and Dalila (997).

This is enough to suggest how rich a field of study the imagery of *Samson Agonistes* provides; and for Milton the

[1] G. Wilson Knight, *Chariot of Wrath*, 1942, pp. 84–7.

abstractions of philosophy and theology were potent for poetry since emotions could play round and be conveyed through them. In his cooler way he was as 'Metaphysical' a poet as Donne.

As for his classical constructions in syntax which often deter modern readers, they were, as Professor M. Y. Hughes writes, 'part of the fibre of his brain'[1] as natural to him as the idioms of ordinary speech were to other men. He has been accused of writing English like a dead language; but it was precisely because English was to him a living language that he modelled it in the manner of Latin with inversions, participial phrases, subordinate clauses, parentheses and ellipses, arranged in periods or long loose aggregations. At a time when poetry, like prose, was turning towards the easy but conventionalised manner of the coffee-house talk which came to its superb climax in Pope's *Epistles*, Milton looked back to the Elizabethan freedom in which words could be used with all their original and acquired colour and the individual author was encouraged to contort his style to the shape of his personality.

Milton's blank verse also shows this individuality and flexibility. It is freer here than in *Paradise Regained*, for he is writing drama, not epic, and as in *Comus* we find occasional feminine endings, many run-on lines, the period placed frequently within the line, and other pauses widely distributed. (Examine lines 187–215 for examples of all these.) It is verse meant to be read aloud, as the blind poet must have recited and heard it. Then the dislocated stresses, the additional syllables, the occasional reduction of five stresses to four (37, 496), a deliberate ruggedness, fall into place in a harmony of music and meaning. These qualities also mark the Choruses, whose paragraphs (strophes), and the rhythmic irregularity of

[1] *Paradise Regained, The Minor Poems and Samson Agonistes*, ed. Merritt Y. Hughes, New York, 1937, p. 425.

the lines (4–12 syllables long, with occasional rhyme) are modelled on the Italian *canzone*. To the last Milton was experimenting, not only in dramatic form, but in verse-technique.

Was Milton a great dramatist? Certainly not in any popular sense, for his gifts were too reflective and didactic to have suited the Stuart theatre either before 1642 or after the reopening in 1660. In *Comus* he wrote for a special occasion a play which in its mingling of Masque, Pastoral, and moral debate, belongs to no one kind of drama, but is unique in itself. *Samson Agonistes* on the other hand is rigorously true to its Greek models. Scholars have argued that it was meant as a counterblast to the 'Heroic' plays in which Dryden and others, during the late sixties, were transferring to the stage the most incredible adventures from the romantic epics of Ariosto and Tasso (beloved by Milton in his youth), and high-pitched sentiment and eloquence about Honour and Love of which Milton could never have approved. It is hard to imagine the old blind Milton sitting through a performance of Dryden's *Conquest of Granada* (played in 1670), but he may have done. His tragedy with its economy and restraint certainly differed extremely from that ten-act episodic romance; and the religious heroism of Samson is utterly unlike the emotional extravagance of Dryden's Almanzor. Milton's classicism cut right across the prevailing current of 'neo-classicism'. He steered by ancient stars, and in so doing wrote one of our greatest poetic dramas.

To read *Comus* and *Samson Agonistes* in rapid succession is a rewarding experience, as one passes from the allegory and the high spirits of the first, almost cocksure in its assurance that virtue is unassailable, to the hard-won trust of the other and its profound study of an individual sinner moving through repentance to victory. In passing from youth to age how far has Milton progressed in knowledge of human nature and its predicament in a world where it is 'Born under one law, to another bound', torn by the conflict of flesh and spirit! Yet there is no essential change in the nature of his religious faith. Unlike the defiant Lady, Samson may despair, but the poet does not; he has himself faced all the questions of his Chorus with invincible trust.

When on his way home from Italy Milton called on the nobleman Camillo Cardoyn at Geneva, he wrote in his host's album these words:

> —if Vertue feeble were
> Heaven it selfe would stoope to her
> Coelum non animum muto dum trans mare curro.[1]
>
> Joannes Miltonius
> Junii 10⁰, 1639   Anglus

Obviously Milton regarded the last two lines of *Comus* as a personal motto. In a sense *Samson* is a play on the same text, since, although no Attendant Spirit appears to rescue Samson, we know that the 'rousing motions' and returning strength which ensure his victory are the inward work of Heaven.

[1] 'I change the sky but not my mind when I cross the sea.'

BOOK LIST

The most essential reference book for students of Milton is the Authorised Version of the Bible. Other useful books are listed below. Those to which we are most indebted are marked with asterisks.

Biographical and critical studies of a comprehensive nature include: D. Masson, *Life of Milton* (1859–94); H. Darbishire, *The Early Lives of Milton* (1932); W. Raleigh, *Milton* (1920); E. M. W. Tillyard, *Milton* (1930)*; D. Daiches, *Milton* (1957).

Studies of particular topics include: R. Bridges, *Milton's Prosody* (1921); W. R. Parker, *Milton's Debt to Greek Tragedy in Samson Agonistes* (1937)*; G. W. Whiting, *Milton's Literary Milieu* (1939); D. H. Wolfe, *Milton and the Puritan Revolution* (1941); J. H. Hanford, *A Milton Handbook* (4th edn., 1946); I. Samuel, *Plato and Milton* (1947); F. M. Krouse, *Milton's Samson and the Christian Tradition* (1949)*; T. H. Banks, *Milton's Imagery* (1950); F. T. Prince, *The Italian Element in Milton's Verse* (1954)*.

Editions: Some of the earliest editions are still valuable, and references are made to them in our Commentary, e.g. T. Warton, *Milton's Minor Poems* (1785); H. J. Todd, *Milton's Poetical Works* (6 vols., 1890)*; D. Masson, *Poetical Works* (3 vols., 1874)*. 'The Columbia Edition' of the Works (1931–1938); M. Y. Hughes, *Milton: Complete Poems and Major Prose* (1957)*.

Textual problems are discussed in editions of the *Poems* by H. Darbishire (2 vols., 1952–5)*; and B. A. Wright (1956)*.

Editions of *Arcades* and *Comus* by A. W. Verity (1891)*; O. Elton (n.d.); P. B. and E. M. W. Tillyard (1952)*.

Editions of *Samson Agonistes* by J. C. Collins (1883); A. W. Verity (1892)*; E. K. Chambers (n.d.)*; F. T. Prince (1957)*.

Arcades

*Part of an Entertainment presented to the Countess Dowager of Derby at
Harefield, by some Noble Persons of her Family, who appear on the
Scene in pastoral habit, moving toward the seat of State, with this Song:*

I. SONG

[margin: Wonderful compliment]
[margin: Pastoral]

Look, Nymphs and Shepherds, look!
What sudden blaze of majesty
Is that which we from hence descry,
Too divine to be mistook?
   This, this is she
To whom our vows and wishes bend:
Here our solemn search hath end.

Fame, that her high worth to raise
Seem'd erst so lavish and profuse,
We may justly now accuse   10
Of detraction from her praise;
   Less than half we find express'd,
   Envy bid conceal the rest.

[margin: Like a pilgrimage]

Mark what radiant state she spreads,
In circle round her shining throne,
Shooting her beams like silver threads.
This, this is she alone,
   Sitting like a Goddess bright
   In the centre of her light.

Might she the wise Latona be,   20
[margin: n.b. Classical imagery.]
Or the tower'd Cybele,
Mother of a hundred gods?
Juno dares not give her odds;

S.D. *presented to*: played before. *habit*: dress. *seat of State*: a throne for
the Countess. *State*: dignity, splendour (cf. 14).   6 *vows*: prayers,
self-dedication.   23 *odds*: advantage.

Arcades

> Who had thought this clime had held
> A deity so unparallel'd?

As they come forward, the Genius of the Wood *appears, and, turning toward them, speaks.*

Genius. Stay gentle Swains, for though in this disguise, *[Blank verse — light yet formal]*
  I see bright honour sparkle through your eyes;
  Of famous Arcady ye are, and sprung
  Of that renowned flood, so often sung,
  Divine Alpheus, who by secret sluice *[Lycidas — 30 same.]*
  Stole under Seas to meet his Arethuse;
  And ye, the breathing Roses of the Wood,
  Fair silver-buskin'd Nymphs, as great and good,
  I know this quest of yours and free intent
  Was all in honour and devotion meant
  To the great Mistress of yon princely shrine,
  Whom with low reverence I adore as mine,
  And with all helpful service will comply
  To further this night's glad solemnity,
  And lead ye where ye may more near behold   40
  What shallow-searching Fame hath left untold;
  Which I full oft amidst these shades alone
  Have sat to wonder at and gaze upon:
  For know, by lot from Jove I am the Pow'r
  Of this fair Wood and live in Oaken bow'r, *[In Comus — a spirit from heaven]*
  To nurse the Saplings tall, and curl the grove
  With Ringlets quaint and wanton windings wove.
  And all my Plants I save from nightly ill
  Of noisome winds, and blasting vapours chill;
  And from the Boughs brush off the evil dew,   50
  And heal the harms of thwarting thunder blue,

24 *clime*: region.   26 *gentle*: well-born (as in 'gentleman'). *Swains*: country youths. The next lines explain their obvious gentility.   30 *secret sluice*: underground channel.   34 *free intent*: liberal purpose. 44 *lot*: command, allotment.   47 *quaint*: pretty.   49 *noisome*: harmful. *blasting*: blighting.   50 *evil dew*: blight.   51 *thwarting*: crossshooting (athwart), hence harmful.

Or what the cross dire-looking Planet smites,
Or hurtful Worm with canker'd venom bites.
When Ev'ning grey doth rise, I fetch my round
Over the mount and all this hallow'd ground,
And early, ere the odorous breath of morn
Awakes the slumbering leaves, or tassell'd horn
Shakes the high thicket, haste I all about,
Number my ranks, and visit every sprout
With puissant words and murmurs made to bless.   60
But else, in deep of night, when drowsiness
Hath lock'd up mortal sense, then listen I
To the celestial Sirens' harmony,
That sit upon the nine infolded Spheres
And sing to those that hold the vital shears
And turn the Adamantine spindle round
On which the fate of gods and men is wound.
Such sweet compulsion doth in music lie,
To lull the daughters of Necessity,
And keep unsteady Nature to her law,   70
And the low world in measur'd motion draw
After the heavenly tune, which none can hear
Of human mould with gross unpurged ear;
And yet such music worthiest were to blaze
The peerless height of her immortal praise
Whose lustre leads us, and for her most fit,
If my inferior hand or voice could hit
Inimitable sounds. Yet, as we go,
Whate'er the skill of lesser gods can show
I will assay, her worth to celebrate,   80
And so attend ye toward her glittering state;

Platonic & Christian theme — musical gravely before conventional compliment [handwritten marginal note]

52 *Planet*: Saturn, the surly, malevolent planet.   53 *canker'd*: disease
that destroys fruit trees.   54 *fetch*: make, take.   57 *tassell'd*: the
huntsman's horn, decorated with tassels.   60 *puissant*: of magic
power. *murmurs*: soft-spoken charms.   62 *mortal sense*: the senses of
mortals. 64 *infolded*: enclosed within each other.   71 *measur'd*: rhyth-
mical. 73 *mould*: form.   74 *blaze*: proclaim (as by heralds with
trumpets).   76 *fit*: suitable.   80 *assay*: attempt, essay.

Where ye may all that are of noble stem
Approach, and kiss her sacred vesture's hem.

II. SONG *delicate, lightly dancing — overtones of Puck & Ariel*

O'er the smooth enamell'd green
Where no print of step hath been,
   Follow me as I sing
   And touch the warbled string:
Under the shady roof
Of branching Elm Star-proof,
   Follow me.   90
I will bring you where she sits
Clad in splendour as befits
   Her deity.
Such a rural Queen
All Arcadia hath not seen.

III. SONG

Nymphs and Shepherds, dance no more
   By sandy Ladon's Lilied banks.
On old Lycæus or Cyllene hoar
   Trip no more in twilight ranks;
Though Erymanth your loss deplore   100
   A better soil shall give ye thanks.
From the stony Mænalus
Bring your Flocks and live with us;
Here ye shall have greater grace,
To serve the Lady of this place.
Though Syrinx your Pan's Mistress were,
Yet Syrinx well might wait on her.
   Such a rural Queen
   All Arcadia hath not seen.

82 *stem*: birth.   84 *enamell'd*: smooth and gay in colour.
87 *warbled*: quivering.

67

"This is an aristocratic art, Elizabethan in feeling, courtly in tone (except where it rises momentarily to mystical contemplation), yet essentially simple in manner". Daiches

A MASKE

PRESENTED

At Ludlow Castle,

1 6 3 4 :

On Michaelmasse night, before the
RIGHT HONORABLE,

IOHN *Earle of Bridgewater*, *Vicount* BRACKLY
Lord President of WALES, And one of
His MAIESTIES most honorable
Privie Counsell.

Eheu quid volui misero mihi ! floribus austrum
Perditus ————

LONDON

Printed for HYMPHREY ROBINSON,
at the signe of the *Three Pidgeons* in
Pauls Church-yard. 1 6 3 7.

[*Comus*]

The Attendant Spirit, afterwards in the habit of **Thyrsis**
Comus with his crew
The Lady
Elder Brother[1]
Second Brother
Sabrina the Nymph

The chief persons which presented were:
   The Lord Brackley
   Mr Thomas Egerton his Brother
   The Lady Alice Egerton

[1] *Milton has* First Brother.

Theme in 'Comus':
"Love virtue; she alone is free"

Comus

The First Scene discovers a wild Wood:

The Attendant Spirit *descends or enters.*

Calm recitative
of formal blank
Verse —

Spirit. Before the starry threshold of Jove's Court
My mansion is, where those immortal shapes
Of bright aërial Spirits live inspher'd
In Regions mild of calm and serene Air,
Above the smoke and stir of this dim spot

Topical?

Which men call Earth, and with low-thoughted care,
Confin'd and pester'd in this pinfold here,
Strive to keep up a frail and Feverish being,
Unmindful of the crown that Virtue gives,
After this mortal change, to her true Servants   10
Amongst the enthron'd gods on Sainted seats.
Yet some there be that by true steps aspire
To lay their just hands on that Golden Key
That opes the Palace of Eternity:
To such my errand is, and but for such
I would not soil these pure Ambrosial weeds
With the rank vapours of this Sin-worn mould.
    But to my task. Neptune, besides the sway
Of every salt Flood and each ebbing Stream,

p. 69 THE PERSONS *presented*: played parts. S.D. *discovers*: reveals,
probably by drawing curtains. 2 *mansion*: home. 3 *aërial*: living
in air. *inspher'd*: in their sphere (of air). 5 *dim spot*: the earth seen
from the heavens is dim with smoke, and small. 7 *pester'd*: encum-
bered, thronged. *pinfold*: pen, sheepfold. 10 *mortal change*: trans-
formation by death (cf. 841). 16 *Ambrosial*: immortal, and with
heavenly perfume. 18 *sway*: rule (over the motions).

70

Took in by lot 'twixt high and nether Jove   20
Imperial rule of all the Sea-girt Isles
That, like to rich and various gems, inlay *χ above*
The unadorned bosom of the Deep;
Which he, to grace his tributary gods,
By course commits to several government,
And gives them leave to wear their Sapphire crowns,
And wield their little tridents. But this Isle,
The greatest and the best of all the main,
He quarters to his blue-hair'd deities;
And all this tract that fronts the falling Sun   30
A noble Peer of mickle trust and power *The Duke of Bridgewater —*
Has in his charge, with temper'd awe to guide *compliment.*
An old and haughty Nation, proud in Arms: *"Lord President of Wales"*
Where his fair offspring, nurs'd in Princely lore,
Are coming to attend their Father's state
And new-entrusted Sceptre. But their way
Lies through the pérplex'd paths of this drear Wood,
The nodding horror of whose shady brows
Threats the forlorn and wandering Passenger;
And here their tender age might suffer peril,   40
But that, by quick command from Sovran Jove,
I was despatch'd for their defence and guard:
And listen why; for I will tell you now
What never yet was heard in Tale or Song,
From old or modern Bard, in Hall or Bow'r.
　　Bacchus, that first from out the purple Grape
Crush'd the sweet poison of misused Wine,
After the Tuscan Mariners transform'd,

20 See Commentary.　　25 *several*: separate.　　27 *this Isle*: Great
Britain.　　29 *quarters to*: assigns to. *blue-hair'd*: Sea gods in masques
often had blue hair.　　30 *all this tract . . . Sun*: Wales or West Britain.
31 *A noble Peer*: the Earl of Bridgewater.　　32 *temper'd awe*: strong rule
tempered by kindness.　　34 *fair offspring*: his children playing in the
masque.　　36 *Sceptre*: the Presidency of Wales.　　37 *pérplex'd*:
tangled. Stress first syllable.　　38 *horror*: horrible waving of foliage,
like hair on the brows of a giant.　　39 *forlorn*: lost and wretched.

71

Comus

Coasting the Tyrrhene shore, as the winds listed,
On Circe's Island fell. (Who knows not Circe,   50
The daughter of the Sun, whose charmed Cup
Whoever tasted lost his upright shape,
And downward fell into a grovelling Swine?)
This Nymph, that gaz'd upon his clustering locks,
With Ivy berries wreath'd, and his blithe youth,
Had by him ere he parted thence, a Son
Much like his Father, but his Mother more,
Whom therefore she brought up and Comus nam'd:
Who, ripe and frolic of his full-grown age,
Roving the Celtic and Iberian fields,   60
At last betakes him to this ominous Wood,
And in thick shelter of black shades embower'd
Excels his Mother at her mighty Art,
Off'ring to every weary Traveller
His orient liquor in a Crystal Glass
To quench the drouth of Phœbus; which as they taste
(For most do taste through fond intemperate thirst)
Soon as the Potion works, their human count'nance,
Th' express resemblance of the gods, is chang'd
Into some brutish form of Wolf or Bear,   70
Or Ounce or Tiger, Hog or bearded Goat,
All other parts remaining as they were;
And they, so perfect is their misery,
Not once perceive their foul disfigurement,
But boast themselves more comely than before,
And all their friends and native home forget,
To roll with pleasure in a sensual sty.
Therefore, when any favour'd of high Jove
Chances to pass through this adventurous glade,

59 *frolic of*: delighting in.   61 *this ominous Wood*: this wood in
Shropshire, dangerous with magic (cf. 207).   65 *orient*: brilliant (like
jewels from the East).   66 *drouth of Phoebus*: thirst caused by the hot
sun.   67 *fond*: foolish.   69 *express*: clearly stamped (L. *expressus*).
71 ***Ounce***: lynx.   79 *adventurous*: perilous.

72

Swift as the Sparkle of a glancing Star   80
I shoot from Heav'n to give him safe convoy,
As now I do. But first I must put off
These my sky-robes spun out of Iris' Woof,
And take the Weeds and likeness of a Swain
That to the service of this house belongs,
Who with his soft Pipe and smooth-dittied Song
Well knows to still the wild winds when they roar
And hush the waving Woods; nor of less faith,
And in this office of his Mountain watch,
Likeliest and nearest to the present aid   90
Of this occasion. But I hear the tread
Of hateful steps; I must be viewless now.

*Comus enters with a Charming-Rod in one hand, his Glass in the
other: with him a rout of Monsters, headed like sundry sorts of wild
Beasts, but otherwise like Men and Women, their Apparel glistering;
they come in making a riotous and unruly noise, with Torches in their
hands.*

Comus. The Star that bids the Shepherd fold,
Now the top of Heav'n doth hold;
And the gilded Car of Day
His glowing Axle doth allay
In the steep Atlantic stream;
And the slope Sun his upward beam
Shoots against the dusky Pole,
Pacing toward the other goal   100
Of his Chamber in the East.
Meanwhile, welcome Joy and Feast,

80 *glancing*: gleaming.   88–91 *Nor of less faith . . . occasion*: 'And
being no less loyal than musical, he is, by the nature of his duty (to
watch sheep on the hills) the most likely—and the nearest—friend to
give the instant aid necessary'.   92 *viewless*: invisible.   93 *The Star*:
Hesperus, the Evening Star.   96 *allay*: steep, quell, cool.   98–9
And the slope Sun . . . Pole: 'And the sun, whose beams have slanted
more and more as it went down below the horizon, shoots a last beam
upwards towards the darkening zenith'.

Midnight shout and revelry,
Tipsy dance and Jollity.
Braid your Locks with rosy Twine,
Dropping odours, dropping Wine.
Rigour now is gone to bed;
And Advice with scrupulous head,
Strict Age, and sour Severity,
With their grave saws in slumber lie.   110
We that are of purer fire
Imitate the Starry Quire,
Who in their nightly watchful Spheres
Lead in swift round the Months and Years.
The Sounds and Seas, with all their finny drove,
Now to the Moon in wavering Morrice move;
And on the Tawny Sands and Shelves
Trip the pert Fairies and the dapper Elves.
By dimpled Brook and Fountain brim
The Wood-Nymphs, deck'd with Daisies trim,   120
Their merry wakes and pastimes keep:
What hath night to do with sleep?
Night hath better sweets to prove;
Venus now wakes, and wakens Love.
Come, let us our rites begin;
'Tis only daylight that makes Sin,
Which these dun shades will ne'er report.
Hail, Goddess of Nocturnal sport,
Dark-veiled Cotytto, t' whom the secret flame
Of midnight Torches burns! mysterious Dame,   130
That ne'er art call'd but when the Dragon womb

making it clear that this is guilty mirth.

105 *rosy Twine*: roses intertwined.   110 *saws*: maxims, proverbs.
Cf. the Justice in *As You Like It*, II. vii. 156, 'full of wise saws'.   112
the Starry Quire: the harmoniously moving stars which make the music
of the spheres.   115 *Sounds*: straits.   116 *wavering Morrice*: the
shifting pattern of the country dance then usually performed on
May-day and at Whitsun.   121 *wakes*: feasting, revels at night
(orig. the watch on the eve of a religious holiday).   131 *call'd*:
invoked.

One of the themes — the distinct 74 between guilty & innocent mirth

Comus

Of Stygian darkness spets her thickest gloom
And makes one blot of all the air! *Movement from revelry to*
Stay thy cloudy Ebon chair *witchcraft.*
Wherein thou rid'st with Hecat', and befriend
Us thy vow'd priests, till utmost end
Of all thy dues be done, and none left out,
Ere the blabbing Eastern scout,
The nice Morn, on th' Indian steep
From her cabin'd loophole peep,   140
And to the tell-tale Sun descry
Our conceal'd Solemnity.
Come, knit hands and beat the ground
In a light fantastic round.

The Measure

Break off, break off! I feel the different pace   *move formal speech*
Of some chaste footing near about this ground.
Run to your shrouds within these Brakes and Trees;
Our number may affright. Some Virgin sure
(For so I can distinguish by mine Art)
Benighted in these Woods! Now to my charms,   150
And to my wily trains. I shall ere long
Be well stock'd with as fair a herd as graz'd
About my Mother Circe. Thus I hurl   *Stage direct^*
My dazzling Spells into the spongy air,
Of power to cheat the eye with blear illusion,
And give it false presentments, lest the place
And my quaint habits breed astonishment,

132 *spets*: spits.   138 *blabbing*: tell-tale.   139 *nice*: squeamish, prudish.   141 *descry*: reveal (L. *describare*).   142 *Solemnity*: ritual. 144 *round*: round dance.   145 *Break off*: The dance breaks off. There is a 'stop of sudden silence' (cf. 552).   147 *shrouds*: shelters. 151 *trains*: tricks or traps (cf. *S.A.* 533).   153–154 Probably Comus flung some coloured powder.   154 *spongy*: receptive, yielding. 155 *blear*: misty, deceptive.   156 *false presentments*: hallucinations. Cf. *Hamlet*. III. iv. 52 'counterfeit presentment' (picture).   157 *quaint habits*: strange dress (L. *habitus*).

75

And put the Damsel to suspicious flight;
Which must not be, for that's against my course.
I, under fair pretence of friendly ends,   160
And well-plac'd words of glozing courtesy,   *cf Satan*
Baited with reasons not unplausible,
Wind me into the easy-hearted man
And hug him into snares. When once her eye
Hath met the virtue of this Magic dust,
I shall appear some harmless Villager
Whom thrift keeps up about his Country gear.
But here she comes; I fairly step aside
And hearken if I may her business hear.

The Lady *enters.*

Flexible verse
with conversat'al   *Lady.* This way the noise was, if mine ears be true,   170
overtones   My best guide now; methought it was the sound
Of Riot and ill-manag'd Merriment,
Such as the jocund Flute or gamesome Pipe
Stirs up among the loose unletter'd Hinds,
When, for their teeming Flocks and granges full,
In wanton dance they praise the bounteous Pan,
she is not condemn- And thank the gods amiss. I should be loth
ing the end only To meet the rudeness and swill'd insolence
the method Of such late Wassailers; yet, O where else
Shall I inform my unacquainted feet   180
In the blind mazes of this tangled Wood?
My Brothers, when they saw me wearied out
With this long way, resolving here to lodge
Under the spreading favour of these Pines,

---

159 *course*: purpose.   161 *glozing*: flattering and deceitful.   163
Wind me . . . man: 'Insinuate myself into the trust of the unsuspic-
ious man'.   165 *virtue*: special power.   167 *gear*: affairs, trade.
168 *fairly*: quietly.   174 *Hinds*: peasants.   175 *granges*: barns,
granaries.   177 *amiss*: in an unsuitable manner.   178 *swill'd*:
drunken.   180 *inform*: direct (cf. *S.A.* 335).   184 *favour*: friendly
shelter.

Stepped, as they said, to the next Thicket-side
To bring me Berries or such cooling fruit
As the kind hospitable Woods provide.
They left me then when the gray-hooded Ev'n, *more stately*
Like a sad Votarist in palmer's weed,
Rose from the hindmost wheels of Phœbus' wain.　190
But where they are, and why they come not back,
Is now the labour of my thoughts. 'Tis likeliest
They had engag'd their wandering steps too far,
And envious darkness, ere they could return,
Had stole them from me: else, O thievish Night, *Milton's nearest*
Why shouldst thou, but for some felonious end, *approach to a con-*
In thy dark lantern thus close up the Stars *cept of the Meta-*
That Nature hung in Heav'n, and fill'd their Lamps *Physical kind*
With everlasting oil, to give due light
To the misled and lonely Traveller?　200
This is the place, as well as I may guess,
Whence even now the tumult of loud Mirth
Was rife and perfect in my listening ear,
Yet nought but single darkness do I find.
What might this be? A thousand fantasies
Begin to throng into my memory,
Of calling shapes, and beckoning shadows dire,
And airy tongues that syllable men's names
On Sands and Shores and desert Wildernesses.
These thoughts may startle well, but not astound　210
The virtuous mind, that ever walks attended
By a strong siding champion, Conscience.
O, welcome, pure-ey'd Faith, white-handed Hope
(Thou hovering Angel girt with golden wings),
And thou unblemish'd form of Chastity!

　189 *sad*: staid, serious. *Votarist*: one performing a vow (L. *votum*)
of pilgrimage.　197 *dark lantern*: a lantern with a shutter to the
light.　203 *rife*: abundant, loud. *perfect in*: filled completely. Milton
wrote 'perfet'.　204 *single*: only.　205 *fantasies*: fancies.　212
siding: going alongside and so defending.

Comus

I see ye visibly, and now believe
That He, the Súpreme Good, to whom all things ill
Are but as slavish officers of vengeance,
Would send a glistering Guardian, if need were,
To keep my life and honour unassail'd.   220
Was I deceiv'd, or did a sable cloud
Turn forth her silver lining on the night?
I did not err; there does a sable cloud
Turn forth her silver lining on the night,
And casts a gleam over this tufted Grove.
I cannot hallo to my Brothers, but
Such noise as I can make to be heard farthest
I'll venture; for my new-enliven'd spirits
Prompt me, and they perhaps are not far off.

SONG

Sweet Echo, sweetest Nymph, that liv'st unseen   230
    Within thy airy shell
  By slow Meander's margent green,
And in the violet-embroider'd vale
    Where the love-lorn Nightingale
Nightly to thee her sad Song mourneth well:
Canst thou not tell me of a gentle Pair
    That likest thy Narcissus are?
      O, if thou have
    Hid them in some flowery Cave,
      Tell me but where,   240
Sweet Queen of Parley, Daughter of the Sphere!
    So mayst thou be translated to the skies,
  And give resounding grace to all Heav'n's Harmonies.

217 *Súpreme*: stress first syllable.   232 *margent*: margin.   241 *Parley*: conversation.   242 *translated*: removed.

78

Comus

Enter Comus.

Comus. Can any mortal mixture of Earth's mould *cf Caliban s*
    Breathe such Divine enchanting ravishment? *attitude to Miranda*
    Sure something holy lodges in that breast
    And with these raptures moves the vocal air
    To testify his hidden residence.
    How sweetly did they float upon the wings
    Of silence, through the empty-vaulted night,   250
    At every fall smoothing the Raven down
    Of darkness till it smil'd! I have oft heard
    My mother Circe with the Sirens three,
    Amidst the flowery-kirtled Naiades,
    Culling their potent herbs and baleful drugs,
    Who, as they sung, would take the prison'd soul
    And lap it in Elysium; Scylla wept
    And chid her barking waves into attention,
    And fell Charybdis murmur'd soft applause.
    Yet they in pleasing slumber lull'd the sense,   260
    And in sweet madness robb'd it of itself; *X Song being used to*
    But such a sacred and home-felt delight, *good & bad ends.*
    Such sober certainty of waking bliss,
    I never heard till now. I'll speak to her,
    And she shall be my Queen.—Hail, foreign wonder!
    Whom certain these rough shades did never breed,
    Unless the Goddess that in rural shrine
    Dwell'st here with Pan or Sylvan, by blest Song
    Forbidding every bleak unkindly Fog
    To touch the prosperous growth of this tall Wood. 270

Lady. Nay, gentle Shepherd, ill is lost that praise
    That is addressed to unattending Ears.

---

244 *mould*: two meanings—dust and form.   247 *raptures*: musical rhapsodies.   248 *his*: an old neuter form for 'its'.   249 *they*: the raptures.   254 *flowery-kirtled*: in tunics wreathed with flowers. 256 *take the prison'd soul*: enchant (and so free) the prisoned soul. 262 *home-felt*: heartfelt, intimate.   271 *ill is lost*: sorely is wasted.

Not any boast of skill, but éxtreme shift
How to regain my sever'd company,
Compell'd me to wake the courteous Echo
To give me answer from her mossy Couch.

Comus. What chance, good Lady, hath bereft you thus?

Lady. Dim darkness and this leavy Labyrinth.

Comus. Could that divide you from near-ushering guides?

Lady. They left me weary on a grassy turf.   280

Comus. By falsehood, or discourtesy, or why?

Lady. To seek i' the valley some cool friendly Spring.

Comus. And left your fair side all unguarded, Lady?

Lady. They were but twain and purpos'd quick return.

Comus. Perhaps forestalling night prevented them.

Lady. How easy my misfortune is to hit!

Comus. Imports their loss beside the present need?

Lady. No less than if I should my brothers lose.

Comus. Were they of manly prime, or youthful bloom?

Lady. As smooth as Hebe's their unrazor'd lips.   290

Comus. Two such I saw, what time the labour'd Ox
In his loose traces from the furrow came,
And the swink'd hedger at his Supper sat.
I saw them under a green mantling vine
That crawls along the side of yon small hill,
Plucking ripe clusters from the tender shoots;

273 *éxtreme*: last (stress first syllable). *shift*: expedient.   279 *near-ushering*: going close in front.   281 *falsehood*: treachery.   285 *prevented*: stopped, with the sense of 'forestalled' (L. *prevenire*). 286 *hit*: guess (cf. *S.A.* 1013–14).   287 'Does losing them matter apart from your present difficulty?'   289 *prime*: early maturity, from 21 to 28 years of age.   291 *what time*: when.   293 *swink'd*: wearied. 294 *mantling*: covering like a mantle (cloak).

Comus

Their port was more than human, as they stood.
I took it for a faery vision
Of some gay creatures of the element,
That in the colours of the Rainbow live   300
And play i' the plighted clouds. I was awe-strook
And, as I pass'd, I worshipp'd. If those you seek,
It were a journey like the path to Heav'n
To help you find them.

Lady.   Gentle villager,
What readiest way would bring me to that place?

Comus. Due west it rises from this shrubby point.

Lady. To find that out, good Shepherd, I suppose,
In such a scant allowance of Starlight,
Would over-task the best Land-Pilot's art
Without the sure guess of well practis'd feet.   310

Comus. I know each lane and every alley green,
Dingle or bushy dell of this wild Wood,
And every bosky bourn from side to side,
My daily walks and ancient neighbourhood;
And if your stray attendance be yet lodg'd
Or shroud within these limits, I shall know
Ere morrow wake or the low-roosted lark
From her thatch'd pallet rouse. If otherwise,
I can conduct you, Lady, to a low
But loyal cottage, where you may be safe   320
Till further quest.

Lady.   Shepherd, I take thy word,

297 *port*: bearing.   298 *vision*: has three syllables.   299 *element*:
air.   300 *Rainbow*: the brothers are probably very brightly dressed.
301 *plighted*: interlaced, embanked.   309 *Land-Pilot's art*: skill of a
guide who goes by the stars.   311 *alley*: shady walk.   312 *Dingle*:
hollow.   313 *bosky bourn*: wood-fringed stream ('Bosky' from L.
boscum, and Fr. *bosquet*—a wood).   315 *stray attendance*: strayed
attendants.   316 *shroud*: sheltering (cf. 147).   318 *thatch'd pallet*:
bed of dry grass.

F   81

And trust thy honest-offer'd courtesy,
Which oft is sooner found in lowly sheds
With smoky rafters than in tap'stry Halls
And Courts of Princes, where it first was nam'd,
And yet is most pretended: In a place
Less warranted than this or less secure
I cannot be, that I should fear to change it.
Eye me blest Providence, and square my trial
To my proportion'd strength! Shepherd, lead on.   330

Enter the Two Brothers.

Elder Bro. Unmuffle, ye faint stars, and thou, fair Moon,
  That wont'st to love the traveller's benison,
  Stoop thy pale visage through an amber cloud,
  And disinherit Chaos, that reigns here
  In double night of darkness and of shades;
  Or if your influence be quite damm'd up
  With black usurping mists, some gentle taper,
  Though a rush Candle from the wicker hole
  Of some clay habitation, visit us
  With thy long levell'd rule of streaming light,   340
  And thou shalt be our star of Arcady,
  Or Tyrian Cynosure.

Second Brother.   Or if our eyes
  Be barr'd that happiness, might we but hear
  The folded flocks penn'd in their wattled cotes,
  Or sound of pastoral reed with oaten stops,
  Or whistle from the Lodge, or village cock

326 *yet*: still.   327 *warranted*: protected safe.   326–8 'I could not be in a place less secure than this, and so I need not fear to go elsewhere!'   329 *square*: adjust, proportion.   332 *benison*: blessing.   334 *disinherit*: dispossess.   336 *influence*: power from the stars exercised upon human fates.   337 *some . . . taper*: may some . . . taper.   338 *wicker hole*: window hole (without glass) framed with wicker.   339 *clay habitation*: wattle-and-daub house.   344 *wattled cotes*: sheep-folds made of interlaced wattle.   346 *Lodge*: small house in the forest.

Count the night watches to his feathery Dames,
'Twould be some solace yet, some little cheering,
In this close dungeon of innumerous boughs.
But O that hapless virgin, our lost sister!   350
Where may she wander now, whither betake her
From the chill dew, amongst rude burs and thistles?
Perhaps some cold bank is her bolster now,
Or 'gainst the rugged bark of some broad Elm
Leans her unpillow'd head fraught with sad fears.
What if in wild amazement and affright,
Or, while we speak, within the direful grasp
Of Savage hunger or of Savage heat?

Elder Brother. Peace, brother; be not over-exquisite
To cast the fashion of uncertain evils;   360
For, grant they be so, while they rest unknown,
What need a man forestall his date of grief,
And run to meet what he would most avoid?
Or if they be but false alarms of Fear,
How bitter is such self-delusion!
I do not think my sister so to seek,
Or so unprincipl'd in virtue's book,
And the sweet peace that goodness bosoms ever,
As that the single want of light and noise
(Not being in danger, as I trust she is not)   370
Could stir the constant mood of her calm thoughts,
And put them into misbecoming plight.
Virtue could see to do what Virtue would
By her own radiant light, though Sun and Moon
Were in the flat Sea sunk. And Wisdom's self
Oft seeks to sweet retired Solitude,

349 *innumerous*: innumerable. 352 *burs*: hairy flowers or seeds
which cling to the clothing. 359 *over-exquisite*: over-subtle, over-
anxious. 360 *cast*: forecast. *fashion*: nature and form. 366 *so to
seek*: so lacking in good sense. 367 *unprincipl'd ... book*: ignorant of
virtuous principles. 368 *bosoms*: bears in its heart. 372 *misbecoming
plight*: unsuitable, unworthy state of mind. 376 *seeks to*: resorts to.

Where, with her best nurse Contemplation,
She plumes her feathers and lets grow her wings,
That in the various bustle of resort
Were all to-ruffled and sometimes impair'd.   380
He that has light within his own clear breast
May sit i' the centre and enjoy bright day;
But he that hides a dark soul and foul thoughts
Benighted walks under the mid-day Sun;   *hence Circe*
Himself is his own dungeon.

Second Brother.   'Tis most true
    That musing meditation most affects
    The Pensive secrecy of desert cell,
    Far from the cheerful haunt of men and herds,
    And sits as safe as in a Senate-house;
    For who would rob a Hermit of his Weeds,   390
    His few Books or his Beads or Maple Dish,
    Or do his gray hairs any violence?
    But Beauty, like the fair Hesperian Tree
    Laden with blooming gold, had need the guard
    Of dragon watch with unenchanted eye,
    To save her blossoms and defend her fruit
    From the rash hand of bold Incontinence.
    You may as well spread out the únsunn'd heaps
    Of Miser's treasure by an outlaw's den,
    And tell me it is safe, as bid me hope   400
    Danger will wink on Opportunity
    And let a single helpless maiden pass
    Uninjur'd in this wild surrounding waste.
    Of night or loneliness it recks me not;
    I fear the dread events that dog them both,

---

378 *plumes*: preens.   380 *to-ruffled*: 'to' is an intensifying prefix to
the participle 'ruffled'.   382 *the centre*: i.e. of the earth.   389 *Senate-
house*: e.g. at Rome, or the English Parliament.   395 *unenchanted*: not
to be enchanted.   397 *Incontinence*: lustful desire.   398 *únsunn'd*: stress
on first syllable.   401 *wink on*: miss seeing.   402 *single*: solitary.
404 *Of . . . not*: 'I am not troubled by her being in the dark alone.'

Lest some ill-greeting touch attempt the person
Of our unowned sister.

Elder Brother.   I do not, brother,
 Infer as if I thought my sister's state
 Secure without all doubt or controversy:
 Yet where an equal poise of hope and fear   410
 Does arbitrate th' event, my nature is
 That I incline to hope rather than fear,
 And gladly banish squint suspicion.
 My sister is not so defenceless left
 As you imagine; she has a hidden strength
 Which you remember not.

Second Brother.   What hidden strength,
 Unless the strength of Heav'n, if you mean that?

Elder Brother. I mean that too, but yet a hidden strength
 Which, if Heav'n gave it, may be term'd her own.
 'Tis chastity, my brother, chastity: 420
 She that has that is clad in cómplete steel,
 And like a quiver'd Nymph with Arrows keen
 May trace huge Forests and unharbour'd Heaths,
 Infamous Hills and sandy perilous wilds,
 Where, through the sacred rays of Chastity,
 No savage fierce, Bandit, or mountaineer
 Will dare to soil her Virgin purity.
 Yea, there where very desolation dwells,
 By grots and caverns shagg'd with horrid shades,
 She may pass on with unblench'd majesty,   430
 Be it not done in pride or in presumption. ✗ Carey thinks this is a hint
 Some say no evil thing that walks by night, of the Lady's weakness.

407 *unowned*: unaccompanied.   408 *Infer*: argue.   410 *poise*:
weight, balance.   411 *arbitrate th' event*: determine the result.   413
squint: squint-eyed, looking all ways at once.   419 *if*: although.
421 *cómplete*: stress first syllable.   423 *trace*: traverse. *unharbour'd*:
without shelter.   426 *mountaineer*: wild man, savage.   429 *horrid*:
bristling (L. *horridus*).   430 *unblench'd*: unshrinking (without losing
her colour).

In fog, or fire, by lake or moorish fen,
Blue meagre Hag, or stubborn unlaid ghost
That breaks his magic chains at curfew time,
No goblin or swart Fairy of the mine,
Hath hurtful power o'er true virginity.
Do ye believe me yet, or shall I call
Antiquity from the old Schools of Greece
To testify the arms of Chastity?   440
Hence had the huntress Dian her dread bow,
(Fair silver-shafted Queen for ever chaste)
Wherewith she tam'd the brinded lioness
And spotted mountain pard, but set at nought
The frivolous bolt of Cupid; gods and men
Fear'd her stern frown, and she was queen o' the Woods.
What was that snaky-headed Gorgon shield
That wise Minerva wore, unconquer'd Virgin,
Wherewith she freez'd her foes to cóngeal'd stone,
But rigid looks of Chaste austerity,   450
And noble grace that dash'd brute violence
With sudden adoration and blank awe?
So dear to Heav'n is Saintly chastity,
That when a soul is found sincerely so,
A thousand liveried Angels lackey her,
Driving far off each thing of sin and guilt,
And in clear dream and solemn vision
Tell her of things that no gross ear can hear,
Till oft converse with heav'nly habitants
Begin to cast a beam on th' outward shape,   460
The unpolluted temple of the mind,
And turns it by degrees to the soul's essence,

433 *fire*: the will-o'-the-wisp.   434 *Blue*: livid with famine or bad blood. *Hag*: evil spirit disguised as a woman.   436 *swart*: dark. 439 *old Schools of Greece*: Greek religion and philosophic teachings. 443 *brinded*: streaked and tawny.   444 *pard*: leopard.   449 *cóngealed*: stress on first syllable.   451 *dash'd*: abashed.   452 *blank*: helplessly amazed.   454 *sincerely so*: wholly chaste.   455 *lackey*: serve, wait on. 461 *temple of the mind*: the body.

Till all be made immortal: but when lust,
By unchaste looks, loose gestures, and foul talk,
But most by lewd and lavish act of sin,
Lets in defilement to the inward parts,
The soul grows clotted by contagion,
Imbodies, and imbrutes, till she quite lose
The divine property of her first being.
Such are those thick and gloomy shadows damp   470
Oft seen in Charnel vaults and Sepulchres,
Lingering and sitting by a new-made grave,
As loth to leave the body that it lov'd,
And link'd itself by carnal sensualty
To a degenerate and degraded state.

Second Brother. How charming is divine Philosophy!
Not harsh and crabbed, as dull fools suppose,
But musical as is Apollo's lute,
And a perpetual feast of nectar'd sweets,
Where no crude surfeit reigns.

Elder Brother.   List, list! I hear   480
Some far-off hallo break the silent Air.

Second Brother. Methought so too: what should it be?

Elder Brother.   For certain,
Either some one like us night-founder'd here,
Or else some neighbour Woodman, or at worst
Some roving Robber calling to his fellows.

Second Bro. Heav'n keep my sister! Again, again, and near!
Best draw, and stand upon our guard.

Elder Brother.   I'll hallo;
If he be friendly, he comes well; if not,
Defence is a good cause, and Heav'n be for us!

465 *lavish*: excessive.   468 *Imbodies, and imbrutes*: becomes grossly
material and brutish.   469 *property*: nature. *first being*: original state.
473 *As loth*: as if such a soul were unwilling ...   476 *divine Philosophy*:
doctrine concerned with the nature of God and the Soul.   480 *crude*:
coarse, undigested.   483 *night-founder'd*: overtaken by night.

Comus

Enter the Attendant Spirit, *habited like a shepherd.*

That hallo I should know. What are you? speak! 490
Come not too near; you fall on iron stakes else.

Spirit. What voice is that? my young Lord? speak again.

Second Brother. O brother, 'tis my father's Shepherd, sure.

Elder Brother. Thyrsis! whose artful strains have oft delay'd
The huddling brook to hear his madrigal,
And sweeten'd every musk-rose of the dale.
How cam'st thou here, good Swain? Hath any ram
Slipp'd from the fold, or young Kid lost his dam,
Or straggling wether the pent flock forsook?
How could'st thou find this dark sequester'd nook? 500

Spirit. O my lov'd master's heir, and his next joy,
I came not here on such a trivial toy
As a stray'd Ewe, or to pursue the stealth
Of pilfering Wolf; not all the fleecy wealth
That doth enrich these Downs is worth a thought
To this my errand, and the care it brought.
But O, my Virgin Lady, where is she?
How chance she is not in your company?

Elder Brother. To tell thee sadly, Shepherd, without blame
Or our neglect, we lost her as we came. 510

Spirit. Ay me unhappy! then my fears are true.

Elder Bro. What fears, good Thyrsis? Prithee briefly shew.

Spirit. I'll tell ye; 'tis not vain or fabulous,
(Though so esteem'd by shallow ignorance)
What the sage Poets, taught by th' heav'nly Muse,
Storied of old in high immortal verse
Of dire Chimeras and enchanted Isles,

491 *iron stakes*: swords.   495 *huddling*: stopping and so massing up.
madrigal: song for several voices (without accompaniment). Lawes
wrote many.   499 *wether*: castrated ram. *pent*: in the fold.   502 *toy*:
slight affair.   506 *To*: compared with.   516 *Storied*: narrated.

And rifted Rocks whose entrance leads to hell;
For such there be, but unbelief is blind.
    Within the navel of this hideous Wood,   520
Immur'd in cypress shades a Sorcerer dwells,
Of Bacchus and of Circe born, great Comus,
Deep skill'd in all his mother's witcheries;
And here to every thirsty wanderer
By sly enticement gives his baneful cup,
With many murmurs mix'd, whose pleasing poison
The visage quite transforms of him that drinks,
And the inglorious likeness of a beast
Fixes instead, unmoulding reason's mintage
Charácter'd in the face. This I have learnt   530
Tending my flocks hard by i' the hilly crofts
That brow this bottom-glade, whence night by night
He and his monstrous rout are heard to howl
Like stabled wolves, or tigers at their prey,
Doing abhorred rites to Hecatë
In their obscured haunts of inmost bowers.
Yet have they many baits and guileful spells
To inveigle and invite th' unwary sense
Of them that pass unweeting by the way.
This evening late, by then the chewing flocks   540
Had ta'en their supper on the savoury Herb
Of Knot-grass dew-besprent and were in fold,
I sat me down to watch upon a bank
With Ivy canopied, and interwove
With flaunting Honeysuckle, and began,
Wrapt in a pleasing fit of melancholy, — ιc P.
To meditate my rural minstrelsy,

520 *navel* centre.   526 *murmurs*: soft incantations.   529–30 *un-moulding . . . face*: 'removing the imprint stamped by reason on the face'. *Charácter'd*: stress second syllable.   532 *brow*: overhang. *bottom glade*: glade in the valley.   534 *stabled*: in their dens.   539 *unweeting*: unsuspecting, unwitting.   540 *by then*: by the time when. 542 *besprent*: sprinkled.   547 *meditate . . . minstrelsy*: practise my pipe.

Till fancy had her fill; but ere a close
The wonted roar was up amidst the Woods,
And fill'd the Air with barbarous dissonance;   550
At which I ceas'd, and listen'd them a while,
Till an unusual stop of sudden silence
Gave respite to the drowsy-flighted steeds
That draw the litter of close-curtain'd Sleep.
At last a soft and solemn breathing sound
Rose like a steam of rich distill'd Perfumes,
And stole upon the Air, that even Silence
Was took ere she was ware, and wish'd she might
Deny her nature and be never more,
Still to be so displac'd. I was all ear,   560
And took in strains that might create a soul
Under the ribs of Death; but O, ere long
Too well I did perceive it was the voice
Of my most honour'd Lady, your dear sister.
Amaz'd I stood, harrow'd with grief and fear,
And 'O poor hapless Nightingale', thought I,
'How sweet thou sing'st, how near the deadly snare!'
Then down the Lawns I ran with headlong haste
Through paths and turnings often trod by day,
Till guided by mine ear I found the place   570
Where that damn'd wizard, hid in sly disguise
(For so by certain signs I knew) had met
Already, ere my best speed could prevent,
The aidless innocent Lady, his wish'd prey;
Who gently asked if he had seen such two,
Supposing him some neighbour villager.
Longer I durst not stay, but soon I guess'd

548 *a close*: a cadence in music, probably at the end of a section.
552 *stop of sudden silence*: the moment when Comus stopped the dance (cf. 145).   558 *took*: taken, enchanted.   560 *Still to be so displac'd*: if her place might always be taken by such music.   568 *Lawns*: open glades in the wood.   573 *prevent*: forestall, anticipate him (cf. 285).

Ye were the two she meant; with that I sprung
Into swift flight till I had found you here,
But further know I not.

Second Brother.   O night and shades,   580
How are ye join'd with hell in triple knot
Against th' unarmed weakness of one Virgin,
Alone and helpless! Is this the confidence
You gave me, Brother?

Elder Brother.   Yes, and keep it still;
Lean on it safely; not a period
Shall be unsaid for me. Against the threats
Of malice or of sorcery, or that power
Which erring men call Chance, this I hold firm:
Virtue may be assail'd, but never hurt,   *View of younger*
Surpris'd by unjust force, but not enthrall'd; *Milton* 590 *(a Tragic*
Yea, even that which mischief meant most harm   *writer like Hardy).*
Shall in the happy trial prove most glory.
But evil on itself shall back recoil   *cf Satan on revenge*
And mix no more with goodness, when at last,
Gather'd like scum, and settl'd to itself,
It shall be in eternal restless change
Self-fed and self-consum'd. If this fail,
The pillar'd firmament is rottenness,
And earth's base built on stubble. But come, let's on.
Against th' opposing will and arm of Heav'n   600
May never this just sword be lifted up.
But for that damn'd magician, let him be girt
With all the grisly legions that troop
Under the sooty flag of Acheron,

581 *knot*: league.   583 *confidence*: assurance.   585 *period*: sentence.
586 *for me*: for my part.   590 *enthrall'd*: enslaved.   591 'Even that
which Evil meant to harm most'.   592 *happy trial*: test which ends
happily. *prove*: achieve.   593–7 'Rebuffed by Goodness, Evil will
cease to interfere with it, but concentrating together in itself it will
exist in its own chaos'.   595 *settl'd to itself*: settling like dregs.
603 *legions*: three syllables.

Harpies and Hydras, or all the monstrous forms
'Twixt Africa and Ind, I'll find him out,
And force him to restore his purchase back,
Or drag him by the curls to a foul death,
Curs'd as his life.

Spirit.　　　　　　Alas, good venturous youth,
I love thy courage yet, and bold Emprise;　　　610
But here thy sword can do thee little stead;
Far other arms and other weapons must
Be those that quell the might of hellish charms.
He with his bare wand can unthread thy joints
And crumble all thy sinews.

Elder Brother.　　　　　Why, prithee Shepherd,
How durst thou then thyself approach so near
As to make this relation?

Spirit.　　　　　　　　Care and utmost shifts
How to secure the Lady from surprisal,
Brought to my mind a certain Shepherd Lad
Of small regard to see to, yet well skill'd　　　620
In every virtuous plant and healing herb
That spreads her verdant leaf to th' morning ray.
He lov'd me well, and oft would beg me sing;
Which when I did, he on the tender grass
Would sit and hearken e'en to ecstasy,
And in requital ope his leathern scrip
And show me simples of a thousand names,
Telling their strange and vigorous faculties.
Amongst the rest a small unsightly root,
But of divine effect, he cull'd me out;　　　630
The leaf was darkish, and had prickles on it,

607 *purchase*: booty.　　610 *yet*: nevertheless. *Emprise*: enterprise.
611 *stead*: service.　　617 *relation*: report.　　620 *regard*: importance.
to see to: to behold.　　621 *virtuous*: with beneficent powers.　　627
simples: herbal medicines.

But in another Country, as he said,
Bore a bright golden flow'r but not in this soil:
Unknown, and like esteem'd, and the dull swain
Treads on it daily with his clouted shoon;
And yet more med'cinal is it than that Moly
That Hermes once to wise Ulysses gave.
He call'd it Hæmony, and gave it me, *faith in God ? œe(n)*
And bade me keep it as of sovran use *grace (True)*
'Gainst all enchantments, mildew blast, or damp, 640
Or ghastly Furies' apparitïon.
I purs'd it up, but little reckoning made,
Till now that this extremity compell'd;
But now I find it true, for by this means
I knew the foul enchanter though disguis'd,
Enter'd the very lime-twigs of his spells,
And yet came off. If you have this about you
(As I will give you when we go) you may
Boldly assault the necromancer's hall;
Where if he be, with dauntless hardihood   650
And brandish'd blade rush on him, break his glass,
And shed the luscious liquor on the ground,
But seize his wand. Though he and his curs'd crew
Fierce sign of battle make and menace high,
Or like the sons of Vulcan vomit smoke,
Yet will they soon retire, if he but shrink.

Elder Brother. Thyrsis, lead on apace; I'll follow thee,
And some good angel bear a shield before us!

The Scene changes to a stately Palace, set out with all manner of *STAGE*
deliciousness: soft Music, Tables spread with all dainties. Comus *DIRECTION*

634 *like esteem'd*: likewise not esteemed.   635 *clouted*: probably has
two meanings, nailed (Fr. *clou*) and patched (M.E. *clouten*, to mend).
639 *sovran*: supremely effective.   640 *mildew blast*: blighting mil-
dew.   641 *Furies'*: evil spirits'.   642 *little reckoning made*: thought
(recked) little of it.   646 *lime-twigs*: traps, twigs smeared with lime
to catch birds.

appears with his rabble, and the Lady *set in an enchanted Chair; to whom he offers his Glass, which she puts by, and goes about to rise.*

Comus. Nay Lady, sit; if I but wave this wand,
  Your nerves are all chain'd up in Alablaster,   660
  And you a statue, or as Daphne was,
  Root-bound, that fled Apollo.

Lady.   Fool, do not boast;
  Thou canst not touch the freedom of my mind
  With all thy charms, although this corporal rind
  Thou hast immanacl'd, while Heav'n sees good.

Comus. Why are you vex'd, Lady? why do you frown?
  Here dwell no frowns, nor anger; from these gates
  Sorrow flies far. See, here be all the pleasures
  That fancy can beget on youthful thoughts,
  When the fresh blood grows lively, and returns   670
  Brisk as the April buds in Primrose-season.
  And first behold this cordial Julep here,
  That flames and dances in his crystal bounds
  With spirits of balm and fragrant Syrups mix'd.
  Not that Nepenthes which the wife of Thone
  In Egypt gave to Jove-born Helena
  Is of such power to stir up joy as this,
  To life so friendly, or so cool to thirst.
  Why should you be so cruel to yourself,
  And to those dainty limbs which Nature lent   680
  For gentle usage and soft delicacy?
  But you invert the cov'nants of her trust
  And harshly deal, like an ill borrower,
  With that which you receiv'd on other terms,

s.d. *puts by*: brushes aside. *goes about*: attempts.   660 *nerves*: sinews. *Alablaster*: alabaster, a white stone used for statues.   664 *corporal rind*: bodily shell.   665 *while*: so long as.   670 *returns*: revives.   672 *cordial*: invigorating. *Julep*: sweet drink (orig. rose-water).   673 *his*: its. *crystal bounds*: goblet.   682 'But you upset the conditions on which She lent them'.

Scorning the unexempt condition
By which all mortal frailty must subsist,
Refreshment after toil, ease after pain,
That have been tir'd all day without repast
And timely rest have wanted; but, fair Virgin,
This will restore all soon.

Lady.   'Twill not, false traitor!   690
'Twill not restore the truth and honesty
That thou hast banish'd from thy tongue with lies.
Was this the cottage and the safe abode
Thou told'st me of? What grim aspécts are these,
These ugly-headed Monsters? Mercy guard me!
Hence with thy brew'd enchantments, foul deceiver!
Hast thou betray'd my credulous innocence
With visor'd falsehood and base forgery,
And wouldst thou seek again to trap me here
With lickerish baits fit to ensnare a brute?   700
Were it a draught for Juno when she banquets,
I would not taste thy treasonous offer. None
But such as are good men can give good things,
And that which is not good is not delicious
To a well-govern'd and wise appetite.

Comus. O foolishness of men! that lend their ears
To those budge doctors of the Stoic Fur,
And fetch their precepts from the Cynic Tub,
Praising the lean and sallow Abstinence.
Wherefore did Nature pour her bounties forth   710
With such a full and unwithdrawing hand,
Covering the earth with odours, fruits, and flocks,
Thronging the Seas with spawn innumerable,
But all to please and sate the curious taste?

685 *unexempt condition*: condition from which nobody is released.
694 *aspécts*: faces. Stress on second syllable.   695 *ugly*: Milton has
'oughly'.   698 *visor'd*: masked. *forgery*: deceit.   700 *lickerish*: sen-
sual.   707 *budge*: solemn, formal.   714 *sate*: satiate. *curious*:
refined, critical.

95

And set to work millions of spinning Worms,
That in their green shops weave the smooth-hair'd silk
To deck her Sons; and that no corner might
Be vacant of her plenty, in her own loins
She hutch'd the all-worshipp'd ore and precious gems
To store her children with. If all the world   720
Should in a pet of temperance feed on Pulse,
Drink the clear stream, and nothing wear but Frieze,
Th' All-giver would be unthank'd, would be unprais'd,
Not half his riches known, and yet despis'd;
And we should serve him as a grudging master,
As a penurious niggard of his wealth,
And live like Nature's bastards, not her sons,
Who would be quite surcharg'd with her own weight,
And strangled with her waste fertility:
Th' earth cumber'd, and the wing'd air dark'd with
    plumes,   730
The herds would over-multitude their Lords,
The Sea o'erfraught would swell, and th' unsought
    diamonds
Would so emblaze the forehead of the Deep
And so bestud with Stars, that they below
Would grow inur'd to light, and come at last
To gaze upon the Sun with shameless brows.
List, Lady; be not coy, and be not cozen'd
With that same vaunted name, Virginity.
Beauty is Nature's coin, must not be hoarded,
But must be current, and the good thereof   740
Consists in mutual and partaken bliss,
Unsavoury in th' enjoyment of itself.

719 *hutch'd*: shut up, boxed.   721 *pet*: brief mood. *Pulse*: peas and
beans.   722 *Frieze*: coarse woollen cloth (orig. from Friesland).
727 'And live as if we were not Nature's legitimate heirs with a right
to use her wealth'.   728 *surcharg'd*: overburdened.   732 *o'erfraught*:
overstocked with fish.   733 *Deep*: centre of the earth.   734 *they
below*: creatures dwelling underground.   737 *cozen'd*: deceived.
740 *current*: in use.   742 *Unsavoury*: savourless, insipid.

Comus

If you let slip time, like a neglected rose
It withers on the stalk with languish'd head.
Beauty is Nature's brag, and must be shown *exactly what she is doing*
In courts, at feasts, and high solemnities,
Where most may wonder at the workmanship.
It is for homely features to keep home;
They had their name thence; coarse complexions
And cheeks of sorry grain will serve to ply   750
The sampler, and to tease the huswife's wool.
What need a vermeil-tinctur'd lip for that,
Love-darting eyes, or tresses like the Morn? *Misuse of rhetoric*
There was another meaning in these gifts; *et PL. Able to express*
Think what, and be advis'd; you are but young yet. *Persuasively views that he (Milton) detested*

Lady. I had not thought to have unlock'd my lips
In this unhallow'd air, but that this Juggler   *lofty rhetorical statement*
Would think to charm my judgment as mine eyes,
Obtruding false rules prank'd in reason's garb.
I hate when Vice can bolt her arguments,   760
And Virtue has no tongue to check her pride.
Impostor! do not charge most innocent Nature,
As if she would her children should be riotous
With her abundance. She, good cateress,
Means her provision only to the good,
That live according to her sober laws
And holy dictate of spare Temperance.
If every just man that now pines with want
Had but a moderate and beseeming share
Of that which lewdly-pamper'd Luxury   770
Now heaps upon some few with vast excess,
Nature's full blessings would be well dispens'd

746 *high solemnities*: stately ceremonies.   750 *grain*: hue (perhaps also 'texture').   751 *tease*: comb out.   752 *vermeil-tinctur'd*: red.
758 *as mine eyes*: as he did my eyes, when disguised.   759 *Obtruding*: advancing. *prank'd*: dressed up.   760 *bolt*: pick and choose ('to bolt' was to sift meal from bran in a flour-mill).   769 *beseeming*: fitting.
772 *dispens'd*: shared out.

Builds up character by devising occasions which call from his characters their most persuasive statements of their position.

Comus

In unsuperfluous even proportion,
And she no whit encumber'd with her store;
And then the Giver would be better thank'd,
His praise due paid; for swinish gluttony
Ne'er looks to Heav'n amidst his gorgeous feast,
But with besotted base ingratitude
Crams, and blasphemes his feeder. Shall I go on?
Or have I said enough? To him that dares   780
Arm his profane tongue with contemptuous words
Against the Sun-clad power of Chastity, *Circe - daughter*
Fain would I something say, yet to what end? *of the sun*
Thou hast not Ear nor Soul to apprehend
The sublime notion, and high mystery
That must be utter'd to unfold the sage
And serious doctrine of Virginity;
And thou art worthy that thou shouldst not know
More happiness than this thy present lot.
Enjoy your dear Wit and gay Rhetoric   790
That hath so well been taught her dazzling fence;
Thou art not fit to hear thyself convinc'd:
Yet should I try, the uncontrolled worth
Of this pure cause would kindle my rapt spirits
To such a flame of sacred vehemence
That dumb things would be mov'd to sympathize,
And the brute Earth would lend her nerves, and shake,
Till all thy magic structures rear'd so high
Were shatter'd into heaps o'er thy false head.

Comus. She fables not; I feel that I do fear   800
Her words, set off by some superior power;
And though not mortal, yet a cold shudd'ring dew
Dips me all o'er, as when the wrath of Jove
Speaks thunder, and the chains of Erebus

774 'And she would in no way be glutted with her own abundance'.
779 *Crams*: gorges himself.   785 *mystery*: hidden wisdom.   791
fence: verbal duelling.   793 *uncontrolled*: irrepressible.   797 *brute*:
dull.   800 *fables not*: tells no lie.   801 *set off*: supported.

98

To some of Saturn's crew. I must dissemble,
And try her yet more strongly.—Come, no more!
This is mere moral babble, and direct
Against the canon laws of our foundation;
I must not suffer this; yet 'tis but the lees
And settlings of a melancholy blood.   810
But this will cure all straight; one sip of this
Will bathe the drooping spirits in delight
Beyond the bliss of dreams. Be wise, and taste.

The Brothers *rush in with Swords drawn, wrest his Glass out of his
hand, and break it against the ground; his rout make sign of resistance,
but are all driven in; The* Attendant Spirit *comes in.*

Spirit. What? have you let the false enchanter scape?
    O, ye mistook; ye should have snatch'd his wand,
    And bound him fast; without his rod revers'd
    And backward mutters of dissevering power,
    We cannot free the Lady that sits here
    In stony fetters fix'd and motionless.
    Yet stay, be not disturb'd; now I bethink me,   820
    Some other means I have which may be us'd,
    Which once of Meliboeus old I learnt,
    The soothest Shepherd that e'er pip'd on plains.
        There is a gentle Nymph not far from hence,
    That with moist curb sways the smooth Severn stream;
    Sabrina is her name, a Virgin pure;
    Whilom she was the daughter of Locrine,
    That had the Sceptre from his father Brute.
    She, guiltless damsel, flying the mad pursuit
    Of her enraged stepdame, Guendolen,   830
    Commended her fair innocence to the flood
    That stay'd her flight with his cross-flowing course.
    The water-Nymphs that in the bottom play'd

808 *canon laws*: laws of our (ungodly) church.   816–17 'Without
reversing his magic wand and saying his charms backwards so as to
undo their spell'.   823 *soothest*: most truthful.

99

Held up their pearled wrists and took her in,
Bearing her straight to aged Nereus' Hall,
Who, piteous of her woes, rear'd her lank head,
And gave her to his daughters to imbathe
In nectar'd lavers strew'd with Asphodil,
And through the porch and inlet of each sense
Dropp'd in Ambrosial Oils, till she reviv'd   840
And underwent a quick immortal change,
Made Goddess of the River. Still she retains
Her maiden gentleness, and oft at Eve
Visits the herds along the twilight meadows,
Helping all urchin blasts and ill-luck signs *comm' p only.*
That the shrewd meddling Elf delights to make,
Which she with precious vial'd liquors heals.
For which the Shepherds at their festivals
Carol her goodness loud in rustic lays,
And throw sweet garland wreaths into her stream   850
Of pansies, pinks, and gaudy Daffodils.
And, as the old Swain said, she can unlock
The clasping charm, and thaw the numbing spell,
If she be right invok'd in warbled Song;
For maidenhood she loves and will be swift
To aid a Virgin, such as was herself,
In hard-besetting need. This will I try
And add the power of some adjuring verse.

SONG

> *Sabrina fair,*
> *Listen where thou art sitting*   860
> *Under the glassy, cool, translucent wave,*
> *In twisted braids of Lilies knitting*
> *The loose train of thy amber-dropping hair;*

836 *lank*: drooping.   838 *lavers*: baths, bowls for washing.   841
immortal change: change to immortality.   845 *urchin blasts*: evil blights.
See Commentary.   846 *shrewd*: malicious.   852 *the old Swain*:
Melibœus.   858 *adjuring*: invoking her to come.   863 *amber-dropping
hair*: yellow hair which seems like scattered amber as it flows loosely.

Comus

Listen for dear honour's sake,
Goddess of the silver lake,
Listen and save!

Listen and appear to us
In the name of great Oceanus;
By the earth-shaking Neptune's mace,
And Tethys' grave majestic pace;   870
By hoary Nereus' wrinkled look
And the Carpathian wizard's hook;
By scaly Triton's winding shell
And old soothsaying Glaucus' spell;
By Leucothea's lovely hands
And her son that rules the strands;
By Thetis' tinsel-slipper'd feet
And the songs of Sirens sweet;
By dead Parthenope's dear tomb,
And fair Ligea's golden comb,   880
Wherewith she sits on diamond rocks
Sleeking her soft alluring locks;
By all the Nymphs that nightly dance
Upon thy streams with wily glance,
Rise, rise, and heave thy rosy head
From thy coral-paven bed,
And bridle in thy headlong wave,
Till thou our summons answer'd have.
          Listen and save!

Sabrina *rises, attended by water-Nymphs, and sings.*

> *By the rushy-fringed bank,*   890
> *Where grows the Willow and the Osier dank,*
> *My sliding Chariot stays,*
> *Thick set with Agate and the azurn sheen*
> *Of Turkis blue and Emerald green,*

864 *honour's*: purity's.   868–84 See Commentary for these water-
deities.   894 *Turkis*: turquoise.

Comus

That in the channel strays;
Whilst from off the waters fleet
Thus I set my printless feet
O'er the Cowslip's Velvet head,
That bends not as I tread.
Gentle swain, at thy request   900
I am here!

Spirit. Goddess dear,
We implore thy powerful hand
To undo the charmed band
Of true Virgin here distrest,
Through the force and through the wile
Of unblest enchanter vile.

Sabrina. Shepherd, 'tis my office best
To help ensnared chastity;
Brightest Lady, look on me: 910
Thus I sprinkle on thy breast
Drops that from my fountain pure
I have kept of precious cure;
Thrice upon thy finger's tip,
Thrice upon thy rubied lip.
Next this marble venom'd seat
Smear'd with gums of glutinous heat
I touch with chaste palms moist and cold.
Now the spell hath lost his hold;
And I must haste ere morning hour   920
To wait in Amphitrite's bower.

"The transit" from a restrictive state of virtue to a positive one is worked out concretely in the poetry"

Sabrina descends, and the Lady *rises out of her seat.*

Clarke

Spirit. Virgin, daughter of Locrine,
Sprung of old Anchises' line,
May thy brimmed waves for this
Their full tribute never miss

897 *printless*: which leave no footprint.   904 *band*: bondage.   916
venom'd seat: the 'enchanted Chair' of the stage direction preceding 659.

"to transform chastity into a positive virtue, a principle of act", not in nature, but in grace?

102

Comus

From a thousand petty rills
That tumble down the snowy hills:
Summer drouth or singed air
Never scorch thy tresses fair,
Nor wet October's torrent flood   930
Thy molten crystal fill with mud;
May thy billows roll ashore
The beryl and the golden ore;
May thy lofty head be crown'd
With many a tower and terrace round,
And here and there thy banks upon
With Groves of myrrh and cinnamon.
   Come Lady, while Heaven lends us grace,
Let us fly this cursed place,
Lest the Sorcerer us entice   940
With some other new device.
Not a waste or needless sound
Till we come to holier ground.
I shall be your faithful guide
Through this gloomy covert wide;
And not many furlongs thence
Is your Father's residence,
Where this night are met in state
Many a friend to gratulate
His wish'd presence, and beside   950
All the Swains that there abide,
With Jigs and rural dance resort.
We shall catch them at their sport,
And our sudden coming there
Will double all their mirth and cheer.
Come let us haste; the Stars grow high,
But Night sits monarch yet in the mid-sky. *Comus' time.*

928 *singed*: scorching.   931 *molten*: liquid.   933 *beryl*: a green,
blue, or yellow crystal.   934 *lofty head*: two meanings (i) mountain
source (ii) the goddess's head, crowned like Cybele's (cf. *Arc.* 21).
949 *gratulate*: give thanks for.   952 *Jigs*: comic dialogues with music
and dancing.

Comus

The Scene changes, presenting Ludlow town and the President's Castle; then come in Country Dancers; after them the Attendant Spirit, *with the two* Brothers *and the* Lady.

SONG

[margin note: true masque ending]

Spirit. *Back, shepherds, back! enough your play* *[margin note: typically Milton]*
　Till next Sunshine holiday.
　Here be, without duck or nod,　　　　　　　　960
　Other trippings to be trod
　Of lighter toes, and such Court guise
　As Mercury did first devise
　With the mincing Dryades
　On the Lawns and on the Leas.

This second Song presents them to their Father and Mother.

　Noble Lord, and Lady bright,
　I have brought ye new delight:
　Here behold so goodly grown
　Three fair branches of your own.
　Heav'n hath timely tried their youth,　　　970
　Their faith, their patience, and their truth,
　And sent them here through hard assays
　With a crown of deathless Praise,
　To triumph in victorious dance
　O'er sensual Folly and Intemperance. *[margin note: Innocent mirth]*

The dances ended, the Spirit *Epiloguizes.*

Spirit. To the Ocean now I fly,
　And those happy climes that lie
　Where day never shuts his eye,
　Up in the broad fields of the sky:
　There I suck the liquid air　　　　　　980
　All amidst the Gardens fair

960 *duck and nod*: rustic equivalents of curtsey and bow.　964 *mincing*: neat-footed.　965 *Leas*: meadows.　970 *timely*: betimes, early.
972 *assays*: trials.　977 *happy climes*: heavenly regions.

Of Hesperus, and his daughters three
That sing about the golden tree:
Along the crisped shades and bowers
Revels the spruce and jocund Spring;
The Graces and the rosy-bosom'd Hours
Thither all their bounties bring.
There eternal Summer dwells,
And West winds with musky wing
About the cedarn alleys fling   990
Nard, and Cassia's balmy smells.
Iris there with humid bow
Waters the odorous banks that blow
Flowers of more mingled hue
Than her purfled scarf can shew;
And drenches with Elysian dew
(List mortals, if your ears be true) *SPIRITUAL MEANING*
Beds of Hyacinth and Roses,
Where young Adonis oft reposes, *of Spenser — Life originates here*
Waxing well of his deep wound   1000
In slumber soft, and on the ground
Sadly sits th'Assyrian Queen. *Venus = earth in mythography*
But far above in spangled sheen
Celestial Cupid, her fam'd son, advanc'd, *Son of earth = Son of man?*
Holds his dear Psyche sweet entranc'd *Soul*
After her wand'ring labours long,
Till free consent the gods among
Make her his eternal Bride, *Ideal of Comus in its*
And from her fair unspotted side *final version is marriage*
Two blissful twins are to be born, *Is there any* 1010
Youth and Joy; so Jove hath sworn. *contradict w this r Lady's*
   But now my task is smoothly done, *doctrine of Virginity 787*
I can fly, or I can run *opposed to the*
pure joy — as
Comus variety

984 *crisped*: curly. 985 *spruce*: trim. 989 *musky*: perfumed.
991 *Nard and Cassia*: sweet spices. 993 *blow*: blossom with. 995
purfled: embroidered at the edge. 997 *true*: attuned (cf. *Arc.* 72).
1004 *advanc'd*: lifted up.

Comus

Quickly to the green earth's end,
Where the bow'd welkin slow doth bend,
And from thence can soar as soon
To the corners of the Moon.
    Mortals that would follow me,
Love Virtue; she alone is free,
She can teach ye how to climb   1020
Higher than the Sphery chime;
Or, if Virtue feeble were,
Heav'n itself would stoop to her.

Miltonic moral. [margin annotation]

1015 *bow'd welkin*: arched vault of heaven.   1017 *corners*: horns.
1021 *Sphery chime*: spheres and their music.

THE END

Freshness, variety, sureness of touch, mastery of different tones show how far Milton had gone in developing high technical skill. [handwritten annotation]

SAMSON AGONISTES,

A

DRAMATIC POEM.

The Author
JOHN MILTON.

Aristot. Poet. Cap. 6.

Τραγῳδία μίμησις πράξεως σπουδαίας, &c.

Tragœdia est imitatio actionis seriæ, &c. *Per misericordiam &*
metum perficiens talium affectuum lustrationem.

LONDON,

Printed by *J. M.* for *John Starkey* at the
Mitre in *Fleetstreet,* near *Temple-Bar.*
MDCLXXI.

I

Of that sort of Dramatic Poem which is called Tragedy

Tragedy, as it was anciently compos'd, hath been
ever held the gravest, moralest, and most profitable
of all other Poems: therefore said by Aristotle to be
of power by raising pity and fear, or terror, to
purge the mind of those and such like passions—
that is, to temper and reduce them to just measure
with a kind of delight, stirr'd up by reading or
seeing those passions well imitated. Nor is Nature
wanting in her own effects to make good his asser-
tion: for so in Physic things of melancholic hue and
quality are us'd against melancholy, sour against
sour, salt to remove salt humours. Hence Philoso-
phers and other gravest Writers, as Cicero, Plu-
tarch, and others, frequently cite out of Tragic
Poets, both to adorn and illustrate their discourse.
The Apostle Paul himself thought it not unworthy
to insert a verse of Euripides into the Text of Holy
Scripture, 1 *Cor.* xv. 33; and Paræus, commenting
on the *Revelation*, divides the whole Book as a
Tragedy, into Acts, distinguish'd each by a Chorus
of Heavenly Harpings and Song between. Here-
tofore Men in highest dignity have labour'd not a
little to be thought able to compose a Tragedy. Of
that honour Dionysius the elder was no less am-
bitious, than before of his attaining to the Tyranny.
Augustus Cæsar also had begun his *Ajax*, but
unable to please his own judgment with what he
had begun, left it unfinish'd. Seneca the Philo-

sopher is by some thought the Author of those
Tragedies (at least the best of them) that go under   30
that name. Gregory Nazianzen, a Father of the
Church, thought it not unbeseeming the sanctity of
his person to write a Tragedy, which he entitl'd,
Christ Suffering. This is mention'd to vindicate
Tragedy from the small esteem, or rather infamy,
which in the account of many it undergoes at this
day with other common Interludes; happ'ning
through the Poet's error of intermixing Comic
stuff with Tragic sadness and gravity; or introdu-
cing trivial and vulgar persons: which by all   40
judicious hath been counted absurd, and brought
in without discretion, corruptly to gratify the
people. And though ancient Tragedy use no Pro-
logue, yet using sometimes, in case of self-defence,
or explanation, that which Martial calls an Epistle,
in behalf of this Tragedy, coming forth after the
ancient manner, much different from what among
us passes for best, thus much beforehand may be
Epistled, that Chorus is here introduc'd after the
Greek manner, not ancient only but modern, and   50
still in use among the Italians. In the modelling
therefore of this Poem, with good reason, the
Ancients and Italians are rather follow'd, as of
much more authority and fame. The measure of
Verse us'd in the Chorus is of all sorts, called by the
Greeks *Monostrophic,* or rather *Apolelymenon,* without
regard had to Strophe, Antistrophe, or Epode,
which were a kind of Stanzas fram'd only for the
Music, then us'd with the Chorus that sung; not
essential to the Poem, and therefore not material: 60
or, being divided into Stanzas or Pauses, they may
be call'd *Allæostropha.* Division into Act and Scene,
referring chiefly to the Stage (to which this work
never was intended), is here omitted.

Samson Agonistes

It suffices if the whole Drama be found not pro-
duc'd beyond the fifth Act. Of the style and
uniformity, and that commonly call'd the Plot,
whether intricate or explicit,—which is nothing
indeed but such economy, or disposition of the
70   fable, as may stand best with verisimilitude and
decorum,—they only will best judge who are not
unacquainted with Æschylus, Sophocles, and
Euripides, the three Tragic Poets unequall'd yet
by any, and the best rule to all who endeavour to
write Tragedy. The circumscription of time
wherein the whole Drama begins and ends, is
according to ancient rule and best example, within
the space of twenty-four hours.

Samson, made Captive, Blind, and now in the Prison at Gaza, there to labour as in a common work-house, on a Festival day, in the general cessation from labour, comes forth into the open Air, to a place nigh, somewhat retir'd, there to sit a while and bemoan his condition. Where he happens at length to be visited by certain friends and equals of his tribe, which make the Chorus, who seek to comfort him what they can; then by his old Father, Manoa, who endeavours the like, and withal tells him his purpose to procure his liberty by ransom; lastly, that this Feast was proclaim'd by the Philistines as a day of Thanksgiving for their deliverance from the hands of Samson— which yet more troubles him. Manoa then departs to prosecute his endeavour with the Philistian Lords for Samson's redemption: who in the meanwhile is visited by other persons, and lastly by a public Officer to require his coming to the Feast before the Lords and People, to play or show his strength in their presence. He at first refuses, dismissing the public Officer with absolute denial to come; at length persuaded inwardly that this was from God, he yields to go along with him, who came now the second time with great threatenings to fetch him. The Chorus yet remaining on the place, Manoa returns full of joyful hope to procure ere long his Son's deliverance; in the midst of which discourse an Ebrew comes in haste, confusedly at first, and afterward more distinctly relating the Catastrophe,—what Samson had done to the Philistines, and by accident to himself; wherewith the Tragedy ends.

"DECORUM IS THE GRAND MASTERPIECE."

THE PERSONS

Samson
Manoa the Father of Samson
Dalila his Wife
Harapha of Gath
Public Officer
Messenger
Chorus of Danites

The scene before the prison in Gaza

Agonistes — means he's in action, also God's champion.
Can't be a chronicle ∴ Unity of Time.
    But how to show he's a tragic hero? Brings his death. B
move — Milton emphasises other things.

The impatience, the humiliation, the questionings of Providenc
go into Samson ∴ the business of tragedy is "by raising
pity & fear, or terror, to purge the mind of those &
such-like passions .... with a kind of delight stirred w
by reading or seeing those passions well imitated.

Samson Agonistes
[handwritten:] Prologue in Gk tragedy ⟶ l. 112.

[handwritten left margin:] why subjective and confused.

Samson. A little onward lend thy guiding hand
To these dark steps, a little further on;
For yonder bank hath choice of Sun or shade.
There I am wont to sit, when any chance
Relieves me from my task of servile toil,
Daily in the common Prison else enjoin'd me,
Where I, a Prisoner chain'd, scarce freely draw
The air imprison'd also, close and damp,
Unwholesome draught: but here I feel amends,
The breath of Heav'n fresh-blowing, pure and sweet,   10
With day-spring born; here leave me to respire.
This day a solemn Feast the people hold
To Dagon their Sea-Idol, and forbid
Laborious works. Unwillingly this rest
Their Superstition yields me; hence with leave
Retiring from the popular noise, I seek
This unfrequented place, to find some ease—
Ease to the body some, none to the mind
From restless thoughts, that like a deadly swarm
Of Hornets arm'd, no sooner found alone,   20
But rush upon me thronging, and present
Times past, what once I was, and what am now.
O wherefore was my birth from Heaven foretold
Twice by an Angel, who at last in sight
Of both my Parents all in flames ascended

[handwritten margin notes:] Sensible ⟶ subjective current about blind. TRAGIC HERO. Prepares audience for catastrophe

2 *dark steps*: blind footsteps.   6 *else enjoin'd*: otherwise enforced on.
11 *day-spring*: day-break (Luke i. 78).   *respire*: breathe freely.   15
Superstition: false religion.   16 *popular*: people's.   20–1 *no . . . But*:
'no sooner do my thoughts find me alone than they . . .'

H   113

From off the Altar, where an Offering burn'd,
As in a fiery column charioting
His Godlike presence, and from some great act
Or benefit reveal'd to Abraham's race?
Why was my breeding order'd and prescrib'd   30
As of a person separate to God,
Design'd for great exploits, if I must die
Betray'd, Captiv'd, and both my Eyes put out,
Made of my Enemies the scorn and gaze,
To grind in Brazen Fetters under task
With this Heav'n-gifted strength? O glorious strength,
Put to the labour of a Beast, debas'd
Lower than bond-slave! Promise was that I
Should Israel from Philistian yoke deliver;
Ask for this great Deliverer now, and find him   40
Eyeless in Gaza at the Mill with slaves,
Himself in bonds under Philistian yoke.
Yet stay; let me not rashly call in doubt
Divine Prediction; what if all foretold
Had been fulfill'd but through mine own default?
Whom have I to complain of but myself,
Who this high gift of strength committed to me,
In what part lodg'd, how easily bereft me,
Under the Seal of silence could not keep,
But weakly to a woman must reveal it,   50
O'ercome with importunity and tears?
O impotence of mind in body strong!
But what is strength without a double share
Of wisdom? vast, unwieldy, burdensome,
Proudly secure, yet liable to fall

28 *and from*: and as if he had.   29 *reveal'd*: prophesied.   31
separate: set apart, dedicated.   34 *gaze*: public spectacle.   35 *under
task*: with a fixed amount of work.   47–9 'could not keep my oath
never to tell where my strength was stored, and how easily it could be
stolen from me'.   50 *woman*: i.e. Dalila.   55 *secure*: careless
(L. *securus*).

114

By weakest subtleties; not made to rule,
But to subserve where wisdom bears command.
God, when he gave me strength, to show withal
How slight the gift was, hung it in my Hair.
But peace! I must not quarrel with the will   60
Of highest dispensation, which herein
Haply had ends above my reach to know:
Suffices that to me strength is my bane,
And proves the source of all my miseries;
So many, and so huge, that each apart
Would ask a life to wail; but chief of all,
O loss of sight, of thee I most complain!
Blind among enemies! O worse than chains,
Dungeon, or beggary, or decrepit age!
Light, the prime work of God, to me is extinct,   70
And all her various objects of delight
Annull'd, which might in part my grief have eas'd,
Inferior to the vilest now become
Of man or worm; the vilest here excel me:
They creep, yet see; I, dark in light, expos'd
To daily fraud, contempt, abuse, and wrong,
Within doors, or without, still as a fool,
In power of others, never in my own;
Scarce half I seem to live, dead more than half.
O dark, dark, dark, amid the blaze of noon,   80
Irrecoverably dark, total Eclipse
Without all hope of day!
O first created Beam, and thou great Word,
'Let there be light, and light was over all,'
Why am I thus bereav'd thy prime decree?
The Sun to me is dark

57 *subserve*: be subordinate.   61 *highest dispensation*: Divine Provi-
dence, disposal (cf. 210).   62 *Haply*: 1671 edn. has 'Happ'ly'.
63 *Suffices*: It suffices.   66 *wail*: bewail.   70 *prime work*: first
creation.   73 *vilest*: lowest.   74 *here*: in having sight.   77 *still . . .
fool*: always treated like an idiot.

Samson Agonistes

And silent as the Moon,
When she deserts the night,
Hid in her vacant interlunar cave.
Since light so necessary is to life,   90
And almost life itself, if it be true
That light is in the Soul,
She all in every part; why was the sight
To such a tender ball as th' eye confin'd,
So obvious and so easy to be quench'd,
And not, as feeling, through all parts diffus'd,
That she might look at will through every pore?
Then had I not been thus exil'd from light,
As in the land of darkness, yet in light,
To live a life half dead, a living death,   100
And buried; but, O yet more miserable!
Myself my Sepulchre, a moving Grave;
Buried, yet not exempt
By privilege of death and burial
From worst of other evils, pains and wrongs;
Yet will not leave But made hereby obnoxious more
To all the miseries of life,
Life in captivity
Among inhuman foes.
Fear of being laughed at – blind among his enemies – helplessness But who are these? for with joint pace I hear *hear chorus* 110
The tread of many feet steering this way;
Perhaps my enemies, who come to stare
At my affliction, and perhaps to insult—
Their daily practice to afflict me more.
?andos – gets them on to the slope *Chorus*. This, this is he; softly a while;
Let us not break in upon him.
O change beyond report, thought, or belief!

89 *vacant*: two senses (i) void of light (ii) when the moon is at leisure
(on vacation!). *interlunar*: between the end of the old moon and the
coming of the new.   95 *obvious*: exposed (L. *obvius*, in the way).
96 *as*: like.   106 *obnoxious*: open, exposed (to injury).   113 *insult*:
exult arrogantly (L. *insultare*).

See how he lies at random, carelessly diffus'd,
With languish'd head unpropt,
As one past hope, abandon'd,   120
And by himself given over;
In slavish habit, ill-fitted weeds
O'er-worn and soil'd.
Or do my eyes misrepresent? Can this be he,
That Heroic, that Renown'd,
Irresistible Samson? whom unarm'd
No strength of man, or fiercest wild beast, could with-
        stand;
Who tore the Lion as the Lion tears the Kid;
Ran on embattl'd Armies clad in Iron,
And, weaponless himself,   130
Made Arms ridiculous, useless the forgery
Of brazen shield and spear, the hammer'd Cuirass,
Chalybean-temper'd steel, and frock of mail
Adamantean Proof;
But safest he who stood aloof,
When insupportably his foot advanc'd,
In scorn of their proud arms and warlike tools,
Spurn'd them to death by Troops. The bold Ascalonite
Fled from his Lion ramp, old Warriors turn'd
Their plated backs under his heel,   140
Or grovelling soil'd their crested helmets in the dust.
Then with what trivial weapon came to hand,
The Jaw of a dead Ass, his sword of bone,
A thousand fore-skins fell, the flower of Palestine,   Violence
In Ramath-lechi, famous to this day:
Then by main force pull'd up, and on his shoulders bore,

118 *at random*: in disorder. *diffus'd*: stretched out.   119 *languish'd*:
drooping. *unpropt*: not held erect.   122 *habit*: *weeds*: clothes.
129 *embattl'd*: in battle order.   131 *forgery*: two senses (i) forging
of metal (ii) pretence.   134 *Adamantean Proof*: impenetrable as
adamant.   136 *insupportably*: irresistibly.   139 *ramp*: rage.   *old*:
experienced.   144 *fore-skins*: the uncircumcised Philistines.

[handwritten top margin: Changeableness of Fortune .: Pathetic. / Free verse - not as onomatopoeic as Lawrence - have more dignit[y] / Effect - v. different to P.L.]

Samson Agonistes

The gates of Azza, Post and massy Bar,
Up to the hill by Hebron, seat of Giants old—
No journey of a Sabbath-day, and loaded so—
Like whom the Gentiles feign to bear up Heav'n.   150
Which shall I first bewail,
Thy Bondage or lost Sight,
Prison within Prison
Inseparably dark?
Thou art become (O worst imprisonment!)
The Dungeon of thyself; thy Soul,
(Which Men enjoying sight oft without cause complain)
Imprison'd now indeed,
In real darkness of the body dwells,
Shut up from outward light   160
To incorporate with gloomy night;
For inward light, alas!
Puts forth no visual beam.
O mirror of our fickle state,
Since man on earth unparallel'd!
The rarer thy example stands,
By how much from the top of wondrous glory,
Strongest of mortal men,
To lowest pitch of abject fortune thou art fall'n.
For him I reckon not in high estate   170
Whom long descent of birth
Or the sphere of fortune raises;
But thee, whose strength, while virtue was her mate,
Might have subdu'd the Earth, *[handwritten: Tragic flaw too]*
Universally crown'd with highest praises.

Samson. I hear the sound of words; their sense the air

[handwritten left margin: Can only appro... indirectly - has cut himself off from the classical allusions. / He's got people of the period talking -... different range from P.L. V. different character though some of the subjects are similar. Someone has sinned]

[handwritten bottom left: First Episode begins - Conversat between Samson & the Chorus]

161 *incorporate with*: become one (body) with.   163 *visual beam*: light to the eyes.   164–5 'Since man came on earth there was never so perfect a reflection (example) of our mutable condition'. 166–9 'You provide a rarer lesson because you have fallen from so high a summit . . . to the lowest depth of fortune'.   173 'But you I regard as having been supremely fortunate whose . . .'   175 '(And been) universally . . .'

[handwritten bottom: Episode = conversat between 2/3 characters on stage]

118

Dissolves unjointed ere it reach my ear.

Chorus. He speaks; let us draw nigh. Matchless in might,
The glory late of Israel, now the grief;
We come, thy friends and neighbours not unknown,   180
From Eshtaol and Zora's fruitful Vale,
To visit or bewail thee; or, if better,
Counsel or Consolation we may bring,
Salve to thy Sores; apt words have power to swage
The tumours of a troubl'd mind,
And are as Balm to fester'd wounds.

Samson. Your coming, Friends, revives me, for I learn
Now of my own experience, not by talk,
How counterfeit a coin they are who 'friends'
Bear in their Superscription (of the most   190
I would be understood). In prosperous days
They swarm, but in adverse withdraw their head,
Not to be found, though sought. Ye see, O friends,
How many evils have enclos'd me round;
Yet that which was the worst now least afflicts me,
Blindness; for had I sight, confus'd with shame,
How could I once look up, or heave the head,
Who like a foolish Pilot have shipwrack'd
My Vessel trusted to me from above,
Gloriously rigg'd, and for a word, a tear,   200
Fool! I have divulg'd the secret gift of God
To a deceitful Woman? Tell me, Friends,
Am I not sung and proverb'd for a Fool
In every street? Do they not say, 'How well
Are come upon him his deserts'? Yet why?
Immeasurable strength they might behold
In me; of wisdom nothing more than mean;

177 *unjointed*: brokenly.   184 *swage*: assuage.   189–90 'who
write themselves down as friends' (like the inscription round a coin).
190–1 (*of . . . understood*): 'I mean this of most men, not all'.   196
confus'd: '(I being) confused'.   203 *proverb'd for*: made a by-word as.
207 *mean*: average.

[Margin annotations:] CHANGE - now he has an audience. Feels the desert of friends. Blames himself - now it is not his blindness but his shame that he finds so dread. Sea

This with the other should at least have pair'd;
These two, proportion'd ill, drove me transverse.

Chorus. Tax not divine disposal; wisest Men   210
Have err'd, and by bad Women been deceiv'd;
And shall again, pretend they ne'er so wise.
Deject not then so overmuch thyself,
Who hast of sorrow thy full load besides;
Yet truth to say, I oft have heard men wonder
Why thou should'st wed <u>Philistian women</u> rather
Than of thine own Tribe fairer, or as fair,
At least of thy own Nation, and as noble.

Samson. The first I saw at Timna, and she pleas'd
Me, not my Parents, that I sought to wed   220
The daughter of an Infidel: they knew not
That what I motion'd was of God; I knew
From intimate impulse, and therefore urg'd
The Marriage on, that by occasion hence
I might begin Israel's Deliverance,
The work to which I was divinely call'd.
She proving false, the next I took to Wife
(O that I never had! fond wish too late!)
Was in the Vale of Sorec, Dálila,
That specious Monster, my <u>accomplish'd</u> snare.   230
I thought it lawful from my former act,
And the same end, <u>still watching to oppress
Israel's oppressors.</u> Of what now I suffer

208 *pair'd*: been equal.   209 *transverse*: off my course.   210 *Tax*: find fault with.   212 *pretend they*: though they claim to be. 213 *Deject*: cast down.   217–18 'Than women of your own tribe who are more or equally beautiful, or if not, at least of Israelite race and not barbarians'.   221 *Infidel*: unbeliever.   222 *motion'd*: purposed.   223 *intimate*: inner.   224 *by occasion hence*: by some opportunity thus afforded.   228 *fond*: foolish.   229 *Dálila*: accent on first syllable.   230 *specious*: deceptively attractive. *accomplish'd*: skilled and completely effective.   231–3 *I thought . . . oppressors*: 'I thought it lawful since I had done it before, and since my aim was the same (to injure the Philistines)'.

Samson Agonistes

She was not the prime cause, but I myself,
Who, vanquish'd with a peal of words (O weakness!),
Gave up my fort of silence to a Woman.

Chorus. In seeking just occasion to provoke
The Philistine, thy Country's Enemy,
Thou never wast remiss, I bear thee witness:
Yet Israel still serves with all his Sons.   240

Samson. That fault I take not on me, but transfer
On Israel's Governors and Heads of Tribes,
Who, seeing those great acts which God had done
Singly by me against their Conquerors,
Acknowledg'd not, or not at all consider'd,
Deliverance offer'd: I on th' other side
Us'd no ambition to commend my deeds;
The deeds themselves, though mute, spoke loud the doer;
But they persisted deaf, and would not seem
To count them things worth notice, till at length   250
Their Lords the Philistines with gather'd powers
Entered Judea seeking me, who then
Safe to the rock of Etham was retir'd,
Not flying, but forecasting in what place
To set upon them, what advantag'd best.
Meanwhile the men of Judah, to prevent
The harass of their Land, beset me round.
I willingly on some conditions came
Into their hands, and they as gladly yield me
To the uncircumcis'd a welcome prey,   260
Bound with two cords; but cords to me were threads
Touch'd with the flame: on their whole Host I flew
Unarm'd, and with a trivial weapon fell'd

235 *peal*: volley (like artillery firing at a fort). 236 *fort*: two senses
(i) stronghold (ii) strength. 237 *provoke*: challenge (L. *provocare*).
240 *still serves*: is still under the Philistine's yoke. 244 *Singly*: single
handed. 245 *consider'd*: valued. 247 *ambition*: canvassing (L.
ambitus, going round to get votes). 251 *powers*: armies. 254 *fore-casting*: planning. 261 *threads*: (like) threads.

Violence

Their choicest youth; they only liv'd who fled.
Had Judah that day join'd, or one whole Tribe,
They had by this possess'd the Towers of Gath,
And lorded over them whom now they serve.
But what more oft, in Nations grown corrupt,
And by their vices brought to servitude,
Than to love Bondage more than Liberty,   270
Bondage with ease than strenuous liberty;
And to despise, or envy, or suspect
Whom God hath of his special favour rais'd
As their Deliverer? If he aught begin,
How frequent to desert him, and at last
To heap ingratitude on worthiest deeds!

Written after the Restorat" – polit-ical significance.

Chorus. Thy words to my remembrance bring
How Succoth and the Fort of Penuel
Their great Deliverer contemn'd,
The matchless Gideon, in pursuit   280
Of Madian, and her vanquish'd Kings:
And how ingrateful Ephraim
Had dealt with Jephtha, who by argument,
Not worse than by his shield and spear,
Defended Israel from the Ammonite,
Had not his prowess quell'd their pride
In that sore battle when so many died
Without Reprieve, adjudg'd to death
For want of well pronouncing *Shibboleth*.

Samson. Of such examples add me to the roll.   290
Me easily indeed mine may neglect,
But God's propos'd deliverance not so.

ode – stasimon sung by chorus between episodes

Chorus. Just are the ways of God, *cf. P.L.*
And justifiable to Men;
Unless there be who think not God at all.

266 *this*: this time.   268 *more oft*: is more frequent.   275 *How
frequent to*: how often they.   291 *mine*: my people.   292 *not so*: not
so easily.   295 *who . . . God*: some who think there is no God.

122

"The Fear of the Lord is the beginning of Wisdom".

If any be, they walk obscure;
For of such Doctrine never was there School,
But the heart of the Fool,
And no man therein Doctor but himself.
Yet more there be who doubt his ways not just,   300
As to his own edicts found contradicting;
Then give the reins to wand'ring thought,
Regardless of his glory's diminution;
Till, by their own perplexities involv'd,
They ravel more, still less resolv'd,
But never find self-satisfying solution.
As if they would confine th' Interminable,
And tie him to his own prescript,
Who made our Laws to bind us, not himself,
And hath full right to exempt
Whomso it pleases him by choice
From National obstriction, without taint
Of sin, or legal debt;
For with his own Laws he can best dispense.

God's right to exempt   310 chosen individuals from moral precepts.

He would not else, who never wanted means,
Nor in respect of the enemy just cause,
To set his people free,
Have prompted this Heroic Nazarite,
Against his vow of strictest purity,
To seek in marriage that fallacious Bride,   320
Unclean, unchaste.
Down Reason, then; at least, vain reasonings down;

296 *obscure*: in darkness.   297 'For there was never any organised philosophical group of Atheists'.   299 *Doctor*: learned master, teacher.   300 'But there are more who are uncertain whether his ways are just or not'.   301 'Considering the contradictions they find in his laws'. *edicts*: stress on second syllable.   302 *wand'ring thought*: thought uncontrolled by faith (hence error).   303 *diminution*: depreciating it in their minds.   303–7 See Commentary.   307 *Interminable*: the limitless, God.   312 *National obstriction*: general rule laid down for the nation.   313 *debt*: fault to be expiated.   315 *else*: otherwise.   320 *fallacious*: deceitful.   322 *Down Reason, then*: keep Reason subservient to faith and Revelation.

Though Reason here aver
That moral verdict quits her of unclean:
Unchaste was subsequent; her stain, not his.
　　But see! here comes <u>thy reverend Sire</u>
With careful step, locks white as down,
Old ⌈Manoa⌉ advise
Forthwith how thou ought'st to receive him.

2nd Episode **Samson.** Ay me! another inward grief, awak'd　　330
　　With mention of that name, renews th' assault.

Manoa. Brethren and men of Dan (for such ye seem,
　　Though in this uncouth place), if old respect,
　　As I suppose, towards your once gloried friend,
　　My Son, now Captive, hither hath inform'd
　　Your younger feet, while mine, cast back with age,
　　Came lagging after, say if he be here.

Chorus. As signal now in low dejected state
　　As erst in highest, behold him where he lies.

Manoa. O miserable change! Is this the man,　　340
　　That invincible Samson, far <u>renown'd</u>,
　　The dread of Israel's foes, who with a strength
　　Equivalent to Angels' walk'd their streets,
　　None offering fight; who, single combatant,
　　Duell'd their Armies rank'd in proud array,
　　Himself an Army—now unequal match
　　To save himself against a coward arm'd
　　At one spear's length? O ever-failing trust
　　In mortal strength! and oh, <u>what not in man</u>
　　<u>Deceivable</u> and vain! Nay, what thing good　　350
　　Pray'd for, but often proves our woe, our bane?

he can a point / Harapha / improvement

324–5 *quits . . . his*: 'acquits her of uncleanliness before marriage;
her unchastity came later and so he was not to blame'.　　327 *careful*:
heavy with care.　　328 *advise*: consider.　　333 *uncouth*: strange, bar-
barous.　　335 *inform'd*: directed.　　345 *Duell'd*: fought single-
handed.　　349–50 *what . . . Deceivable*: 'what in man is not deceptive'.

I pray'd for Children, and thought barrenness
In wedlock a reproach; I gain'd a Son,
And such a Son as all Men hail'd me happy.
Who would be now a Father in my stead?
Oh, wherefore did God grant me my request,
And as a blessing with such pomp adorn'd?
Why are his gifts desirable, to tempt
Our earnest Prayers, then, giv'n with solemn hand
As Graces, draw a Scorpion's tail behind?   360
For this did the Angel twice descend? for this
Ordain'd thy nurture holy, as of a Plant;
Select and Sacred, Glorious for a while,
The miracle of men; then in an hour
Ensnar'd, assaulted, overcome, led bound,
Thy Foes' derision, Captive, Poor and Blind,
Into a Dungeon thrust, to work with Slaves?
Alas! methinks whom God hath chosen once
To worthiest deeds, if he through frailty err,
He should not so o'erwhelm, and as a thrall   370
Subject him to so foul indignities,
Be it but for honour's sake of former deeds.

Samson. Appoint not heav'nly disposition, Father.
Nothing of all these evils hath befall'n me
But justly; I myself have brought them on;
Sole Author I, sole cause: if aught seem vile,
As vile hath been my folly, who have profan'd
The mystery of God, giv'n me under pledge
Of vow, and have betray'd it to a woman,
A Canaanite, my faithless enemy.   380
This well I knew, nor was at all surpris'd,
But warn'd by oft experience. Did not she
Of Timna first betray me, and reveal

354 *as*: that.   357 *pomp*: ceremony.   360 *Graces*: favours (**L.**
gratiae).   364 *miracle*: wonder.   370 *thrall*: slave.   373 'Do not
blame God's ordering of things'.   376 *vile*: base, unworthy.   377
As: so.   *profan'd*: (L. sense) sacrilegiously revealed.

The secret wrested from me in her highth
Of Nuptial Love profess'd, carrying it straight
To them who had corrupted her, my Spies
And Rivals? In this other was there found
More Faith, who also in her prime of love,
Spousal embraces, vitiated with Gold,
Though offer'd only, by the scent conceiv'd   390
Her spurious first-born, Treason against me?
Thrice she assay'd with flattering prayers and sighs
And amorous reproaches, to win from me
My capital secret, in what part my strength
Lay stor'd, in what part summ'd, that she might know:
Thrice I deluded her, and turn'd to sport
Her importunity, each time perceiving
How openly and with what impudence
She purpos'd to betray me, and (which was worse
Than undissembl'd hate) with what contempt   400
She sought to make me Traitor to myself.
Yet the fourth time, when must'ring all her wiles,
With blandish'd parleys, feminine assaults,
Tongue-batteries, she surceas'd not day nor night
To storm me, over-watch'd and wearied out.
At times when men seek most repose and rest,
I yielded, and unlock'd her all my heart,
Who, with a grain of manhood well resolv'd,
Might easily have shook off all her snares;

384-5 *in . . . profess'd*: 'at the height of her professedly great love for her husband'.   389 *vitiated*: corrupted.   390-1 'As soon as gold was offered, the mere scent of it made her conceive the first-born child of her brain, Treachery against me'. *conceiv'd*: in the double sense of (i) an idea (ii) a child.   392 *assay'd*: tried.   394 *capital*: a triple pun (i) principal (ii) about my head (hair) (iii) fatal.   394-5 *in . . . know*: inverted—that she might know where in my body my strength was stored and concentrated.   402 *must'ring*: gathering like troops.   403 *blandish'd parleys*: speeches full of blandishments.   405 *overwatch'd*: tired out by having to keep vigilant.   408 *well resolv'd*: truly resolute.

Adam - fondly o'ercome with female charm.

Samson Agonistes

But foul effeminacy held me yok'd   410
Her Bond-slave. O indignity, O blot
To Honour and Religion! servile mind
Rewarded well with servile punishment!
The base degree to which I now am fall'n,
These rags, this grinding, is not yet so base
As was my former servitude, ignoble,
Unmanly, ignominious, infamous,
True slavery; and that blindness worse than this,
That saw not how degenerately I serv'd.

Manoa. I cannot praise thy Marriage-choices, Son;   420
Rather approv'd them not; but thou didst plead
Divine impulsion prompting how thou might'st
Find some occasion to infest our Foes.
I state not that; this I am sure, our Foes
Found soon occasion thereby to make thee
Their Captive, and their triumph; thou the sooner
Temptation found'st, or over-potent charms,
To violate the sacred trust of silence
Deposited within thee, which to have kept
Tacit, was in thy power. True; and thou bear'st   430
Enough and more the burden of that fault;
Bitterly hast thou paid, and still art paying,
That rigid score. A worse thing yet remains:
This day the Philistines a popular Feast
Here celebrate in Gaza, and proclaim
Great Pomp, and Sacrifice, and Praises loud,
To Dagon, as their God who hath deliver'd
Thee, Samson, bound and blind into their hands—
Them out of thine, who slew'st them many a slain.

414 _degree_: rank, state (cf. 1607).   421 _Rather . . . not_: 'Indeed I
never approved of them'.   423 _infest_: plague.   424 _I state not that_:
'I shall not go into details of that'.   426 _their triumph_: their means
of victory.   433 _rigid score_: debt (penalty) which must be fully paid.
434 _popular_: for the general populace.   436 _Pomp_: festive ceremony
(L. _pompa_, festival procession).   439 _thine_: thy hands. _them_: of them.

127

So Dagon shall be magnifi'd, and God,   440
Besides whom is no God, compar'd with Idols,
Disglorifi'd, blasphem'd, and had in scorn
By th' Idolatrous rout amidst their wine;
Which to have come to pass by means of thee,
Samson, of all thy sufferings think the heaviest,
Of all reproach the most with shame that ever
Could have befall'n thee and thy Father's house.

Samson. Father, I do acknowledge and confess
  That I this honour, I this pomp, have brought
  To Dagon, and advanc'd his praises high   450
  Among the Heathen round; to God have brought
  Dishonour, obloquy, and op'd the mouths
  Of Idolists, and Atheists; have brought scandal
  To Israel, diffidence of God, and doubt
  In feeble hearts, propense enough before
  To waver, or fall off and join with Idols:
  Which is my chief affliction, shame and sorrow,
  The anguish of my Soul, that suffers not
  Mine eye to harbour sleep, or thoughts to rest.
  This only hope relieves me, that the strife   460
  With me hath end: all the contést is now
  'Twixt God and Dagon. Dagon hath presum'd,
  Me overthrown, to enter lists with God,
  His Deity comparing and preferring
  Before the God of Abraham. He, be sure,
  Will not connive, or linger, thus provok'd,
  But will arise and his great name assert:
  Dagon must stoop, and shall ere long receive
  Such a discomfit as shall quite despoil him

440 *magnifi'd*: glorified.   441 *compar'd with*: reduced to equality
with.   444 'That this has come to pass through thee'.   446 'The
most shameful of all disgraces'.   453 *Idolists*: idolaters.   454 *diffi-
dence*: distrust.   455 *propense*: inclined.   461 *with . . . end*: may
mean: 'that through me the strife comes to its climax'. *contést*: stress
on second syllable.   466 *connive*: shut His eyes (L. *connivere*, wink).
469 *discomfit*: discomfiture.

Of all these boasted Trophies won on me,   470
And with confusion blank his Worshippers.

Manoa. With cause this hope relieves thee; and these words
  I as a Prophecy receive; for God
  (Nothing more certain) will not long defer
  To vindicate the glory of his name
  Against all competition, nor will long   *Play proves this — but in*
  Endure it doubtful whether God be Lord   *what a way.*
  Or Dagon. But for thee what shall be done?
  Thou must not in the meanwhile, here forgot,
  Lie in this miserable loathsome plight   480
  Neglected. I already have made way
  To some Philistian Lords, with whom to treat
  About thy ransom: well they may by this
  Have satisfi'd their utmost of revenge
  By pains and slaveries, worse than death, inflicted
  On thee, who now no more canst do them harm.

Samson. Spare that proposal, Father; spare the trouble
  Of that solicitation; let me here,
  As I deserve, pay on my punishment,   *cf Satan in P.L. egotism.*
  And expiate, if possible, my crime,   490
  Shameful garrulity. To have reveal'd
  Secrets of men, the secrets of a friend,
  How heinous had the fact been, how deserving
  Contempt and scorn of all—to be excluded
  All friendship, and avoided as a blab,
  The mark of fool set on his front!
  But I God's counsel have not kept, his holy secret
  Presumptuously have publish'd, impiously,
  Weakly at least, and shamefully—a sin
  That Gentiles in their Parables condemn   500

471 *blank*: make pale.   477 *God be Lord*: our God be master (the
Almighty).   481–482 *made way To*: approached.   483 *by this*: now.
484 *utmost*: utmost desire.   488 *solicitation*: appeal, petition.   489
pay on: go on paying.   493 *heinous*: odious. *fact*: deed.   495 *blab*:
blabber.   496 *front*: forehead.

I   129

Samson Agonistes

To their abyss and horrid pains confin'd.

Manoa. Be penitent, and for thy fault contríte,
But act not in thy own affliction, Son.
Repent the sin, but if the punishment
Thou canst avoid, self-preservation bids;
Or th' execution leave to high disposal,
And let another hand, not thine, exact
Thy penal forfeit from thyself. Perhaps
God will relent, and quit thee all his debt;
Who ever more approves and more accepts   510
(Best pleas'd with humble and filial submission)
Him who, imploring mercy, sues for life,
Than who, self-rigorous, chooses death as due;
Which argues over-just, and self-displeas'd
For self-offence more than for God offended.
Reject not then what offer'd means, who knows
But God hath set before us, to return thee
Home to thy country and his sacred house,
Where thou may'st bring thy off'rings, to avert
His further ire, with prayers and vows renew'd.   520

Samson. His pardon I implore; but as for life,
To what end should I seek it? When in strength
All mortals I excell'd, and great in hopes,
With youthful courage and magnanimous thoughts
Of birth from Heav'n foretold and high exploits,
Full of divine instinct, after some proof
Of acts indeed heroic, far beyond

501 'Confining the sinner in their Hell with its dreadful torments'.
502 *contríte*: stress second syllable.   505 *bids*: bids thee avoid it.
507–8 *exact . . . forfeit*: demand from you the penalty you must pay.
509 *quit . . . debt*: remit all the debt you owe him.   513 *self-rigorous*: severe against himself.   514–15 'Such severity proves a
man to be too harsh a judge, and more displeased with his offence
against himself than with his sin against God'.   516–17 'Do not
reject whatever opportunities are offered, which (who knows) God
may have granted us in order to return thee . . .'   524 *magnanimous*:
great-minded, heroic.   526 *instinct*: impulse.

130

The Sons of Anak, famous now and blaz'd,
Fearless of danger, like a petty God
I walk'd about, admir'd of all, and dreaded 530
On hostile ground, none daring my affront.
Then, swoll'n with pride, into the snare I fell
Of fair fallacious looks, venereal trains,
Soften'd with pleasure and voluptuous life,
At length to lay my head and hallow'd pledge
Of all my strength in the lascivious lap
Of a deceitful Concubine, who shore me,
Like a tame Wether, all my precious fleece,
Then turn'd me out ridiculous, despoil'd,
Shav'n, and disarm'd among my enemies. 540

Chorus. Desire of wine and all delicious drinks,
Which many a famous Warrior overturns,
Thou could'st repress; nor did the dancing Ruby,
Sparkling out-pour'd, the flavour, or the smell,
Or taste that cheers the heart of Gods and men,
Allure thee from the cool Crystalline stream.

Samson. Wherever fountain or fresh current flow'd
Against the Eastern ray, translucent, pure
With touch ethereal of Heav'n's fiery rod,
I drank, from the clear milky juice allaying 550
Thirst, and refresh'd; nor envied them the grape
Whose heads that turbulent liquor fills with fumes.

Chorus. O madness! to think use of strongest wines
And strongest drinks our chief support of health,
When God with these forbidd'n made choice to rear
His mighty Champion, strong above compare,
Whose drink was only from the liquid brook!

528 *blaz'd*: proclaimed (trumpeted) everywhere.   531 *my affront*:
to meet me.   533 *venereal trains*: snares of love.   535 *pledge*: symbol,
i.e. his hair.   537 *shore me*: clipped from me.   538 *Wether*: castrated
ram.   543 *dancing Ruby*: wine (cf. *Com.* 673).   549 *fiery rod*: the sun's
ray.   550 *milky juice*: water sweet as milk.   557 *liquid*: clear, trans-
parent.

Samson. But what avail'd this temperance, not complete
Against another object more enticing?
What boots it at one gate to make defence,   560
And at another to let in the foe,
Effeminately vanquish'd? by which means,
Now blind, dishearten'd, sham'd, dishonour'd, quell'd,
To what can I be useful? wherein serve
My Nation, and the work from Heav'n impos'd?
But to sit idle on the household hearth,
A burdenous drone; to visitants a gaze,
Or pitied object; these redundant locks,
Robustious to no purpose, clust'ring down,
Vain monument of strength; till length of years   570
And sedentary numbness craze my limbs
To a contemptible old age obscure.
Here rather let me drudge and earn my bread,
Till vermin or the draff of servile food
Consume me, and oft-invocated death
Hasten the welcome end of all my pains.

Manoa. Wilt thou then serve the Philistines with that gift
Which was expressly giv'n thee to annoy them?
Better at home lie bed-rid, not only idle,
Inglorious, unemploy'd, with age outworn.   580
But God, who caus'd a fountain at thy prayer
From the dry ground to spring, thy thirst to allay
After the brunt of battle, can as easy
Cause light again within thy eyes to spring,
Wherewith to serve him better than thou hast.
And I persuade me so: why else this strength
Miraculous yet remaining in those locks?
His might continues in thee not for naught,
Nor shall his wondrous gifts be frustrate thus.

560 *What boots it*: of what use is it.   568 *redundant*: flowing (L. *redundans*).   569 *Robustious*: powerful (L. *robustus*).   571 *craze*: weaken or break.   574 *draff . . . food*: refuse given as food to slaves. 578 *annoy*: hurt.   586 *And . . . so*: and I am convinced it will be so.

Samson. All otherwise to me my thoughts portend— 590
That these dark orbs no more shall treat with light,
Nor th' other light of life continue long,
But yield to double darkness nigh at hand:
So much I feel my genial spirits droop,
My hopes all flat; nature within me seems
In all her functions weary of herself;
My race of glory run, and race of shame,
And I shall shortly be with them that rest.

Manoa. Believe not these suggestions which proceed
From anguish of the mind and humours black 600
That mingle with thy fancy. I, however,
Must not omit a Father's timely care
To prosecute the means of thy deliverance
By ransom or how else: meanwhile be calm,
And healing words from these thy friends admit.

                                                          [*Exit*]

Samson. O that torment should not be confin'd
To the body's wounds and sores,
With maladies innumerable
In heart, head, breast, and reins;
But must secret passage find 610
To th' inmost mind,
There exercise all his fierce accidents,
And on her purest spirits prey,
As on entrails, joints, and limbs,
With answerable pains, but more intense,
Though void of corporal sense!
    My griefs not only pain me
As a ling'ring disease,
But finding no redress, ferment and rage;

---

590 *portend*: foretell.   591 *treat with*: have dealings with.   593
double darkness: i.e. blindness and death.   594 *genial spirits*: vital
powers.   600 *humours black*: melancholy.   603 *prosecute*: pursue.
609 *reins*: kidneys or loins.   612 *accidents*: unfavourable symptoms,
pains.   615 *answerable*: corresponding.

Nor less than wounds immedicable   620
Rankle, and fester, and gangrene,
To black mortification.
Thoughts, my Tormentors, arm'd with deadly stings,
Mangle my apprehensive tenderest parts,
Exasperate, exulcerate, and raise
Dire inflammation, which no cooling herb
Or med'cinal liquor can assuage,
Nor breath of Vernal Air from snowy Alp.
Sleep hath forsook and giv'n me o'er
To death's benumbing Opium as my only cure.   630
Thence faintings, swoonings of despair,
And sense of Heav'n's desertion.
   I was his nursling once and choice delight,
His destin'd from the womb,
Promis'd by Heavenly message twice descending.
Under his special eye
Abstemious I grew up and thriv'd amain;
He led me on to mightiest deeds
Above the nerve of mortal arm,
Against the uncircumcis'd, our enemies.   640
But now hath cast me off as never known,
And to those cruel enemies,
Whom I by his appointment had provok'd,
Left me all helpless with th' irreparable loss
Of sight, reserv'd alive to be repeated
The subject of their cruelty or scorn.
Nor am I in the list of them that hope;
Hopeless are all my evils, all remediless;
This one prayer yet remains—might I be heard,

620 *immedicable*: incurable.   622 'Till they turn black and die'.
624 *apprehensive tenderest parts*: conscious mind, the senses and imagin-
ation.   625 *Exasperate*: irritate. *exulcerate*: cause ulcers.   628 *Alp*:
mountain.   635 *message*: messenger.   637 *Abstemious*: abstaining
from wine (L. *abstemius*).   639 *nerve*: sinew (L. sense) hence 'strength'.
643 *appointment*: command.   645 *repeated*: repeatedly.

No long petition—speedy death,   *negative wish.*   **650**
The close of all my miseries and the balm.

__Chorus.__ Many are the sayings of the wise   *2nd choric ode.*
In ancient and in modern books enroll'd,
Extolling Patience as the truest fortitude, *the last thing S. is*
And to the bearing well of all calamities,
All chances incident to man's frail life,
Consolatories writ
With studied argument, and much persuasion sought,
Lenient of grief and anxious thought.
But with th' afflicted in his pangs their sound   **660**
Little prevails, or rather seems a tune
Harsh, and of dissonant mood from his complaint;
Unless he feel within
Some source of consolation from above,
Secret refreshings, that repair his strength
And fainting spirits uphold.
    God of our Fathers! what is Man,
That thou towards him with hand so various
(Or might I say contrarious?)
Temper'st thy providence through his short course, **670**
Not evenly, as thou rul'st
Th'Angelic orders and inferior creatures mute,
Irrational and brute?
Nor do I name of men the common rout,
That, wand'ring loose about,
Grow up and perish as the summer fly,
Heads without name no more remember'd;
But such as thou hast solemnly elected,
With gifts and graces eminently adorn'd
To some great work, thy glory,   **680**

651 *balm*: cure.   657–8 'Consoling discourses (i.e. by the wise, 652) written with careful arguments and much ingenious (sought-for) persuasion'.   659 *Lenient*: likely to soothe (L. *leniens*).   662 *mood*: in mood and in measure.   670 *Temper'st*: regulatest.   677 *Heads*: so many people.   678 *elected*: chosen specially and . . .

And people's safety, which in part they effect:
Yet towards these, thus dignifi'd, thou oft
Amidst their highth of noon
Changest thy countenance and thy hand, with no regard
Of highest favours past
From thee on them, or them to thee of service.
 Nor only dost degrade them, or remit
To life obscur'd, which were a fair dismission,
But throw'st them lower than thou didst exalt them high—
Unseemly falls in human eye,   690
Too grievous for the trespass or omission;
Oft leav'st them to the hostile sword
Of Heathen and profane, their carcasses
To dogs and fowls a prey, or else captiv'd,
Or to the unjust tribunals, under change of times,
And condemnation of the ungrateful multitude.
If these they scape, perhaps in poverty
With sickness and disease thou bow'st them down,
Painful diseases and deform'd,
In crude old age;   700
Though not disordinate, yet causeless suff'ring
The punishment of dissolute days. In fine,
Just or unjust alike seem miserable,
For oft alike both come to evil end.
 So deal not with this once thy glorious Champion,
The Image of thy strength, and mighty minister.
What do I beg? how hast thou dealt already!
Behold him in this state calamitous, and turn
His labours, for thou canst, to peaceful end.
 But who is this? what thing of Sea or Land— 710

681 *effect*: accomplish.   682 *dignifi'd*: elevated as worthy (Med.
L. *dignificare*).   687 *remit*: send back.   688 *obscur'd*: private, not in
the public eye.   690 'To depths which to human minds are un-
fitting' (disproportionate).   700 *crude*: premature (L. *crudus*, unripe).
701–2 'Though they have not lived irregular lives, yet, without
cause, they suffer the punishment due to the dissolute'.   702 *In
fine*: In conclusion.   705 *So*: Thus.   706 *minister*: servant.

Female of sex it seems—
That so bedeck'd, ornate, and gay,
Comes this way sailing
Like a stately Ship
Of Tarsus, bound for th' Isles
Of Javan or Gadier,
With all her bravery on, and tackle trim,
Sails fill'd, and streamers waving,
Courted by all the winds that hold them play;
An Amber scent of odorous perfume   720
Her harbinger, a damsel train behind?
Some rich Philistian Matron she may seem;
And now at nearer view no other certain
Than Dalila thy wife.

Samson. My Wife! my Traitress! let her not come near me.

Chorus. Yet on she moves; now stands and eyes thee fix'd,
About t' have spoke; but now, with head declin'd,
Like a fair flower surcharg'd with dew, she weeps,
And words address'd seem into tears dissolv'd,
Wetting the borders of her silken veil: 730
But now again she makes address to speak.

Dalila. With doubtful feet and wavering resolution
I came, still dreading thy displeasure, Samson,
Which to have merited, without excuse
I cannot but acknowledge; yet if tears *— he was overcome by a tear — unfortunate*
May expiate (though the fact more evil drew
In the perverse event than I foresaw), *she didn't know he'd go blind*
My penance hath not slacken'd, though my pardon

717 *bravery*: finery. *tackle trim*: rigging neatly arranged.   719 *hold them play*: sport with them.   720 *Amber scent*: scent of ambergris.
721 *harbinger*: forerunner.   728 *surcharg'd*: weighed down.   729 *address'd*: prepared.   732 *doubtful*: hesitant.   734–5 'Which I cannot but admit (without offering any excuses) that I have deserved'.
736–7 (*though . . . foresaw*): 'though my action brought more evil in its unhappy results than I foresaw'. *perverse*: adverse.   738 *penance*: penitence.

137

No way assur'd. But conjugal affection,
Prevailing over fear and timorous doubt,   740
Hath led me on, desirous to behold
Once more thy face, and know of thy estate,
If aught in my ability may serve
To lighten what thou suffer'st, and appease
Thy mind with what amends is in my power—
Though late, yet in some part to recompense
My rash but more unfortunate misdeed.

Samson. Out, out, Hyæna! these are thy wonted arts,
And arts of every woman false like thee,
To break all faith, all vows, deceive, betray;   750
Then, as repentant, to submit, beseech,
And reconcilement move with feign'd remorse,
Confess, and promise wonders in her change;
Not truly penitent, but chief to try
Her husband, how far urg'd his patience bears,
His virtue or weakness which way to assail:
Then with more cautious and instructed skill
Again transgresses, and again submits;
That wisest and best men, full oft beguil'd,
With goodness principl'd not to reject   760
The penitent, but ever to forgive,
Are drawn to wear out miserable days,
Entangl'd with a poisonous bosom-snake,
If not by quick destruction soon cut off,
As I by thee, to Ages an example.

Dalila. Yet hear me, Samson; not that I endeavour
To lessen or extenuate my offence,

739 *No way assur'd*: by no means sure.   742 *estate*: condition.
744 *appease*: pacify.   746 'Amends which though coming late may
somewhat atone for . . .'   754 *try*: test.   755–6 'how far his
patience will bear being provoked, and in which way she may best
attack his strength or weakness'.   757 *instructed*: experienced.   759
That: so that.   760 'Yet instructed in the good principle never to
reject . . .'

But that, on th' other side, if it be weigh'd *Points out the warmth of*
By itself, with aggravations not surcharg'd, *a sinner as she—may be true but irrelevant.*
Or else with just allowance counterpois'd,   770
I may, if possible, thy pardon find
The easier towards me, or thy hatred less.
First granting, as I do, it was a weakness
In me, but incident to all our sex,   *LIE.*
Curiosity, inquisitive, importune
Of secrets, then with like infirmity
To publish them—both common female faults:
Was it not weakness also to make known *This is his own argument*
For importunity, that is for naught,   *to himself*
Wherein consisted all thy strength and safety?   780
To what I did thou show'dst me first the way.
But I to enemies reveal'd, and should not.
Nor should'st thou have trusted that to woman's frailty:
Ere I to thee, thou to thyself wast cruel.
Let weakness then with weakness come to parle,
So near related, or the same of kind;
Thine forgive mine, that men may censure thine
The gentler, if severely thou exact not
More strength from me than in thyself was found.
And what if Love, which thou interpret'st hate,   790
The jealousy of Love, powerful of sway
In human hearts, nor less in mine towards thee,
Caus'd what I did? I saw thee mutable
Of fancy; fear'd lest one day thou would'st leave me,   *TRUE (partly)*
As her at Timna; sought by all means therefore,
How to endear and hold thee to me firmest:
No better way I saw than by importuning

---

769 *with . . . surcharg'd*: not overburdened with exaggeration.   770
'Or else with proper allowances made which counterbalance it'.
774 *incident to*: likely to be found in.   775 *importune*: persistently
wanting to be told.   782 *But*: But (you'll say).   785 *parle*: agree-
ment.   786 *kind*: nature.   787 *Thine*: Thy weakness.   793 *mutable*:
fickle.   794 *fancy*: affection.   795 *As her*: as you did her.

To learn thy secrets, get into my power
Thy key of strength and safety. Thou wilt say,
'Why then reveal'd?' I was assur'd by those   800
Who tempted me, that nothing was design'd
Against thee but safe custody and hold:
That made for me; I knew that liberty
Would draw thee forth to perilous enterprises,
While I at home sat full of cares and fears,
Wailing thy absence in my widow'd bed;
Here I should still enjoy thee day and night,
Mine and Love's prisoner, not the Philistines',
Whole to myself, unhazarded abroad,
Fearless at home of partners in my love.   810
These reasons in Love's law have pass'd for good,
Though fond and reasonless to some perhaps:
And Love hath oft, well meaning, wrought much woe,
Yet always pity or pardon hath obtain'd.
Be not unlike all others, not austere
As thou art strong, inflexible as steel.
If thou in strength all mortals dost exceed,
In uncompassionate anger do not so.

Samson. How cunningly the sorceress displays
Her own transgressions, to upbraid me mine!   820
That malice, not repentance, brought thee hither,
By this appears. I gave, thou say'st, th' example,
I led the way—bitter reproach, but true;
I to myself was false ere thou to me.
Such pardon therefore as I give my folly
Take to thy wicked deed; which when thou seest
Impartial, self-severe, inexorable,
Thou wilt renounce thy seeking, and much rather
Confess it feign'd. Weakness is thy excuse,
And I believe it, weakness to resist   830

803 *That made for me*: That was in my favour, for . . .   809 *Whole*:
wholly.   826 *which*: the pardon I give myself.   827 'Is no pardon
at all but an impartial, ruthless self-punishment'.

Samson Agonistes

Philistian gold. If weakness may excuse,
What Murtherer, what Traitor, Parricide,
Incestuous, Sacrilegious, but may plead it?
All wickedness is weakness; that plea therefore,
With God or Man will gain thee no remission.
But Love constrain'd thee! Call it furious rage
To satisfy thy lust. Love seeks to have Love;
My love how could'st thou hope, who took'st the way
To raise in me inexpiable hate,
Knowing, as needs I must, by thee betray'd?   840
In vain thou striv'st to cover shame with shame,
Or by evasions thy crime uncover'st more.

Dalila. Since thou determin'st weakness for no plea
In man or woman, though to thy own condemning,
Hear what assaults I had, what snares besides,
What sieges girt me round, ere I consented;
Which might have aw'd the best-resolv'd of men,
The constantest, to have yielded without blame.
It was not gold, as to my charge thou lay'st,
That wrought with me: thou know'st the Magistrates
And Princes of my country came in person,   851
Solicited, commanded, threaten'd, urg'd,
Adjur'd by all the bonds of civil Duty
And of Religion, press'd how just it was,
How honourable, how glorious, to entrap
A common enemy, who had destroy'd
Such numbers of our Nation: and the Priest
Was not behind, but ever at my ear,
Preaching how meritorious with the gods
It would be to ensnare an irreligious   860
Dishonourer of Dagon. What had I
To oppose against such powerful arguments?

832 *Parricide*: slayer of his father.   836 'You say you were driven by Love . . .'   838 *hope*: hope for.   840 'Knowing that I was betrayed by thee'.   841 *shame*: i.e. lies.   843 *determin'st*: judgest (to be no excuse).   847 *aw'd*: subdued.   853 *Adjur'd*: urged.

Only my love of thee held long debate,
And combated in silence all these reasons
With hard contest. At length that grounded maxim,
So rife and celebrated in the mouths
Of wisest men, that to the public good
Private respects must yield, with grave authority
Took full possession of me, and prevail'd;
Virtue, as I thought, truth, duty, so enjoining.   870

Samson. I thought where all thy circling wiles would end—
In feign'd Religion, smooth hypocrisy!
But, had thy love, still odiously pretended,
Been, as it ought, sincere, it would have taught thee
Far other reasonings, brought forth other deeds.
I, before all the daughters of my Tribe
And of my Nation, chose thee from among
My enemies, lov'd thee, as too well thou knew'st,
Too well; unbosom'd all my secrets to thee,
Not out of levity, but overpower'd   880
By thy request, who could deny thee nothing;
Yet now am judg'd an enemy. Why then
Didst thou at first receive me for thy husband,
Then, as since then, thy country's foe profess'd?
Being once a wife, for me thou wast to leave
Parents and country; nor was I their subject,
Nor under their protection, but my own;
Thou mine, not theirs. If aught against my life
Thy country sought of thee, it sought unjustly,
Against the law of nature, law of nations;   890
No more thy country, but an impious crew
Of men conspiring to uphold their state
By worse than hostile deeds, violating the ends

865 *grounded*: firmly established.   866 *rife*: widespread. *celebrated*:
proclaimed (as in L. *celebratus*).   868 *respects*: considerations, wishes.
871 *circling*: circuitous, evasive.   880 *levity*: trivial irresponsibility.
884 'Then, as always since, an avowed foe'.   887 *but my own*: but
under the protection of my own country and parents.

For which our country is a name so dear;
Not therefore to be obey'd. But zeal mov'd thee;
To please thy gods thou didst it! Gods unable
To acquit themselves and prosecute their foes
But by ungodly deeds, the contradiction
Of their own deity, Gods cannot be;
Less therefore to be pleas'd, obey'd, or fear'd.   900
These false pretexts and varnish'd colours failing,
Bare in thy guilt how foul must thou appear!

Dalila. In argument with men a woman ever
Goes by the worse, whatever be her cause.

Samson. For want of words no doubt, or lack of breath!
Witness when I was worried with thy peals.

Dalila. I was a fool, too rash, and quite mistaken
In what I thought would have succeeded best.
Let me obtain forgiveness of thee, Samson;
Afford me place to show what recompense   910
Towards thee I intend for what I have misdone,
Misguided. Only what remains past cure
Bear not too sensibly, nor still insist
To afflict thyself in vain. Though sight be lost,
Life yet hath many solaces, enjoy'd
Where other senses want not their delights,
At home, in leisure and domestic ease,
Exempt from many a care and chance to which
Eyesight exposes daily men abroad.
I to the Lords will intercede, not doubting   920
Their favourable ear, that I may fetch thee
From forth this loathsome prison-house, to abide

895 *zeal*: religious zeal (you say).   897 *To acquit themselves*: to do
their duties (as tribal gods).   898–9 'Except by ungodly deeds
which contradict . . .'   900 *Less*: all the less therefore.   901 *varnish'd
colours*: bright superficial excuses, false pleas.   904 *Goes . . . worse*:
gets the worst of it.   906 *peals*: noisy chatterings.   910 *place*:
opportunity.   913 *too sensibly*: too passionately.   916 *want*: lack.
921 *ear*: hearing.

143

With me, where my redoubl'd love and care,
With nursing diligence, to me glad office,
May ever tend about thee to old age,
With all things grateful cheer'd, and so supplied
That what by me thou hast lost thou least shalt miss.

Samson. No, no; of my condition take no care;
It fits not; thou and I long since are twain;
Nor think me so unwary or accurst   930
To bring my feet again into the snare
Where once I have been caught. I know thy trains,
Though dearly to my cost, thy gins, and toils.
Thy fair enchanted cup and warbling charms
No more on me have power; their force is null'd;
So much of Adder's wisdom I have learnt,
To fence my ear against thy sorceries.
If in my flower of youth and strength, when all men
Lov'd, honour'd, fear'd me, thou alone could hate me
Thy Husband, slight me, sell me, and forgo me,   940
How would'st thou use me now, blind, and thereby
Deceivable, in most things as a child
Helpless, thence easily contemn'd, and scorn'd,
And last neglected! How would'st thou insult,
When I must live uxorious to thy will
In perfect thraldom! how again betray me,
Bearing my words and doings to the Lords
To gloss upon, and censuring, frown or smile!
This gaol I count the house of Liberty
To thine, whose doors my feet shall never enter.   950

Dalila. Let me approach at least, and touch thy hand.

Samson. Not for thy life, lest fierce remembrance wake

924 *office*: duty.   926 *grateful*: pleasant (L. *gratus*).   932 *trains*: cf.
533 note.   933 *gins*: snares.   *toils*: hunters' nets.   935 *null'd*: can-
celled, made void.   940 *forgo*: forsake, give up.   943 *contemn'd*:
held in contempt.   944 *last*: finally.   *insult*: exult.   945 *uxorious*:
submissive to a wife (L. *uxor*).   948 *gloss*: comment.   *censuring*: sitting
in judgment.

My sudden rage to tear thee joint by joint.
At distance I forgive thee, go with that;
Bewail thy falsehood, and the pious works
It hath brought forth to make thee memorable
Among illustrious women, faithful wives:
Cherish thy hasten'd widowhood with the gold
Of Matrimonial treason: so farewell.

Dalila. I see thou art implacable, more deaf
  To prayers than winds and seas; yet winds to seas
Are reconcil'd at length, and Sea to Shore:
Thy anger, unappeasable, still rages,
Eternal tempest never to be calm'd.
Why do I humble thus myself, and suing
For peace, reap nothing but repulse and hate,
Bid go with evil omen, and the brand
Of infamy upon my name denounc'd?
To mix with thy concernments I desist
Henceforth, nor too much disapprove my own.
Fame, if not double-fac'd, is double-mouth'd,
And with contrary blast proclaims most deeds;
On both his wings, one black, th' other white,
Bears greatest names in his wild aery flight.
My name perhaps among the Circumcis'd
In Dan, in Judah, and the bordering Tribes,
To all posterity may stand defam'd,
With malediction mention'd, and the blot
Of falsehood most unconjugal traduc'd.
But in my country, where I most desire,
In Ecron, Gaza, Asdod, and in Gath,
I shall be nam'd among the famousest
Of Women, sung at solemn festivals,

960 *(handwritten marginal note:* Then she changes but this is really getting the last word sth N insisted on Eve's doing*)*

970

975 *(handwritten marginal note:* Public & private morality interweave. *)*

980

954 *go*: go away satisfied.   958–9 'Enjoy, with the gold won by
treachery to your husband, the widowhood you have prematurely
hastened'.   967 *Bid go*: bidden to go.   969 *concernments*: affairs.
972 *contrary blast*: contradictory reports.   975 *the Circumcis'd*: the
Israelites.   979 *traduc'd*: slandered.   980 *desire*: desire it.

K   145

ironic – they all killed

Living and dead recorded, who to save
Her country from a fierce destroyer, chose
Above the faith of wedlock-bands; my tomb
With odours visited and annual flowers;
Not less renown'd than in Mount Ephraim

Good point. Israelite god condones this kind of violence

Jael, who, with inhospitable guile
Smote Sisera sleeping, through the Temples nail'd. 990
Nor shall I count it heinous to enjoy
The public marks of honour and reward
Conferr'd upon me for the piety
Which to my country I was judg'd to have shown.
At this whoever envies or repines,
I leave him to his lot, and like my own.   [*Exit*]

Chorus. She's gone, a manifest Serpent by her sting
    Discover'd in the end, till now conceal'd.

Samson. So let her go. God sent her to debase me,
    And aggravate my folly, who committed   1000
    To such a viper his most sacred trust
    Of secrecy, my safety, and my life.

it understands it knows how painful it must have been for Samson

Chorus. Yet beauty, though injurious, hath strange power,
    After offence returning, to regain   *he can't see her. Ma*
    Love once possess'd, nor can be easily   *this is why he can w*
    Repuls'd without much inward passion felt,   *her this time*
    And secret sting of amorous remorse.

Samson. Love-quarrels oft in pleasing concord end;
    Not wedlock-treachery endangering life.

3rd Stasimon – Choric Ode.

Chorus. It is not virtue, wisdom, valour, wit,   1010
    Strength, comeliness of shape, or amplest merit,
    That woman's love can win or long inherit;
    But what it is hard is to say,

984 *who to save*: who chose (985) to save . . .   986 'Rather than keep faith with her husband . . .'   987 *odours*: ritual burning of spices.   998 *Discover'd*: revealed.   1000 *aggravate*: to increase (as in L.).   1006 *passion*: suffering (L. *passio*).   1007 *remorse*: sorrow, pity.   1012 *inherit*: possess (cf. Luke xviii. 18. 'to inherit eternal life').

Harder to hit,
(Which way soever men refer it)
Much like thy riddle, Samson, in one day
Or seven, though one should musing sit.
    If any of these, or all, the Timnian bride
Had not so soon preferr'd
Thy Paranymph, worthless to thee compar'd,   1020
Successor in thy bed,
Nor both so loosely disallied
Their nuptials, nor this last so treacherously
Had shorn the fatal harvest of thy head.
Is it for that such outward ornament
Was lavish'd on their Sex, that inward gifts
Were left for haste unfinish'd, judgment scant,
Capacity not rais'd to apprehend
Or value what is best
In choice, but oftest to affect the wrong?   1030
Or was too much of self-love mix'd,
Of constancy no root infix'd,
That either they love nothing, or not long?
    Whate'er it be, to wisest men and best
Seeming at first all heavenly under virgin veil,
Soft, modest, meek, demure,
Once join'd, the contrary she proves, a thorn
Intestine, far within defensive arms
A cleaving mischief, in his way to virtue
Adverse and turbulent; or by her charms   1040
Draws him awry, enslav'd

1014 *hit*: be sure of.   1015 ('No matter how men may consider it').   1016–17 'As hard as your riddle, though one sat trying to solve it for one whole day, or even seven'.   1018 *if . . . all*: If any of the virtues in 1010–11 could hold a woman's love.   1020 *Thy Paranymph*: the 'best man' at your wedding.   1022 *both*: both of your wives. *disallied*: broken.   1025 *for that*: because.   1027 *for haste*: through (Nature's) haste. *scant*: left scanty.   1030 *affect*: desire, prefer.   1037 *join'd*: i.e. in wedlock.   1038 *intestine*: internal, intimate. *far . . . arms*: 'having got within a man's defences'.

With dotage, and his sense deprav'd
To folly and shameful deeds, which ruin ends.
What Pilot so expert but needs must wreck,
Embark'd with such a Steers-mate at the Helm?
  Favour'd of Heav'n who finds
One virtuous (rarely found)
That in domestic good combines!
Happy that house! his way to peace is smooth:
But virtue which breaks through all opposition,   1050
And all temptation can remove,
Most shines and most is acceptable above.
  Therefore God's universal Law
Gave to the man despotic power
Over his female in due awe,
Nor from that right to part an hour,
Smile she or lour:
So shall he least confusion draw
On his whole life, not sway'd
By female usurpation, nor dismay'd.   1060
  But had we best retire? I see a storm.

4th Episode

Samson. Fair days have oft contracted wind and rain.

Chorus. But this another kind of tempest brings.

Samson. Be less abstruse; my riddling days are past.

Chorus. Look now for no enchanting voice, nor fear
  The bait of honey'd words; a rougher tongue
  Draws hitherward; I know him by his stride,
  The Giant Harapha of Gath, his look
  Haughty as is his pile high-built and proud.
  Comes he in peace? What wind hath blown him hither

1043 *which . . . ends*: of which ruin is the end.   1046–8 'He is
favour'd by Heaven who marries one of those (rarely-found) good
women who join with their husbands in domestic harmony'.   1057
lour: frown.   1059 *not sway'd*: by not being overruled.   1062
contracted: brought together (L. *contrahere*).   1069 *his pile high-built*:
his bulk (like a lofty building).

148

I less conjecture than when first I saw   1071
  The sumptuous Dalila floating this way:
  His habit carries peace, his brow defiance.

Samson. Or peace or not, alike to me he comes.

Chorus. His fraught we soon shall know; he now arrives.

Harapha. I come not, Samson, to condole thy chance,
  As these perhaps, yet wish it had not been,
  Though for no friendly intent. I am of Gath;
  Men call me Harapha, of stock renown'd
  As Og or Anak and the Emims old   1080
  That Kiriathaim held: thou know'st me now,
  If thou at all art known. Much I have heard
  Of thy prodigious might and feats perform'd,
  Incredible to me, in this displeas'd,
  That I was never present on the place
  Of those encounters, where we might have tried
  Each other's force in camp or listed field;
  And now am come to see of whom such noise
  Hath walk'd about, and each limb to survey,
  If thy appearance answer loud report.   1090

Samson. Thy way to know were not to see, but taste.

Harapha. Dost thou already single me? I thought
  Gyves and the Mill had tam'd thee. O that fortune
  Had brought me to the field where thou art fam'd
  To have wrought such wonders with an Ass's Jaw!
  I should have forc'd thee soon wish other arms,
  Or left thy carcase where the Ass lay thrown:
  So had the glory of Prowess been recover'd

1073 *His . . . peace*: i.e. he is not dressed for battle.   1075 *fraught*:
freight, business.   1076 *chance*: misfortune.   1077 *these*: the Chorus.
1078 *intent*: wish, reason.   1087 *camp*: field of battle (L. *campus*).
listed field: field of tournament.   1088 *noise*: fame, rumour.   1091
taste: learn by trial.   1092 *single*: challenge to single combat.   1093
Gyves: fetters.

To Palestine, won by a Philistine
From the unforeskinn'd race, of whom thou bear'st   1100
The highest name for valiant Acts. That honour,
Certain to have won by mortal duel from thee,
I lose, prevented by thy eyes put out.

Samson. Boast not of what thou would'st have done, but do
  What then thou would'st; thou seest it in thy hand.

Harapha. To combat with a blind man I disdain,
  And thou hast need much washing to be touch'd.

Samson. Such usage as your honourable Lords
  Afford me, assassinated and betray'd;
  Who durst not with their whole united powers   1110
  In fight withstand me single and unarm'd,
  Nor in the house with chamber-ambushes
  Close-banded durst attack me, no, not sleeping,
  Till they had hir'd a woman with their gold,
  Breaking her Marriage-Faith to circumvent me.
  Therefore, without feign'd shifts, let be assign'd
  Some narrow place enclos'd, where sight may give thee,
  Or rather flight, no great advantage on me;
  Then put on all thy gorgeous arms, thy Helmet
  And Brigandine of brass, thy broad Habergeon,   1120
  Vant-brass and Greaves and Gauntlet; add thy Spear,
  A Weaver's beam, and seven-times-folded Shield;
  I only with an Oaken staff will meet thee,
  And raise such outcries on thy clatter'd Iron,
  Which long shall not withhold me from thy head,
  That in a little time, while breath remains thee,
  Thou oft shalt wish thyself at Gath, to boast

1100 *unforeskinn'd*: circumcised, Jewish.   1102 *mortal*: to the death. 1105 *in thy hand*: within reach of thy hand.   1109 *assassinated*: treacherously struck down.   1113 *Close-banded*: banded secretly together.   1116 *feign'd shifts*: evasive pretences.   1120 *Brigandine*: coat armoured with metal rings. *Habergeon*: chain-mail covering neck and breast.   1121 *Vant-brass*: armour for the forearm, vambrace (Fr. *avant-bras*). *Greaves*: leg-armour. *Gauntlet*: mailed glove.

Again in safety what thou would'st have done
To Samson, but shalt never see Gath more.

Harapha. Thou durst not thus disparage glorious arms
    Which greatest Heroes have in battle worn,   1130
    Their ornament and safety, had not spells
    And black enchantments, some Magician's Art,
    Arm'd thee or charm'd thee strong, which thou from Heaven
    Feign'dst at thy birth was giv'n thee in thy hair,
    Where strength can least abide, though all thy hairs
    Were bristles rang'd like those that ridge the back
    Of chaf'd wild Boars, or ruffled Porcupines.

Samson. I know no Spells, use no forbidden Arts;
    My trust is in the living God, who gave me   1140
    At my Nativity this strength, diffus'd
    No less through all my sinews, joints and bones,
    Than thine, while I preserv'd these locks unshorn,
    The pledge of my unviolated vow.
    For proof hereof, if Dagon be thy god,
    Go to his Temple, invocate his aid
    With solemnest devotion, spread before him
    How highly it concerns his glory now
    To frustrate and dissolve these Magic spells,
    Which I to be the power of Israel's God   1150
    Avow, and challenge Dagon to the test,
    Offering to combat thee, his Champion bold,
    With th' utmost of his Godhead seconded:
    Then thou shalt see, or rather to thy sorrow
    Soon feel, whose God is strongest, thine or mine.

Harapha. Presume not on thy God, what'er he be;
    Thee he regards not, owns not, hath cut off
    Quite from his people, and deliver'd up
    Into thy Enemies' hand; permitted them

1138 *chaf'd*: angry (cf. 1246).   1147 *spread*, lay, explain.

To put out both thine eyes, and fetter'd send thee 1160
Into the common Prison, there to grind
Among the Slaves and Asses, thy comrádes,
As good for nothing else, no better service
With those thy boist'rous locks; no worthy match
For valour to assail, nor by the sword
Of noble Warrior, so to stain his honour,
But by the Barber's razor best subdu'd.

Samson. All these indignities, for such they are
From thine, these evils I deserve and more,
Acknowledge them from God inflicted on me 1170
Justly, yet despair not of his final pardon
Whose ear is ever open, and his eye
Gracious to re-admit the suppliant;
In confidence whereof I once again
Defy thee to the trial of mortal fight,
By combat to decide whose god is God,
Thine, or whom I with Israel's Sons adore.

Harapha. Fair honour that thou dost thy God, in trusting
He will accept thee to defend his cause,
A Murtherer, a Revolter, and a Robber! 1180

Samson. Tongue-doughty Giant, how dost thou prove me
these?

Harapha. Is not thy Nation subject to our Lords?
Their Magistrates confess'd it when they took thee
As a League-breaker, and deliver'd bound
Into our hands: for hadst thou not committed
Notorious murder on those thirty men
At Ascalon, who never did thee harm,
Then like a Robber stripp'dst them of their robes?
The Philistines, when thou hadst broke the league,

1162 *comrádes*: accent second syllable.   1169 *From thine*: from thy
people.   1177 *whom*: He whom.   1181 *Tongue-doughty*: valiant in
words.   1184 *League-breaker*: treaty-breaker.

Went up with armed powers thee only seeking;   1190
To others did no violence nor spoil.

Samson. Among the Daughters of the Philistines
  I chose a Wife, which argu'd me no foe,
  And in your City held my Nuptial Feast:
  But your ill-meaning Politician Lords,
  Under pretence of Bridal friends and guests,
  Appointed to await me thirty spies,
  Who, threat'ning cruel death, constrain'd the bride
  To wring from me, and tell to them, my secret,
  That solv'd the riddle which I had propos'd.   1200
  When I perceiv'd all set on enmity,
  As on my enemies, wherever chanc'd,
  I us'd hostility, and took their spoil
  To pay my underminers in their coin.
  My Nation was subjected to your Lords!
  It was the force of Conquest; force with force
  Is well ejected when the Conquer'd can.
  But I, a private person, whom my Country
  As a League-breaker gave up bound, presum'd
  Single Rebellion, and did Hostile Acts!   1210
  I was no private, but a person rais'd,
  With strength sufficient and command from Heav'n,
  To free my Country. If their servile minds
  Me, their Deliverer sent, would not receive,
  But to their Masters gave me up for naught,
  Th' unworthier they; whence to this day they serve.
  I was to do my part from Heav'n assign'd,
  And had perform'd it if my known offence
  Had not disabled me, not all your force.

1193 *argu'd*: proved.   1195 *Politician*: intriguing.   1204 *my underminers*: those who worked secretly against me.   1207 *well*: rightly.   1208 *But*: But (you say) . . . *private person*: not officially recognised.   1210 *Single*: singlehanded.   1214 *sent*: Heaven-sent.   1217 *I . . . do*: It was my duty to do . . .   1218 *known*: well-known, admitted.

These shifts refuted, answer thy appellant,   1220
Though by his blindness maim'd for high attempts,
Who now defies thee thrice to single fight,
As a petty enterprise of small enforce.

Harapha. With thee, a Man condemn'd, a Slave enroll'd,
Due by the Law to capital punishment?
To fight with thee no man of arms will deign.

Samson. Cam'st thou for this, vain boaster, to survey me,
To descant on my strength, and give thy verdict?
Come nearer, part not hence so slight inform'd;
But take good heed my hand survey not thee.   1230

Harapha. O Baal-zebub! can my ears unus'd
Hear these dishonours, and not render death?

Samson. No man withholds thee; nothing from thy hand
Fear I incurable; bring up thy van;
My heels are fetter'd, but my fist is free.

Harapha. This insolence other kind of answer fits.

Samson. Go baffled coward, lest I run upon thee,
Though in these chains, bulk without spirit vast,
And with one buffet lay thy structure low,
Or swing thee in the Air, then dash thee down   1240
To the hazard of thy brains and shatter'd sides.

Harapha. By Astaroth, ere long thou shalt lament
These braveries in Irons loaden on thee.   [*Exit*]

Chorus. His Giantship is gone somewhat crestfall'n,
Stalking with less unconscionable strides,
And lower looks, but in a sultry chafe.

1220 *appellant*: challenger to a combat (in medieval chivalry).
1221 *maim'd . . . attempts*: made incapable of heroic enterprises.
1223 *of small enforce*: easy to fulfil.   1228 *descant*: sing variations
on. *verdict*: Milton has 'verdit'.   1234 *van*: first line of battle;
vanguard.   1237 *baffled*: disgraced (a chivalric term).   1238 *bulk
. . . vast*: vast spiritless bulk.   1243 *braveries*: boasts.   1245 *unconscionable*: excessive.

By the end of the 4th Episode - Sampson far more sensible - speaks well against one so despicable. Harapha does it, bring[?] the good out of Samson, Chorus particularly joyful Movement towards final catastrophe.

Samson Agonistes

Samson. I dread him not, nor all his Giant-brood,
  Though Fame divulge him Father of five Sons,
  All of Gigantic size, Goliah chief.

Chorus. He will directly to the Lords, I fear,   1250
  And with malicious counsel stir them up
  Some way or other yet further to afflict thee.

Samson. He must allege some cause, and offer'd fight
  Will not dare mention, lest a question rise
  Whether he durst accept the offer or not;
  And that he durst not plain enough appear'd.
  Much more affliction than already felt
  They cannot well impose, nor I sustain,
  If they intend advantage of my labours,
  The work of many hands, which earns my keeping,   1260
  With no small profit daily to my owners.
  But come what will, my deadliest foe will prove
  My speediest friend, by death to rid me hence;
  The worst that he can give, to me the best.
  Yet so it may fall out, because their end
  Is hate, not help to me, it may with mine
  Draw their own ruin who attempt the deed.

Chorus. Oh how comely it is, and how reviving   *4th Stasimon (Choric Ode)*
  To the Spirits of just men long opprest,
  When God into the hands of their deliverer   1270
  Puts invincible might
  To quell the mighty of the Earth, th' oppressor,
  The brute and boist'rous force of violent men,
  Hardy and industrious to support
  Tyrannic power, but raging to pursue
  The righteous, and all such as honour Truth!
  He all their Ammunition
  And feats of War defeats,

1248 *divulge*: proclaim (L. *divulgare*).   1253 *offer'd fight*: the fight I offered.   1260 *work of*: work equal to that of . . .   1265 *because*: that because . . .   1266 *with mine*: with my ruin.

Private individual a public fate.
Each person is his own deliverer.

With plain Heroic magnitude of mind
And celestial vigour arm'd;   1280
Their Armouries and Magazines contemns,
Renders them useless, while
With winged expedition
Swift as the lightning glance he executes
His errand on the wicked, who, surpris'd,
Lose their defence, distracted and amaz'd.
    But patience is more oft the exercise
Of Saints, the trial of their fortitude,
Making them each his own Deliverer,
And Victor over all   1290
That tyranny or fortune can inflict.
Either of these is in thy lot,
Samson, with might endu'd
Above the Sons of men; but sight bereav'd
May chance to number thee with those
Whom Patience finally must crown.

Does he ever attain this state?
5th Episode

    This Idol's day hath been to thee no day of rest,
Labouring thy mind
More than the working day thy hands;
And yet perhaps more trouble is behind;   1300
For I descry this way
Some other tending; in his hand
A Sceptre or quaint staff he bears,
Comes on amain, speed in his look.
By his habit I discern him now
A Public Officer, and now at hand.
His message will be short and voluble.

Officer.) Ebrews, the Pris'ner Samson here I seek.

1281 *Magazines*: stores of ammunition.   1283 *expedition*: speed.
1286 *defence*: power to defend themselves.   *amaz'd*: confused.   1292
Either: Both patience and fortitude.   1300 *behind*: still to come.
1302 *some other tending*: someone else approaching.   1303 *quaint*:
ornamented (cf. *Arc.* 47; *Com.* 157).   1307 *voluble*: quickly de-
livered.

156

Chorus. His manacles remark him; there he sits.

Officer. Samson, to thee our Lords thus bid me say: 1310
  This day to Dagon is a solemn Feast,
  With Sacrifices, Triumph, Pomp, and Games;
  Thy strength they know surpassing human rate,
  And now some public proof thereof require
  To honour this great Feast, and great Assembly.
  Rise therefore with all speed and come along,
  Where I will see thee hearten'd and fresh clad,
  To appear as fits before th' illustrious Lords.

Samson. Thou know'st I am an Ebrew; therefore tell them
  Our Law forbids at their Religious Rites   1320
  My presence; for that cause I cannot come.

Officer. This answer, be assur'd, will not content them.

Samson. Have they not Sword-players, and ev'ry sort
  Of Gymnic Artists, Wrestlers, Riders, Runners,
  Jugglers and Dancers, Antics, Mummers, Mimics,
  But they must pick me out, with shackles tir'd,
  And over-labour'd at their public Mill,
  To make them sport with blind activity?
  Do they not seek occasion of new quarrels,
  On my refusal to distress me more,   1330
  Or make a game of my calamities?
  Return the way thou cam'st; I will not come.

Officer. Regard thyself; this will offend them highly.

Samson. Myself? my conscience, and internal peace.
  Can they think me so broken, so debas'd
  With corporal servitude, that my mind ever

1309 *remark*: denote, mark him out.   1312 *Triumph*: festival of
victory. *Pomp*: procession (cf. 436).   1313 *rate*: calculation, meas-
ure.   1317 *hearten'd*: refreshed.   1323 *Sword-players*: professional
fencers.   1324 *Gymnic*: gymnastic.   1325 *Antics*: clowns grotesquely
dressed. *Mummers*: actors in dumb show.   1333 *Regard thyself*: Look
to thyself; beware.

Will condescend to such absurd commands?
Although their drudge, to be their fool or jester,
And in my midst of sorrow and heart-grief,
To show them feats, and play before their god—   1340
The worst of all indignities, yet on me
Join'd with extreme contempt? I will not come.

Officer. My message was impos'd on me with speed,
Brooks no delay: is this thy resolution?

Samson. So take it with what speed thy message needs.

Officer. I am sorry what this stoutness will produce.

Samson. Perhaps thou shalt have cause to sorrow indeed.
                                             [*Exit* Officer]

Chorus. Consider, Samson; matters now are strain'd
Up to the heighth, whether to hold or break.
He's gone, and who knows how he may report   1350
Thy words by adding fuel to the flame?
Expect another message more imperious,
More Lordly thund'ring than thou well wilt bear.

Samson. Shall I abuse this Consecrated gift
Of strength, again returning with my hair
After my great transgression, so requite
Favour renew'd, and add a greater sin
By prostituting holy things to Idols;
A Nazarite, in place abominable
Vaunting my strength in honour to their Dagon?   1360
Besides how vile, contemptible, ridiculous,
What act more execrably unclean, profane?

Chorus. Yet with this strength thou serv'st the Philistines,
Idolatrous, uncircumcis'd, unclean.

1342 *Join'd*: enjoined, imposed.   1344 *Brooks*: permits.   1346
sorry what: sorry (to think) what. *stoutness*: courage, obstinacy.   1348
matters: i.e. the relations between Samson and the Philistines, now
reaching a climax.   1360 *Vaunting*: displaying proudly.   1362
unclean: against the Mosaic law.

Samson. Not in their Idol-worship, but by labour
   Honest and lawful to deserve my food
   Of those who have me in their civil power.

Chorus. Where the heart joins not, outward acts defile not.

Samson. Where outward force constrains, the sentence
      holds:
   But who constrains me to the Temple of Dagon,   1370
   Not dragging? The Philistian Lords command:
   Commands are no constraints. If I obey them,
   I do it freely, venturing to displease
   God for the fear of Man, and Man prefer,
   Set God behind; which in his jealousy
   Shall never, unrepented, find forgiveness.
   Yet that he may dispense with me, or thee,
   Present in Temples at Idolatrous Rites
   For some important cause, thou need'st not doubt.

Chorus. How thou wilt here come off surmounts my reach.

Samson. Be of good courage; I begin to feel   1381
   Some rousing motions in me which dispose
   To something extraordinary my thoughts.
   I with this Messenger will go along,
   Nothing to do, be sure, that may dishonour
   Our Law, or stain my vow of Nazarite.
   If there be aught of presage in the mind,
   This day will be remarkable in my life
   By some great act, or of my days the last.   1389

Chorus. In time thou hast resolv'd; the man returns.

Officer. Samson, this second message from our Lords
   To thee I am bid say: Art thou our Slave,

   1369 *sentence holds*: the maxim holds good (L. *sententia*).   1375
which: an act which.   1376 *unrepented*: if not repented of.   1377–
1378 'Yet that he may give me or thee a dispensation (permission) to
be present . . . at idolatrous rites . . .'   1380 *come off*: escape safely.
1382 *rousing motions*: stirrings of excitement.

Our Captive, at the public Mill our drudge,
And dar'st thou at our sending and command
Dispute thy coming? Come without delay;
Or we shall find such Engines to assail
And hamper thee, as thou shalt come of force,
Though thou wert firmlier fasten'd than a rock.

Samson. I could be well content to try their Art,
  Which to no few of them would prove pernicious; 1400
  Yet knowing their advantages too many,
  Because they shall not trail me through their streets
  Like a wild Beast, I am content to go.
  Masters' commands come with a power resistless
  To such as owe them absolute subjection;
  And for a life who will not change his purpose?
  (So mutable are all the ways of men!)
  Yet this be sure, in nothing to comply
  Scandalous or forbidden in our Law.

Officer. I praise thy resolution. Doff these links: 1410
  By this compliance thou wilt win the Lords
  To favour, and perhaps to set thee free.

Samson. Brethren, farewell. Your company along
  I will not wish, lest it perhaps offend them
  To see me girt with Friends; and how the sight
  Of me, as of a common Enemy
  So dreaded once, may now exasperate them,
  I know not. Lords are Lordliest in their wine;
  And the well-feasted Priest then soonest fir'd
  With zeal, if aught Religion seem concern'd: 1420
  No less the people on their Holy-days
  Impetuous, insolent, unquenchable.

1396 *Engines*: devices, instruments. 1397 *hamper*: bind, constrain. *of force*: perforce. 1399 *Art*: skill (in subduing me). 1400 *pernicious*: deadly. 1402 *Because*: so that. 1406 *for a life*: to save his life. 1410 *Doff*: take off. 1418 *Lordliest*: most arrogant. 1420 *if aught*: if at all.

Samson Agonistes

Happen what may, of me expect to hear
Nothing dishonourable, impure, unworthy
Our God, our Law, my Nation, or myself;
The last of me or no I cannot warrant.

[*Exeunt* Samson *and* Officer]

Chorus. Go, and the Holy One
    Of Israel be thy guide
To what may serve his glory best, and spread his name
Great among the Heathen round: 1430
Send thee the Angel of thy Birth, to stand
Fast by thy side, who from thy Father's field
Rode up in flames after his message told
Of thy conception, and be now a shield
Of fire; that Spirit that first rush'd on thee
In the Camp of Dan,
Be efficacious in thee now at need!
For never was from Heaven imparted
Measure of strength so great to mortal seed,
As in thy wondrous actions hath been seen.   1440
But wherefore comes old Manoa in such haste
With youthful steps? Much livelier than erewhile
He seems: supposing here to find his Son,
Or of him bringing to us some glad news?

Manoa. Peace with you, brethren! My inducement hither
Was not at present here to find my Son,
By order of the Lords new-parted hence
To come and play before them at their Feast.
I heard all as I came; the City rings,
And numbers thither flock; I had no will,   1450
Lest I should see him forc'd to things unseemly.
But that which mov'd my coming now was chiefly

1426 'I cannot be sure whether or not this will be the last you hear
of me' (cf. 1423).   1431 *Send thee*: May God send thee.   1433 *after
... told*: after speaking his message.   1445 *My ... hither*: what led me
here.   1447 *new parted*: just departed.   1450 *no will*: no will to go
'thither'.

To give ye part with me what hope I have
With good success to work his liberty.

Chorus. That hope would much rejoice us to partake
With thee. Say, reverend Sire; we thirst to hear.

Manoa. I have attempted one by one the Lords,
Either at home, or through the high street passing,
With supplication prone and Father's tears,
To accept of ransom for my Son, their pris'ner. 1460
Some much averse I found and wondrous harsh,
Contemptuous, proud, set on revenge and spite,
That part most reverenc'd Dagon and his Priests:
Others more moderate seeming, but their aim
Private reward, for which both God and State
They easily would set to sale: a third
More generous far and civil, who confess'd
They had enough reveng'd, having reduc'd
Their foe to misery beneath their fears;
The rest was magnanimity to remit, 1470
If some convenient ransom were propos'd.
What noise or shout was that? It tore the Sky.

Chorus. Doubtless the people shouting to behold
Their once great dread, captive and blind before them,
Or at some proof of strength before them shown.

Manoa. His ransom, if my whole inheritance
May compass it, shall willingly be paid
And number'd down: much rather I shall choose
To live the poorest in my Tribe, than richest
And he in that calamitous prison left. 1480
No, I am fix'd not to part hence without him.
For his redemption all my Patrimony,

1453 *To . . . me*: to let you share with me.   1457 *attempted*: tried
to persuade.   1469 *beneath their fears*: too low for them to need fear
him.   1470 'It would be generous to remit the rest of their re-
venge'.   1478 *number'd down*: counted out.   1481 *fix'd*: resolute.

If need be, I am ready to forgo
And quit: not wanting him, I shall want nothing.

Chorus. Fathers are wont to lay up for their Sons;
  Thou for thy Son art bent to lay out all:
  Sons wont to nurse their Parents in old age;
  Thou in old age car'st how to nurse thy Son,
  Made older than thy age through eye-sight lost.

Manoa. It shall be my delight to tend his eyes,   1490
  And view him sitting in the house, ennobl'd
  With all those high exploits by him achiev'd,
  And on his shoulders waving down those locks
  That of a Nation arm'd the strength contain'd.
  And I persuade me God had not permitted
  His strength again to grow up with his hair
  Garrison'd round about him like a Camp
  Of faithful Soldiery, were not his purpose
  To use him further yet in some great service—
  Not to sit idle with so great a gift   1500
  Useless, and thence ridiculous, about him.
  And since his strength with eye-sight was not lost,
  God will restore him eye-sight to his strength.

Chorus. Thy hopes are not ill founded, nor seem vain,
  Of his delivery, and thy joy thereon
  Conceiv'd, agreeable to a Father's love;
  In both which we, as next, participate.

Manoa. I know your friendly minds, and—O, what noise!
  Mercy of Heav'n! what hideous noise was that?
  Horribly loud, unlike the former shout.   1510

Chorus. Noise call you it, or universal groan,
  As if the whole inhabitation perish'd?

1483 *forgo*: do without.   1484 *quit*: give up. *wanting*: lacking.
1486 *bent*: willing, resolved.   1503 *to his strength*: as well as strength.
1506 *agreeable to*: in accordance with.   1507 *as next*: as kinsmen, being of the same tribe.

Blood, death, and deathful deeds are in that noise,
Ruin, destruction at the utmost point.

Manoa. Of ruin indeed methought I heard the noise.
Oh! it continues; they have slain my Son.

Chorus. Thy Son is rather slaying them: that outcry
From slaughter of one foe could not ascend.

Manoa. Some dismal accident it needs must be.
  What shall we do, stay here, or run and see?   1520

Chorus. Best keep together here, lest, running thither,
We unawares run into danger's mouth.
This evil on the Philistines is fall'n:
From whom could else a general cry be heard?
The sufferers then will scarce molest us here;
From other hands we need not much to fear.
What if, his eye-sight (for to Israel's God
Nothing is hard) by miracle restor'd,
He now be dealing dole among his foes,
And over heaps of slaughter'd walk his way?   1530

Manoa. That were a joy presumptuous to be thought.

Chorus. Yet God hath wrought things as incredible
For his people of old; what hinders now?

Manoa. He can, I know, but doubt to think he will;
Yet Hope would fain subscribe, and tempts Belief.
A little stay will bring some notice hither.

Chorus. Of good or bad so great, of bad the sooner;
For evil news rides post, while good news baits.
And to our wish I see one hither speeding,
An Ebrew, as I guess, and of our Tribe.   1540

1514 *at . . . point*: in the extreme.   1515 *ruin*: falling buildings (L. *ruina*).   1529 *dole*: grief, pain.   1535 *fain subscribe*: gladly assent to (it).   1536 *stay*: wait. *notice*: news.   1537 'The news will be very great, whether good or bad; if bad, it will come sooner'.   1538 *rides post*: travels fast. *baits*: pauses to feed (bait) the horses.

Samson Agonistes

[*Enter* Messenger]

Messenger. O whither shall I run, or which way fly
The sight of this so horrid spectacle,
Which erst my eyes beheld, and yet behold?
For dire imagination still pursues me.
But providence or instinct of nature seems,
Or reason, though disturb'd and scarce consulted,
To have guided me aright, I know not how,
To thee first, reverend Manoa, and to these
My Countrymen, whom here I knew remaining,
As at some distance from the place of horror,   1550
So in the sad event too much concern'd.

Manoa. The accident was loud, and here before thee
With rueful cry; yet what it was we hear not.
No Preface needs; thou seest we long to know.

Messenger. It would burst forth; but I recover breath
And sense distract, to know well what I utter.

Manoa. Tell us the sum; the circumstance defer.

Messenger. Gaza yet stands, but all her Sons are fall'n,
All in a moment overwhelm'd and fall'n.

Manoa. Sad! but thou know'st to Israelites not saddest   1560
The desolation of a Hostile City.

Messenger. Feed on that first; there may in grief be surfeit.

Manoa. Relate by whom.

Messenger.   By Samson.

Manoa.   That still lessens
The sorrow, and converts it nigh to joy.

Messenger. Ah, Manoa, I refrain too suddenly

1543 *erst*: just now.   1550 *As . . . So*: Though . . . yet.   1552
accident: happening, what happened (L. *accidere*).   1553 *rueful cry*:
dismal noise.   1554 *No Preface needs*: No need for preliminaries;
get to the point.   1557 *the sum*: the general effect, gist. *circumstance*:
details.   1562 *may . . . surfeit*: may later be excess of grief.

165

Samson Agonistes

To utter what will come at last too soon,
Lest evil tidings, with too rude irruption
Hitting thy aged ear, should pierce too deep.

Manoa. Suspense in news is torture; speak them out.

Messenger. Take then the worst in brief: Samson is dead.

Manoa. The worst indeed! O, all my hope's defeated 1571
To free him hence! but death who sets all free
Hath paid his ransom now and full discharge.
What windy joy this day had I conceiv'd,
Hopeful of his Delivery, which now proves
Abortive as the first-born bloom of spring
Nipt with the lagging rear of winter's frost!
Yet ere I give the reins to grief, say first
How died he? death to life is crown or shame.
All by him fell, thou say'st: by whom fell he?   1580
What glorious hand gave Samson his death's wound?

Messenger. Unwounded of his enemies he fell.

Manoa. Wearied with slaughter then, or how? explain.

Messenger. By his own hands.

Manoa.   Self-violence? What cause
Brought him so soon at variance with himself
Among his foes?

Messenger.   Inevitable cause,
At once both to destroy and be destroy'd;
The Edifice, where all were met to see him,
Upon their heads and on his own he pull'd.

Manoa. O lastly over-strong against thyself!   1590
A dreadful way thou took'st to thy revenge.
More than enough we know; but while things yet
Are in confusion, give us if thou canst,

  1574 *windy*: empty.   1585 *at variance*: in conflict.

166

Eye-witness of what first or last was done,
Relation more particular and distinct.

Messenger. Occasions drew me early to this City;
  And as the gates I enter'd with Sun-rise,
  The morning Trumpets Festival proclaim'd
  Through each high street. Little I had dispatch'd,
  When all abroad was rumour'd that this day   1600
  Samson should be brought forth, to show the people
  Proof of his mighty strength in feats and games.
  I sorrow'd at his captive state, but minded
  Not to be absent at that spectacle.
  The building was a spacious Theatre,
  Half round on two main Pillars vaulted high,
  With seats where all the Lords, and each degree
  Of sort, might sit in order to behold;
  The other side was op'n, where the throng
  On banks and scaffolds under Sky might stand;   1610
  I among these aloof obscurely stood.
  The Feast and noon grew high, and Sacrifice
  Had fill'd their hearts with mirth, high cheer, and wine,
  When to their sports they turn'd. Immediately
  Was Samson as a public servant brought,
  In their state Livery clad; before him Pipes
  And Timbrels; on each side went armed guards;
  Both horse and foot before him and behind,
  Archers and Slingers, Cataphracts and Spears.
  At sight of him the people with a shout   1620
  Rifted the Air, clamouring their god with praise,

1594 *Eye-witness*: as an eyewitness.   1595 *Relation*: report.
1596 *Occasions*: my affairs.   1599 *Little . . . dispatch'd*: I had done
little business.   1603 *minded*: decided.   1608 *sort*: quality, kind.
in order: according to their rank.   1610 *banks*: benches. *scaffolds*:
temporary platforms.   1612 'It was high noon and the feast was at
its height . . .'   1616 *state Livery*: uniform of a state retainer.   1617
Timbrels: tambourines.   1619 *Cataphracts*: men and horses both clad
in armour.   *Spears*: spearmen.   1621 *Rifted*: rent, tore (cf. 1472).
clamouring: shouting to.

Who had made their dreadful enemy their thrall.
He, <u>patient but undaunted</u>, where they led him,
Came to the place; and what was set before him,
Which without help of eye might be assay'd,
To heave, pull, draw, or break, he still perform'd
All with incredible, stupendious force,
None daring to appear Antagonist.
At length, for intermission sake, they led him
Between the pillars; he his guide requested   1630
(For so from such as nearer stood we heard),
As over-tir'd, to let him lean a while
With both his arms on those two massy Pillars,
That to the arched roof gave main support.
He unsuspicious led him; which when Samson
Felt in his arms, with head a while inclin'd,
And eyes fast fix'd, he stood, as one who pray'd,
Or some great matter in his mind revolv'd.
At last with head erect thus cried aloud:—
'Hitherto, Lords, what your commands impos'd   1640
I have perform'd, as reason was, obeying,
Not without wonder or delight beheld.
Now of my own accord such other trial
I mean to show you of my strength, yet greater,
As with amaze shall strike all who behold.'
This utter'd, straining all his nerves, he bow'd;
As with the force of winds and waters pent
When Mountains tremble, those two massy Pillars
With horrible convulsion to and fro
He tugg'd, he shook, till down they came, and drew   1650
The whole roof after them with burst of thunder
Upon the heads of all who sat beneath,
Lords, Ladies, Captains, Counsellors, or Priests,
Their choice nobility and flower, not only
Of this, but each Philistian City round,
Met from all parts to solemnize this Feast.

1626 *still*: every time.   1629 *intermission*: interval, pause.

Samson, with these immix'd, inevitably
Pull'd down the same destruction on himself;
The vulgar only scap'd, who stood without.

Chorus. O dearly-bought revenge, yet glorious!   1660
  Living or dying thou hast fulfill'd
  The work for which thou wast foretold
  To Israel, and now liest victorious
  Among thy slain self-kill'd;
  Not willingly, but tangled in the fold
  Of dire necessity, whose law in death conjoin'd
  Thee with thy slaughter'd foes, in number more
  Than all thy life had slain before.

Semichorus. While their hearts were jocund and sublime,
  Drunk with Idolatry, drunk with Wine   1670
  And fat regorg'd of Bulls and Goats,
  Chaunting their Idol, and preferring
  Before our living Dread, who dwells
  In Silo his bright Sanctuary,
  Among them he a spirit of frenzy sent,
  Who hurt their minds,
  And urg'd them on with mad desire
  To call in haste for their destroyer.
  They, only set on sport and play,
  Unweetingly importun'd   1680
  Their own destruction to come speedy upon them.
  So fond are mortal men,
  Fall'n into wrath divine,
  As their own ruin on themselves to invite,
  Insensate left, or to sense reprobate,
  And with blindness internal struck.

1659 *the vulgar*: the common folk.   1666 *necessity*: fate.   1669
sublime: elated (L. *sublimis*).   1671 *regorg'd*: gorged to excess.   1672
preferring: boasting his superiority.   1680 *Unweetingly*: ignorantly.
1685 'Left without understanding, or capable only of perverted
thinking'.

Semichorus. But he, though blind of sight,
　　Despis'd and thought extinguish'd quite,
　　With inward eyes illuminated,
　　His fiery virtue rous'd　　　　　　　　　　　1690
　　From under ashes into sudden flame,
　　And as an ev'ning Dragon came,
　　Assailant on the perched roosts
　　And nests in order rang'd
　　Of tame villatic Fowl; but as an Eagle
　　His cloudless thunder bolted on their heads.
　　So virtue, giv'n for lost,
　　Depress'd and overthrown, as seem'd,
　　Like that self-begotten bird,
　　In the Arabian woods embost,　　　　　　　1700
　　That no second knows nor third,
　　And lay erewhile a Holocaust,
　　From out her ashy womb now teem'd,
　　Revives, reflourishes, then vigorous most
　　When most unactive deem'd;
　　And though her body die, her fame survives,
　　A secular bird, ages of lives.

Manoa. Come, come; no time for lamentation now,
　Nor much more cause. Samson hath quit himself
　Like Samson, and heroicly hath finish'd　　　1710
　A life Heroic, on his Enemies
　Fully reveng'd; hath left them years of mourning,
　And lamentation to the Sons of Caphtor
　Through all Philistian bounds; to Israel

1690 *virtue*: excellence of soul and body.　1692 *Dragon*: serpent
(L. *draco*).　1695 *villatic*: farmyard (L. *villa*, farm).　1696 *bolted*:
shot like a 'bolt (arrow) from the blue'.　1697 *giv'n for*: given up
for.　1699 *that . . . bird*: the Phoenix.　1700 *embost*: enclosed,
embosked (Fr. *embusquer*) in woods.　1702 *Holocaust*: whole burnt
offering.　1703 *teem'd*: brought to birth.　1707 *A secular bird*: a
bird living through many ages (L. *saeculum*).　1709 *Nor . . . cause*: i.e.
than there is time.　*quit*: acquitted.　1714 *Philistian bounds*: the
borders of Philistia.

Honour hath left, and freedom, let but them
Find courage to lay hold on this occasion;
To himself and Father's house eternal fame;
And, which is best and happiest yet, all this
With God not parted from him, as was fear'd,
But favouring and assisting to the end.   1720
Nothing is here for tears, nothing to wail
Or knock the breast; no weakness, no contempt,
Dispraise, or blame; nothing but well and fair,
And what may quiet us in a death so noble.
Let us go find the body where it lies
Soak'd in his enemies' blood, and from the stream
With lavers pure and cleansing herbs wash off
The clotted gore. I with what speed the while
(Gaza is not in plight to say us nay),
Will send for all my kindred, all my friends,   1730
To fetch him hence and solemnly attend,
With silent obsequy and funeral train,
Home to his Father's house. There will I build him
A Monument, and plant it round with shade
Of Laurel ever green, and branching Palm,
With all his Trophies hung, and Acts enroll'd
In copious Legend, or sweet Lyric Song.
Thither shall all the valiant youth resort,
And from his memory inflame their breasts
To matchless valour and adventures high;   1740
The Virgins also shall on feastful days
Visit his Tomb with flowers, only bewailing
His lot unfortunate in nuptial choice,
From whence captivity and loss of eyes.

Chorus. All is best, though we oft doubt Final statement —rather like
a sonnet but hasn't the length
of line.

1722 *knock the breast*: i.e. as a Jewish sign of mourning.   1727
lavers: vessels for washing (cf. *Com.* 838).   1728 *with what speed*:
with what speed I can.   1729 *plight*: condition.   1732 *obsequy*:
funeral rites. *train*: procession.   1737 *In . . . Legend*: inscribing his
story fully there.

171

Samson Agonistes

(handwritten margin note: complicated rhyme-scheme)

What th' unsearchable dispose
Of Highest Wisdom brings about,
And ever best found in the close.
Oft He seems to hide his face,
But unexpectedly returns,   1750
And to his faithful Champion hath in place
Bore witness gloriously; whence Gaza mourns,
And all that band them to resist
His uncontrollable intent.
His servants He, with new acquist
Of true experience from this great event,
With peace and consolation hath dismiss'd,
And calm of mind, all passion spent.

1746 *dispose*: disposition, ordering.   1748 *close*: final outcome.
1751 *in place*: in this place, and at the right moment.   1753 *band them*: combine.   1755 *acquist*: acquisition, increase.   1756 *event*: result, outcome (L. *eventum*).   1758 *passion spent*: mental agitation purged.

(handwritten notes:)
v. slow, v. heroic, v tragic. Moral a psychological
The end is v much resolved

THE END

Do we like to be left with sth more horrific.

Yet not a tragedy — its hero recovers & does God's w[?]
No disproport between sin a punishment, no tempora[?]
dislocat of the universal order, no sense of waste o[?]
even "the pity of it"

From one point of view a Christian tragedy is a
contradiction in terms ∴ there can be no injustice o[?]
disproportion where God is in control.

172

TEXTUAL NOTE

ARCADES AND COMUS

The Cambridge Manuscript

Much more of Milton's handwriting survives than of Shakespeare's. Trinity College, Cambridge, possesses a manuscript containing drafts of many minor poems and suggestions for larger works, with corrections made at various times between 1631 and 1658. *Arcades* and *Comus* are in this working-notebook. From it he made a copy of *Comus* for Henry Lawes's performance at Ludlow, entering into the earlier draft the corrections needed. Before the masque was printed in 1637 he revised it again, and finally before the publication of his 1645 *Poems* he entered new corrections. To work out the order of all these alterations is a difficult task.

The Bridgewater Manuscript

A copy of *Comus* was made by a professional scribe for the Earl of Bridgewater from the acting-copy used at Ludlow. It shows the adjustments made for the performance, e.g. the shifting of part of the Epilogue to make an introductory Song, the division between the Brothers of the later part of the invocation to Sabrina, and the omission of 215 lines of dialogue to shorten the piece, and maybe to reduce the amount of moralising. About 60 lines were cut from the Lady's part.

The 1637 Edition

In 1637 the poem was published separately and anonymously, with a dedicatory letter to Lord Brackley in which Lawes wrote: 'Although not openly acknowledg'd by the Author, yet it is a legitimate offspring, so lovely, and so much desir'd that the often Copying of it hath tir'd my Pen to give my severall friends satisfaction, and brought me now to a necessity of producing it to the publike view. . . .' The title is simply 'A Maske presented at Ludlow Castle, 1634' and in full the title-page runs: A Maske / presented / At Ludlow Castle / 1634: / On Michaelmasse night, before the / Right Honorable, / John Earle of

Bridgewater Vicount Brackly, / Lord Præsident of Wales, And one of / His Maiesties most honorable / Privie Councell. / Motto / *Eheu quid volui misero mihi! floribus austrum* / *Perditus.*

For this edition Milton cut out some extravagances and made other corrections, e.g. 'And hold a counterpoint to all Heav'n's Harmonies' (Cambridge MS.) becomes 'And give resounding grace, &c.' The moral is stressed by inserting lines 679–87, and the Lady's praise of Chastity at 779–99.

The 1645 Edition

In the 1645 edition of the *Poems Comus* has a separate title-page: A / Mask / Of the same / Author / Presented / At Ludlow-Castle / 1634 / Before / The Earl of Bridgwater / Then President of Wales / Anno Dom. 1645. No Motto. Henry Lawes's letter is followed by a letter from Sir Henry Wotton to Milton dated 13 April 1638 in which the famous diplomat and connoisseur thanks him for 'a dainty peece of entertainment . . . Wherin I should much commend the Tragical part, if the Lyrical did not ravish me with a certain Dorique delicacy in your Songs, and Odes, wherunto I must plainly confess to have seen yet nothing parallel in our Language: *Ipsa mollities.*' For this edition Milton made a few textual changes of a Doric (austere) nature; e.g. 'Angel girt with flittering wings' (Cambridge MS.) became 'Angel girt with hovering wings'.

The 1673 Edition. This followed 1645 closely.

SAMSON AGONISTES

Only one edition appeared in Milton's lifetime: in 1671, when it was added to *Paradise Regained*. The printer, John Starkey, was not as careful as the printer of *Paradise Lost*, who had followed the blind poet's instructions faithfully in spelling and punctuation.

THIS EDITION

Our text of *Arcades* and *Comus* is based on the 1645 edition and of *Samson* on the 1671 edition but spelling and punctuation have been modernised. The seventeenth-century use of capital letters has been retained not only because they give the page something of the effect of the original edition, but also because they seem to have been used, though without great consistency, to stress important nouns. Milton's notebook (Cambridge MS.)

has few capitals, even at the beginning of lines, and his spelling
at first was old-fashioned, with its frequent use of the final -e;
but he was already tending to spell as he pronounced, and,
probably when a schoolmaster he began to systematise his
spelling and punctuation according to principles which have
been discussed by Miss Helen Darbishire in her edition of the
Poetical Works, vol. i, 1952, pp. ix–xxxv, and by B. A. Wright in
his Textual Introduction to the *Poems*, 1956 (Everyman
Library). In modernising we have printed 'd where final -ed
should not be pronounced and we have marked unusual
stresses and some elisions.

COMMENTARY

ARCADES

Arcades. The title means 'dwellers in Arcadia', the Greek
state in the Peloponnese whose simple shepherds were idealised
and celebrated in pastoral romances and poems during the
Renaissance, e.g. in Sidney's *Arcadia* and Tasso's *Aminta*. The
piece contains references to the Arcadian rivers, Alpheus (30)
and Ladon (97) and the Arcadian mountains Cyllene (98),
Erymanthus (100), and Maenalus (102). In this region Ovid
laid the story of Pan's courtship of the nymph Syrinx (106).

Countess Dowager. The Countess Dowager, now an old lady of
over seventy, was a daughter of Sir John Spencer of Althorpe
in Northamptonshire. She had been married twice. By her first
husband, Lord Strange, she had three daughters before he died
in 1594, a year after becoming the Earl of Derby. His death was
mentioned by Edmund Spenser (a very distant relation) in
Colin Clout's Come Home Again (1595), where she is given the
pastoral name 'Amaryllis'. He had already dedicated *The Tears
of the Muses* (1591) to her. In 1600 she married a widower,
Sir Thomas Egerton, Lord Keeper of the Great Seal (who had
had the poet Donne as his secretary), and Egerton was made
Viscount Brackley just before he died in 1617. The Countess
lived at Harefield in Middlesex with her widowed daughter

Commentary

Lady Chandos who had several children. Her second daughter Frances had married Egerton's son John (who was therefore the Countess's son-in-law and also her stepson). He was made Earl of Bridgewater, and (before *Comus* was written) President of the Council of Wales. He lived at Ashridge in Hertfordshire not far from Harefield, and no doubt his family attended the festivities during which *Arcades* was 'presented to' the Countess Dowager.

seat of State. The Countess's throne would be in the centre facing the actors.

1. *Song*. This introduces the theme: praise of the Countess, picking her out from the rest of the company and directing compliments towards her.

1. *Nymphs and Shepherds*: the Arcadians.

6. *vows*: vows of loyalty and affection.

7. *search*. The theme of the piece is the coming of Arcadian shepherds in search of the Countess, attracted by rumours of her glory.

14–19. This stanza suggests that the Countess's seat was surrounded with candles or lamps, hence the aptness of the imagery of lines 18–19.

20. *Latona*: mother of Apollo and Diana. She was a goddess of spiritual concord.

21. *Cybele*: wife of Saturn and mother of Jupiter, Juno and many other gods. Virgil says a hundred (*Aeneid*, vi. 786). She taught men to build cities and so her crown bore turrets (*Aeneid*, x. 252–3). Spenser wrote of

> Old Cybele . . .
> Wearing a diademe embattild wide
> With hundred turrets   (*Faerie Queene*, IV. xi. 28).

The reference is to the Countess's many grandchildren, some of whom no doubt took part in *Arcades*.

23. *Juno*: queen of the gods. She dare not give the Countess any advantage, e.g. by setting aside her divinity and meeting her on equal terms.

25. *unparallel'd*. Shakespeare's Cleopatra is 'a lass unparallel'd' (*Antony and Cleopatra*, v. ii. 314).

176

Arcades

s.d. *Genius of the Wood*. Masques often included the Spirit of the place. Here the Spirit acts as 'Presenter', telling who the masquers are and taking them to do homage. Probably Henry Lawes took this part.

30. *Alpheus*: the god of a river in Arcadia. Ovid (*Metamorphoses*, v. 574–641) tells how the nymph Arethusa, when pursued by Alpheus, was transformed into a stream by Diana and escaped under the Adriatic Sea to Sicily where Alpheus joined her.

32. *breathing*: living (Nymphs).

33. *silver-buskin'd*. The actresses wore boots (buskins) like the huntress Diana and her nymphs.

63. *celestial Sirens*: the Muses, heavenly counterparts of the Sirens who sang to Odysseus. The Muses defeated the Sirens in singing and thereafter wore their feathers.

63–73. Milton takes this account of the machinery of the universe from Plato's vision of Er in the *Republic*, x. 616–17. According to this, the universe is bound together by light, but its revolving motion is caused by a distaff of adamant held by Necessity. The whorl is hollow and contains other whorls of similar shape one within the other, so that there are eight whorls altogether, which spin with the movement of the distaff on the knees of Necessity. 'Upon each of its circles stands a siren, who travels round with the circle, uttering one note in one tone; and from all the eight notes there results a single harmony. At equal distances around sit three other personages, each on a throne. These are the daughters of Necessity, the Fates, Lachesis, Clotho, Atropos; who clothed in white robes, with garlands on their heads, chant to the music of the sirens, Lachesis the events of the past, Clotho those of the present, Atropos those of the future. Clotho with her right hand takes hold of the outermost rim of the distaff, and twirls it altogether, at intervals; and Atropos with her left hand twirls the inner circles in like manner; while Lachesis takes hold of each in turn with either hand' (trans. Davies and Vaughan, pp. 365–6).

68–9. Milton imagines that the harsh unstable Fates are kept quiet by the Sirens' music and their own singing.

72–3. Cf. Lorenzo, in *The Merchant of Venice* (v. i. 64–5), speaking of the music of the spheres:

Commentary

> But while this muddy vesture of decay
> Doth grossly close it in, we cannot hear it.

75. Milton's compliment to the Countess is sheer hyperbole.

ii. *Song*: sung by Lawes to the lute as the masquers moved forward towards the throne. The varied lines of the songs well fitted them to be set to music.

89. Cf. Spenser, *Faerie Queene* (i. i. 7), a grove 'not perceable with power of any starre'.

iii. *Song*. Between the songs the masquers would make their obeisance and then dance their formal dances. No description of them is given, but they are hinted at in 96–9.

98–102. See note on title.

106. *Syrinx . . . Pan.* Pan (born on Mount Lycaeus, 98) was the goat-footed god of flocks and herds; also of all sub-human nature. Syrinx, the lovely daughter of Ladon, was pursued by him. She fled into the river and was changed into a reed from which Pan made his pipe.

COMUS

s.d. *The Attendant Spirit*. In the Cambridge MS. he is 'a guardian spirit or demon'. Cf. *Antony and Cleopatra*, ii. iii. 19, 'Thy demon, that's thy spirit which keeps thee'.

1–92. The Attendant Spirit's Prologue. When acted, Comus opened with a song by the Spirit made from lines 976–99 of our text. The Prologue, like those of Euripides, is divided into an introduction (1–17) and an exposition of the setting and situation (18–92). A compliment to the Earl is introduced (18–36) which shows the formal occasion of the masque.

3. *aërial . . . inspher'd*. At once Milton takes us high in the Ptolemaic universe in which there were ten spheres revolving round the earth. Seven of them carried the planets (including the Moon and Sun); then came the sphere of fixed stars, the crystalline sphere, and the Primum Mobile (first moved) which moved the whole. Many men thought that each sphere and planet had its own guiding spirit. Below the Moon was the region of the four elements, earth, water, air and fire; above it was aether. Henry More thought that the Soul's home

before birth was 'these immense tracts of pure and quiet aether that are above Saturn'.

4. *In Regions mild*: like the home of the gods in Homer's *Odyssey* (vi. 43, 44) 'shaken by no winds, drenched by no showers and invaded by no snows, it is set in a cloudless sea of limpid air with a white radiance playing over all' (Rieu's translation).

5. This is an echo of Horace, *Odes*, III. xxix. 12, 'the smoke and luxury and noise of Rome'.

11. Cf. Revelation, iv. 4. 'And round about the throne were four and twenty seats', and Giles Fletcher, *Christ's Victorie*, iii. 53 has

> glad Spirits, that now sainted sit
> On your celestial thrones in glory drest.

13. *Golden Key*: this is St. Peter's. Cf. *Lycidas*, 111, 'The golden opes, the iron shuts amain'.

16–17. Angels were thought to have aetherial bodies but they assumed bodies of thickened air in order to be visible to men. Donne writes of the difference 'twixt Aire and Angells' puritie'. Cf. *P.L.* vi. 330–53.

20. In *Iliad*, xv. 190–3, Poseidon says that he was given the sea, Zeus the sky, Hades the underworld.

33. *proud in Arms*: a compliment to the Welsh people who thought themselves to be descended from the Romans; translated from Virgil's description of the Romans (*Aeneid*, i. 21).

34. This may allude to the princely descent of the children —from Henry VII.

45. *Hall or Bow'r*: the men's hall and ladies' chamber of a castle, often referred to in romances. Spenser speaks of Sir Philip Sidney, 'Merrily masking both in bowre and hall' (*Astrophel*, 28).

48. Ovid, *Metamorphoses*, iii. 670–86, describes the voyage of Bacchus (god of wine) along the Tyrrhene shore (coast of Etruria), his seizure by pirate sailors and their transformation into dolphins for their violence to the god.

50. Circe was the daughter of the sun god (Helios) and lived on Aeaea. Homer, *Odyssey*, x, tells how Odysseus was wrecked on her island and his comrades changed into swine. In Ariosto's

Commentary

Orlando Furioso (canto vi), Alcina has a magic cup and transforms Astolpho.

54–7. In *L'Allegro* (16) 'Ivy-crowned Bacchus' was (perhaps) father of 'heart-easing Mirth' by Venus. Here, by Circe, he fathers another seductive but more sinister offspring. For Comus see Introduction. T. Dekker, in *Gull's Hornbook* (1609), calls on 'Comus, thou Clarke of Gluttonies kitchen'.

60. *Celtic and Iberian fields*: France and Spain, wine countries appropriate to Bacchus.

69. *Th' express . . . gods*. Cf. Genesis i. 27 'God created man in his own image'.

70. Alcina's victims in Ariosto were 'chang'd . . . Into some brutish beast, some stone or tree' (*Orlando Furioso*, vi. 52).

72–6. According to Homer, Circe changed the whole bodies of her victims but Milton changes only the heads. Unlike Homer, he makes the people transformed by Comus think themselves more beautiful. This points a moral.

76. Astolpho, enchanted by Alcina, 'Neither remembered France nor anything else' (*Orlando Furioso*, vi. 47).

83. *Iris' Woof*: rainbow stuff (Iris was the goddess of the rainbow). Cf. the Archangel's dress in *P.L.* xi. 244, 'Iris had dipped the woof'. Between lines 92 and 93 the Genius must don shepherd's clothes.

85. Henry Lawes, who played the part, was music-master to the Earl of Bridgewater's family ('service of this house'). There would be piquancy in his disguising himself thus.

87. Henry Lawes later borrowed this idea in praising his dead brother William's music: 'He could allay the murmurs of the wind' (*Choice Psalmes*, 1648).

s.d. 93. *headed . . . Beasts*. Circe's victims became entirely beastlike. Alcina's, according to Harington, are a 'monstrous band, of which some have heads like dogs, some have countenances and gestures of apes'. (*Allegorie* to his trans.) Milton's monsters were masked. They must dance the Antimasque.

95–7. This is the Greek idea of the sun in his golden chariot cooling its wheels in the evening in the *Atlantic stream* (Oceanus) which was believed to flow round the earth.

102–6. Milton had used such barely-personified abstractions in his *Nativity Ode*, 136–44. But here he probably drew on the Latin *Comus* of Puteanus: 'Meanwhile Comus enters in a throng of riot and excess; . . . The Hours strewed the sweetest summer odours and every bright flower. Love was followed by the Graces, Delights, Wit and other lawless forms of Hilarity: Voluptuous Laughter and Jest. With Satiety came his sister Drunkenness . . .'

104. *Jollity*. Jollity and Laughter were two characters in Shirley's *Triumph of Peace* (February, 1634).

107–10. Cf. the Ode in Puteanus: 'Now it is right to banish the marks and blemishes of severity from mind and face. Begone grim care. Here are excitement, youth and mirth.'

111. *fire*. The Ancients believed that everything was composed of four elements—earth, water, fire and air. Cf. *Antony and Cleopatra*, v. ii. 287) 'I am fire and air'.

112–14. *the Starry Quire*: the harmoniously moving stars which make the music of the spheres and the cosmic dance. There is a reference to the Spirits or Platonic Sirens who guide them in dance-like revolutions (rounds), which mark for men on earth the periods of time.

129. *Cotytto*: Thracian goddess of wantonness whose rites were held at night.

132. *Stygian darkness*: like the darkness of the underworld. The river Styx flowed through Hades.

135. *Hecat'*: Hecate, goddess of night and witchcraft.

143–4. Cf. Puteanus' Ode: 'Let him learn to beat the ground with broken step', but the idea is found in Horace, Jonson, Fletcher, etc.
fantastic. Cf. *L'Allegro*, 34, 'light, fantastic toe'.
round: defined as 'When men dance and sing, taking hands round' (Barret's *Alvearie*, 1580).

s.d. *The Measure*. This was usually a formal, stately dance but in the Cambridge MS. Milton described it as 'a wild, rude, wanton antick'.

176. *Pan*: the pastoral god of all things.

177. *amiss*: in an unsuitable manner, i.e. not with Christian

Commentary

reverence. The Lady does not approve of the Harvest Home customs described by Herrick and later by Thomas Hardy.

179. *Wassailers*. At Christmas mummers used to go from house to house playing and drinking healths; hence tipsy revellers.

189. *palmer*: a pilgrim bearing a palm-branch in proof of having visited the Holy Land. Robert Greene wrote of a pilgrim: 'In a surcoat all of grey'.

197. *In thy dark lantern*. Night is like a thief with a dark lantern (darkness) and the stars are the light inside, which he shuts off by twisting the shutter. While declaring that this image is rather absurd Warton admired Milton's 'wild and romantick imagery' in *Comus*. Such 'conceits', daring, homely, slightly grotesque, were a feature of Caroline poetry.

195–225 *else . . . Grove*. These lines are not in the Bridgewater MS., perhaps so that the Lady should not have so much to memorise.

205–9. Cf. the night-fears dismissed by Clorin in John Fletcher's *Faithful Shepherdess*, i. i. 114–20, including 'voices calling me in dead of night'. Shelley recalled this in his 'shapes that haunt thoughts' wildernesses' (*Prometheus Unbound*).

210–11. Cf. Fletcher's Clorin who knows herself safe 'if I keep my virgin-flower uncropt, pure, chaste and fair'.

215. Cf. Fletcher
then, strong Chastity,
Be thou my strongest guard.

221–5. The audience would see this too. Cloud and moon effects were common in the masques.

228. *new-enliven'd*: by the proof given by the moon that God will send a 'glistring guardian'.

230. *Echo*: a nymph who fell hopelessly in love with Narcissus and pined away until only her voice remained (Ovid, *Metamorphoses*, iii. 370–400). Echo songs, in which the last words of a line were repeated or varied to answer the singer, were a feature of pastoral drama from Guarini onwards. The popular theatre made lavish use of them. Milton invokes Echo but she does not reply.

231. *airy shell*: cavern of air. Jonson who mocks at Echo songs in *Cynthia's Revels*, I. i. makes Mercury invoke Echo, to learn in what cavern of the earth her airy spirit is contained. Milton's image is of the hollow air acting like a cavern wall, or sea-shell throwing back sound. The Cambridge MS. reads 'cell' in margin.

232. *Meander*: the Phrygian river whose winding course gave the word 'meander' (wander).

237. *Narcissus*: the son of a river-god, who, falling in love with his own reflection, was changed into a flower (Ovid, *Metamorphoses*, iii. 410–510).

241. *Queen of Parley*: because she answers when spoken to.
Daughter of the Sphere: because her music is airy and elusive like that of the spheres. Cf. *At a Solemn Music* (2): 'Sphere-born harmonious sisters, Voice and Verse'.

243. The Cambridge MS. has 'and hold a counterpoint to all Heav'n's Harmonies'. Milton cut out the technical, musical reference.

244–8. A compliment to Lady Alice Egerton who had just sung.

251. *fall*: musical cadence. Cf. Orsino in *Twelfth Night* (I. i. 4): 'That strain again, it had a dying fall'.

251–2. *Raven . . . darkness*. Cf. *L'Allegro*, 6, 7:

> Where brooding Darkness spreads his jealous wings,
> And the night-raven sings.

253–5. A pleasant fancy: of Circe paying a call on the Sirens while her Nymphs gather drugs! In Homer's *Odyssey* (bk. xii) Circe warns Odysseus against the Sirens who with the music of their song cast their spell upon passing sailors.

254. *Naiades*: water nymphs. In Homer (*Odyssey*, x) Circe's four handmaidens are the 'daughters of Springs . . . and the sacred Rivers that flow out into the sea' (Rieu).

257. *Scylla . . . Charybdis*: the rock and whirlpool opposite one another on the Italian and Sicilian coasts and also the monsters inhabiting these places. Scylla had the body of a woman, six heads, and barked like a dog. She snatched sailors from passing ships and devoured them, while Charybdis, three

times a day, sucked in the waters of the straits and spat them out again in a whirlpool. (*Odyssey*, bk. xii.)

263. A wonderful phrase to describe good music.

268. *Sylvan*: Sylvanus, originally god of fields and woods, later identified with Pan.

271–2. She thinks him a shepherd and mildly reproves him for his extravagant praise. She pays no attention to it.

277–90. This is the Greek rhetorical device 'stichomythia'— rapid question and answer. See *S.A.* 1552 ff.

290. *Hebe*: a youthful cupbearer of the gods.

291–2. Both Virgil (*Eclogues*, ii. 66–7) and Homer use the unyoking of oxen to signify the approach of evening.

325. The Lady rightly derives 'courtesy' from 'court' but she disagrees with Spenser (*Faerie Queene*, VI. i. 1)

> Of Court, it seems, men Courtesie do call,
> For that it there most useth to abound.

and agrees with Harington's translation of Ariosto:

> As courtesie oft-times in simple bowres
> Is found as great as in the stately towres (XIX. 52).

331. *Unmuffle*: unveil. Cf. *Romeo and Juliet*, v. iii. 21: 'Muffle me, night awhile'.

333. *Stoop*: bend down and show.

> And oft as if her head she bowed,
> Stooping through a fleecy cloud (*Il Penseroso*, 71–2)

334. Chaos is (1) the confusion of elements before creation and (2) the god who ruled over them. Cf. *P.L.* ii. 894–910.

335. *double night*. The temporary darkness of night is added to the permanent and sinister darkness of shady places. Cf. *S.A.* 593.

338. *rush Candle*. This was the poor man's light, made by dipping a rush in tallow.

341. *star of Arcady*. 'Calisto the daughter of Lycaon, king of Arcadia, was changed into the Greater Bear . . . and her son Arcas into the Lesser, called also Cynosura, by observing of which the Tyrians and Sidonians steered their course, as the

Grecian mariners did by the other' (Newton). The Pole Star is in the Lesser Bear.

345. *pastoral reed*: the shepherd's pipe usually made of reed, cane or hemlock stems. By a mistranslation of Virgil's 'tenui avena' (*Eclogues*, i. 2) which might mean any stalk, Spenser gave 'Oaten reedes, Avena'. Hence 'Oaten stops'.

373–5. Cf. the Red Cross Knight's encouragement to Una (*Faerie Queene*, I. i. 12): 'Virtue gives herself light through darkness for to wade': also Jonson, in *Pleasure Reconcil'd to Virtue*:

> She, she it is in darkness shines,
> 'Tis she that still herself refines,
> By her own light, to every eye.

375. *flat Sea*. Cf. 'the level brine' in *Lycidas* (98).

377. Contrast *Il Penseroso*, 54, 'the Cherub Contemplation'.

381. *Light . . . breast*. Contrast *S.A.* 160–3, where Samson grieves for the loss of 'inward light'.

383–5. Cf. *P.L.* i. 254–5.

> The mind is its own place, and in itself
> Can make a Heaven of Hell, a Hell of Heaven.

384–5. The Cambridge MS. has:

> Walks in black vapours, though the noontyde brand
> blaze in the summer solstice . . .

385. Cf. *S.A.* 153.

393. *Hesperian Tree*: the golden-fruited tree given by Earth to Hera at her marriage to Zeus and guarded by the nymphs (Hesperides) and a sleepless, hundred-headed dragon. One of the labours of Hercules was to slay the dragon and get the fruit.

399–403. This recalls Rosalind in *As You Like It*, i. iii, before going into the forest:

> Alas! What danger will it be to us,
> Maids as we are, to travel forth so far!
> Beauty provoketh thieves sooner than gold.

413. *squint suspicion*. Cf. Spenser's Suspicion in *Faerie Queene*, III. xii. 15:

> But he was foul, ill-favoured, and grim,
> Under his eyebrows looking still askance.

Commentary

420–1. Amarillis in Guarini's *Pastor Fido*, III. 3, declares

> For She that is protected by her honour,
> Scorns there should be a safer guard upon her.

and St. Ambrose: 'Virginity is guarded by a wall of chastity and defended sevenfold with divine protection.'

421. Todd's note is amusing: 'This phrase is supposed to be borrowed from *Hamlet*. Critics must show their reading, in quoting books, but I think it was a common expression for "armed from head to foot".' (He then cites many books.)

425. This recalls the confidence of Clorin in *Faithful Shepherdess*, cf. 210 note.

435. Cf. *King Lear*, III. iv. 112–13, 'the foul fiend . . . begins at curfew, and walks till the first cock'.

436. *swart Fairy of the mine*. It was a common belief that goblins lived in mines. One, the 'pukka', gave his name to Shakespeare's Puck.

441. *Dian*. Diana, goddess of the moon, of chastity and of hunting, had silver arrows.

447. *snaky-headed Gorgon shield*. The Gorgon Medusa, whose glance turned men to stone, was killed by Perseus who looked at her in a mirror. She had snakes instead of hair.

448. *Minerva*: the virgin Athene, goddess of wisdom. The head of Medusa was represented on her shield.

455–75. This is one of Milton's central doctrines throughout his life.

455. Cf. St. Ambrose *On Virgins*: 'Nor wonder if Angels fight on your behalf who war in the virtuous ways of angels . . .'

457–8. But the good angels also teach the virtuous soul by dreams.

458. Cf. *Arc.* 72: but Milton here means not only the harmony of the Spheres but the mystical truths of religion.

459–63. See Introduction, p. 26.

463–73. On the other hand indulgence in sensuality assimilates the soul to matter, hence, as Plato writes in *Phaedo*, para. 81, such a soul 'if it departs polluted and impure from the body . . . having served and loved it . . . will be impressed by that which is corporeal . . . and is weighed down and drawn

186

Comus

again into the visible world through dread of the invisible and
of Hades, wandering, as it is said, amongst monuments and
tombs, about which, indeed, certain shadow phantoms of souls
have been seen. . . . These are the souls . . . of the wicked, which
are compelled to wander about such places, paying the penalty
of their former [evil] conduct . . . ; and they wander about so
long, until, through the desire of the corporeal nature that
accompanies them, they are again united to a body; and they
are united, as is probable, to animals having the same habits
as those they have given themselves up to during life. . . . For
instance, those who have given themselves up to gluttony,
wantonness and drinking, and having put no restraint on them-
selves, will probably be clothed in the form of asses and brutes
of that kind' (Cary's trans.).

468. *Imbodies, and imbrutes*: becomes material and animal. So
Satan regrets having to become a serpent:

mix'd with bestial slime,
This essence to incarnate and imbrute.   *P.L.* ix. 165.

476. Warton noted the difference in maturity between the
two Brothers, and adds: 'The whole dialogue, which is indeed
little more than a solitary declamation in blank verse, much
resembles the manner of our author's Latin *Prolusions*, where
philosophy is enforced by pagan fable and poetical allusion.'
'Philosophy' here means the knowledge about man's nature
and relation to God and the Universe.

477–80. Later Milton praised 'a virtuous and noble educa-
tion, laborious indeed at the first ascent, but also so smooth,
so green, so full of goodly prospect and melodious sounds, that
the harp of Orpheus was not more charming' (*Tractate on
Education*, 1644). Here the music is that of Apollo, god of string-
music and of the intellect.

483. *night-founder'd*. Cf. *P.L.* i. 204, 'pilot of some small night-
founder'd Skiff'.

494. *Thyrsis*: a traditional name for a shepherd in pastoral
literature; used later by Matthew Arnold in his Elegy on
Clough.

494–6. *whose . . . dale*: a compliment to Henry Lawes as a
singer and a composer of madrigals.

187

Commentary

495–512. Eighteen lines whose rhyming couplets enforce their orthodox pastoralism. The passage also 'relieves the tension of the excitingly dramatic episode which has just occurred' (Tillyard), before the long narrative by the Spirit.

515. Milton himself is 'taught by the heav'nly Muse' in *P.L.* iii. 19.

517. *Chimeras*: fire-breathing monsters, part lion, part dragon, part goat. *enchanted Isles*: refers to the 'Wand'ring Islands' of the *Faerie Queene*, II. xii. 11 ff. Belief in the existence of these mysterious islands was common.

529. *reasons' mintage*. Reason meant the powers of intellect and spiritual aspiration distinguishing man from (as Hamlet put it) 'a beast, that wants discourse of reason' (*Hamlet*, I. ii. 150).

534–5. Circe 'prays to Hecate with magic howls' in Ovid, *Metamorphoses*, xiv. 405. Cf. Introduction, p. 24.

544. Cf. *Midsummer Night's Dream*, II. i. 251; 'Quite over-canopied with luscious woodbine'.

546. *melancholy*: not gloom but the quiet meditation of *Il Penseroso*, 12.

547. The line comes from Virgil: 'Silvestrem tenui musam meditaris avena.' Cf. *Lycidas*, in a different mood, 'And strictly meditate the thankless Muse'.

553. *drowsy-flighted*. This, the Cambridge MS. reading, is more satisfactory than the 'drowsy-frighted' of the Bridgewater MS. and early editions. *Henry VI*, pt. 2, IV. i refers to the 'jades' of Night 'with their drowsy, slow, and flagging wings'.

554. *close-curtain'd Sleep*. Cf. *Macbeth*, II. i. 51, 'curtain'd sleep'.

561–2. *strains . . . Death*: 'music beautiful enough to put a new soul into the skeleton Death of medieval tombs or paintings'. An Emblem in Hugo's *Pia Desideria* (1624) shows a skeleton with a child-like soul inside it trying to get free. Quarles used the picture in his *Emblems* (1635), bk. v. no. 8.

588. So-called Chance is either the Devil's work, or God's Providence; here the former.

592. *the happy trial*. Milton believed that virtue must prove

188

Comus

itself by testing and temptation. Cf. 'that which purifies us is trial, and trial is by what is contrary' (*Areopagitica*).

595–6. This image has been thought to come from Renaissance astronomers' theories about sunspots 'which they suppose to be the scum of that fiery matter, which first breeds it [the scum] and then breaks through and consumes it' (Warburton).

604. *sooty flag*. Cf. Phineas Fletcher's poem *Locusts* (2. 39), 'All hell run out, and sooty flags display'. *Acheron*: one of the four rivers of Hades; here it means hell itself.

605. *Harpies*: monstrous birds with female faces who swoop down and defile banquets (cf. Virgil, *Aeneid*, iii. 214–18).

Hydras: snake-like beast with many heads, slain by Hercules, though two new heads grew whenever one was cut off.

606. *Ind*. For the Mediterranean peoples, India stood for the far east and Africa the far west.

619. Refers maybe to Milton's medical friend Diodati.

620–2. This recalls both Shakespeare's Friar Lawrence (*Romeo and Juliet*, II. iii) and Fletcher's Clorin who collects healing herbs (*Faithful Shepherdess*, I. 1).

636. *Moly*: a plant with a white flower and black root given to Odysseus by Hermes as a protection against the spells of Circe (*Odyssey*, x).

638. *Haemony*. The name is Milton's invention, derived from Haemonia (Thessaly) the land of magic. He means Faith in God.

651. *brandish'd blade*. Cf. *Odyssey*, x. 294–5 where Hermes advises Odysseus 'when Circe strikes you with her long wand, you must draw your sword from your side and rush at her' (Rieu).

651–2. So Sir Guyon (Temperance) in *Faerie Queene*, II. xii. 57, snatching her golden goblet from the hand of Excess

> The cup to ground did violently cast,
> That all in pieces it was broken fond,
> And with the liquor stained all the lond.

655. *sons of Vulcan*. Cacus, son of Vulcan (god of fire) was squeezed to death by Hercules though he vomited fire and smoke (Virgil, *Aeneid*, viii. 194 ff.).

s.d. 659. The banquet is a symbol of fleshly delights used in

189

Commentary

many romantic tales and dramas, e.g. the 'several strange shapes bringing in a banquet, and inviting the king to eat' in *The Tempest*, III. iii. Milton used the device again, *P.R.* ii. 337 ff.

660. Cf. Prospero's threat to paralyse Ferdinand in *The Tempest*, I. ii. 484–5.

> Thy nerves are in their infancy again,
> And have no vigour in them.

661–2. *Root-bound*. The nymph, Daphne, was changed into a laurel tree as she fled from Apollo, her arms becoming the branches and her feet the roots (Ovid, *Metamorphoses*, i. 547–52).

675. *Nepenthes*: a pain-lulling drug. This was the opiate given to Telemachus by Helen (to whom it had been given by Polydama, wife of Thone) to allay his grief for his father.

679. Cf. Shakespeare, urging his friend to marry: 'Thyself thy foe, to thy sweet self so cruel' (Sonnet I).

683. 'In dealing harshly with your beauty you behave like a debtor who uses what he borrows against the terms of the loan.' Cf. Shakespeare's Sonnet IV.

707. *budge*: formal. Budge meant also the fur used for academic hoods; and so was used of the men who wore it. 'Budge-bachelors' (B.A.s) walked in the Lord Mayor's procession. Here 'budge doctors' means 'formal furred doctors'—in ridicule.

707–8. *Stoic . . . Cynic*: two Schools of Greek philosophy. Both rejected sensual pleasure. The great Cynic Diogenes lived in a tub to show his contempt for comfort and orthodoxy.

710–36. Comus expounds a common argument for Epicurean hedonism, the gospel of pleasure. Earth's creatures were made for man's enjoyment.

721. Cf. Daniel i. 10–15, and Introduction, p. 35.

727. Cf. Hebrews xii. 8, and Introduction, p. 35.

737–55. These lines, absent from the Bridgewater MS., were not spoken in performance.

739–40. Shakespeare uses similar imagery from money which is meant to be used, in Sonnets IV and VI.

Comus

743. Cf. *Midsummer Night's Dream*, I. i. 76–8.

> But earthlier happy is the rose distill'd,
> Than that which, withering on the virgin thorn,
> Grows, lives and dies in single blessedness.

745–7. Michael Drayton in the *Epistle* in which King John tempts Matilda uses this argument:

> Why, heaven made beauty, like herself, to view,
> Not to be shut up in a smoky mew.

748. Cf. *Two Gentlemen of Verona*, I. i. 2: 'Home-keeping youth have ever homely wits'.

755. *You . . . yet*: 'Young enough to need advice, and to take advantage of it.'

760. *bolt*: 'Curiously to discuss . . . the truth in reasoning' (Barret's *Alvearie*, 1580).

768–76. In *King Lear* (IV. i. 67–72) Gloucester gives the outcast Edgar his purse, saying

> Heavens, deal so still!
> Let the superfluous and lust-dieted man,
> . . . feel your power quickly;
> So distribution should undo excess,
> And each man have enough.

779–806. *Shall I . . . more strongly*: not in the Cambridge and Bridgewater MSS. Probably added before publication to bring out the central doctrine of the poem.

784. Cf. 997. Comus has a 'gross unpurged ear' (*Arc.* 73).

787. In his *Smectymnuus* Milton explains that Scripture unfolds 'those chaste and high mysteries, . . . that the body is for the Lord, and the Lord for the body'.

792. *convinc'd*: convicted of error.

803–5. 'As when wrathful Jove speaks in thunder and pronounces on Saturn's followers the doom of imprisonment in Erebus (an underground cavern).'
Saturn: Jove's father, the Titan, against whom he made war, and, triumphing, imprisoned him under the earth.

808. Milton ironically treats Comus's realm as (like the Church) an endowed institution (foundation) with fixed rules (canon laws).

Commentary

809–10. Cf. T. Nashe, *Terrors of the Night* (1594), of melancholy. It 'sinketh down to the bottom like the lees of wine, corrupteth all the blood, and is the cause of lunacy'.

811–13. The promised effect is like that of the deadly fountain of Armida in Tasso's *Jerusalem Delivered*, xiv. 74.

816–19. Circe's charms were undone when her rod was reversed and her formula of words said backwards (Ovid, *Metamorphoses*, xiv. 300–1). In *The Faerie Queene*, II. xii. 49 Sir Guyon breaks the magic staff of the porter of Pleasure, and throws down his bowl. In *The Faerie Queene*, III. xii. 36 Amoret was released when Britomart read from Busyrane's magic book 'his charms back to reverse'.

822. *Meliboeus*. The shepherds Meliboeus and Tityrus appear in Virgil's first Eclogue. Milton (following Spenser's example) called Chaucer 'Tityrus' in *Mansus* 34. Here by Meliboeus he means Spenser, who told the legend of Sabrina in *The Faerie Queene*, II. x. 14–19.

824–41. According to the legend, Locrine was the son of Brutus, grandson of Aeneas, and inherited from him the throne of England, his brothers receiving Wales and Scotland. He married Guendolen, daughter of Corineus, king of Cornwall, but deserted her for Estrildis, by whom he had a daughter Sabra (in Spenser, Sabrina). Guendolen attacked them, slew Locrine and threw Estrildis and Sabra into a river which was afterwards called Sabrina or Severn. Milton alters the legend here: says nothing of Sabrina's guilty mother; makes Guendolen her stepdame; and Sabrina alone is drowned in the river by accident in her flight from Guendolen. She is received by the 'water Nymphs'—the fifty Nereids, daughters of Nereus (really a sea-god).

834. *pearled wrists*: telling the story in *Polyolbion* v, Drayton wrote

> where she meant to go,
> The path was strew'd with *pearl*.

838. *Asphodil*: asphodel, a plant which grew in the meadows of Elysium where Odysseus found the souls of dead heroes. It became a symbol of immortality.

839. Cf. *Hamlet*, I. v. 61–4, 'thy uncle . . . in the porches of mine ears did pour . . . leprous distilment'.

840. Ambrosia, the food of the gods, gave immortality.

843-7. Cf. Clorin in *Faithful Shepherdess*, I. i.

> Of all green wounds I know the remedies
> In men or cattle; be they stung with snakes,
> Or charm'd with powerful words of wicked art.

845. *urchin blasts*: malignant breaths of the hedgehog. In English folklore the hedgehog was a harmful animal with magical properties. Mischievous fairies assumed its form. Caliban says that Prospero may order his spirits to 'Fright me with urchin-shows, pitch me i' the mire' and appear 'Like hedgehogs' i.e. to prick his feet. (*The Tempest*, II. ii. 5–12).

846. Robin Goodfellow was 'that shrewd and knavish sprite' (*Midsummer Night's Dream*. II. i. 33).

863. *amber-dropping*: transparent gold. In *P.L.* iii. 358–9,

> the river of bliss, through midst of Heav'n
> Rolls o'er Elysian flow'rs her amber stream.

The sun has 'amber locks' in Sylvester's *Dubartas*.

868. *Oceanus*: the stream which was thought to encircle the earth. In the list of water gods, Milton keeps the epithets of classical usage, e.g. 'great' Oceanus, 'earth-shaking' Neptune.

870. *Tethys*: the wife of Oceanus.

871. *hoary Nereus*: the aged Nereus (835), as in Virgil, *Georgics*, iv. 392.

872. *Carpathian wizard*: Proteus, the 'Old Man of the Sea', who according to Virgil lived on Carpathos, a Mediterranean island. He carries a hook because he was sea-shepherd to Neptune; he is a 'wizard' because he could prophesy.

873. *Triton*: a sea-god with the tail of a fish. Ovid refers to him as the herald of the sea who announced Neptune's decrees with his conch shell (*Metamorphoses*, i. 333).

874. *Glaucus*: a fisherman who became immortal; he taught Apollo the art of prophecy.

875. *Leucothea*. Ino, with her son Melicertes, fled from her insane husband Athamas and threw herself into the sea where she was changed into a sea-deity called Leucothea. Melicertes became a sea-god, hence 'rules the strands' (Ovid, *Fasti*, vi. 545).

Commentary

877. *Thetis*: a Nereid, the mother of Achilles. Homer called her 'silver-footed'.

879–80. *Parthenope, Ligea*: Sirens. Parthenope's tomb was at Naples.

890–2. In Fletcher's *Faithful Shepherdess* (III. i) the God of the River tells how

> twixt two banks with osiers set
> That only prosper in the wet,
> Through the meadows do [I] glide.

893–4. In *Polyolbion*, v, Drayton gives Sabrina an

> imperial chair
> Of crystal richly wrought.

911–13. Cf. Fletcher's River-God:

> If thou be'st a virgin pure,
> I can give a present cure:
> Take a drop into thy wound
> From my watery locks   (III. i).

921. *Amphitrite*: wife of Neptune. Drayton's Sabrina wears a garment 'Which as a princely gift great Amphitrite gave'.

923. *Anchises*: father of Aeneas and an ancestor of Locrine. See 824 note.

924–7. Milton knew that the Severn often floods when the snows melt on Plinlimmon.

933. Gold was mined in Wales, and the Severn was said to contain the metal.

S.D. 958. *Country Dancers*. Carew had country dances in his masque *Coelum Britannicum* (1633).

Song. The Attendant Spirit dismisses the Country Dancers (Shepherds).

958–9. Cf. *L'Allegro*, 97–8:

> And young and old come forth to play
> On a sunshine holiday.

961–2. Referring to the courtly dances which follow the presentation.

963–5. *Mercury*: the winged-footed messenger of the gods. In Jonson's *Pan's Anniversary* nymphs sing of

Comus

Pan,
that leads the Naiads and the Dryads forth,
And to their dances more than Hermes can.

966–75. The Spirit's second Song is addressed to the Earl and Countess of Bridgewater.

976–1011. This is often compared with Ariel's song in *The Tempest*, v. i. Milton uses the old legend of a western paradise popular since Homer's *Odyssey*. Warton writes, 'This luxuriant imagery Milton has dressed anew, from the classical gardens of antiquity, from Spenser's gardens of Adonis "fraught with pleasures manifold", from the same gardens in Marino's *L'Adone*, Ariosto's garden of Paradise, Tasso's garden of Armida, and Spenser's Bower of Blisse'.

976–99. These lines were set to music by Lawes and transferred to the opening of the masque when performed.

982. See 393 note.

986. *Graces*: three goddesses, Thalia (Youth), Aglaia (Beauty), and Euphrosyne (Joy). *Hours*: three sister-goddesses of the seasons spring, summer and winter.

992. Cf. 83 and note.

997. Cf. *Arc.* 72. Milton warns the reader that the myths which follow have a spiritual meaning.

999. *Adonis*. Beloved by Aphrodite ('th'Assyrian Queen', 1002), he was killed by a boar, but allowed to spend half the year with her and half in the underworld. Cf. Spenser, *Faerie Queene*, III. vi. 29–49, where the union of Adonis ('the Father of all Forms') with Venus represents the creative energy of divine love.

1003–8. Apuleius tells how Psyche (the Soul) was loved by Cupid but lost him by rash curiosity and was reunited to him only after many trials and wandering in the Underworld. Jove gave her divinity at Cupid's request. In *The Faerie Queene*, III. vi. 49–51, Cupid and Psyche live with Adonis.

1009–11. *twins*: In *The Faerie Queene* Psyche and Cupid have a daughter, Pleasure; but in Spenser's *Hymne of Love*, Love (Cupid) is said to live in 'a paradise of all delight' with Hercules and Hebe (Youth) and other of 'Venus darlings'; they make innocent Pleasure 'their Goddess and their Queen'. Milton has adapted these myths.

1015. Cf. Sylvester's *Dubartas*, 'heav'n's bow'd arches'.

1012–23. The Spirit concludes like Puck in *Midsummer Night's Dream* and Prospero in *The Tempest*. Fletcher's ministering Satyr in *The Faithful Shepherdess* offers fanciful services; Milton recalls us to his moral message.

SAMSON AGONISTES

PREFACE

Of that sort of Dramatic Poem which is called Tragedy

3. *by Aristotle.* On the title page Milton gave a passage from Aristotle's *Poetics* in Greek and Latin: 'Tragedy is the imitation of a serious action . . . achieving through pity and fear a purgation of those and similar passions.' Pity and Fear were dangerous and unmanly passions, hence the need to temper them by pleasurable imitations. The authority of Aristotle would satisfy most learned doubters of Tragedy's worth.

7–8. *by reading or seeing.* This play is not meant for the stage.

10. *so in Physic.* Not content with Aristotle's authority he explains how tragedy operates. The analogy from the medical practice (homœopathy) of Paracelsus and others had been given by Minturno (1564). W. R. Parker points out that the Latin 'lustratio' on the title page meant a ritual purification—so Milton insists on the spiritual as well as the biological effect (cf. 1775–8).

12–34. *Hence . . . Suffering.* He now cites great men both pagan and Christian who loved tragedy or wrote it.

16. *Paul.* The quotation 'Evil communications corrupt good manners' was probably taken from a proverb, not from Euripides.

18. *Paræus.* The German David Paræus was one of Milton's favourite modern theologians; he had quoted his description of the Apocalypse of St. John as 'a high and stately tragedy', in his *Reason of Church Government* (bk. ii, preface).

Samson Agonistes

24. *Dionysius.* 431–367 B.C. He was Tyrant of Syracuse and a patron of the arts. The Athenians awarded him a prize for his tragedy.

26. *Augustus Cæsar.* Milton got the tale from Suetonius (ii. 85).

28. *Seneca.* Most scholars now believe that the Stoic moralist also wrote the ten tragedies which influenced Renaissance tragedy.

31. *Gregory Nazianzen.* A.D. 325–90. He was Bishop of Constantinople, and the *Christus Patiens* (wrongly ascribed to him) was much read by humanists of the Renaissance, who wanted to see a school of Christian tragedy. Milton is in that tradition.

35. *small esteem.* Tragedy had two main classes of opponents: Puritans like Stephen Gosson who disliked all stage plays because of the violent passions and often sinful acts represented, as well as the unseemly behaviour of audiences; and the classically minded literary critics (such as Sir Philip Sidney) who objected to *modern* tragedies because they broke decorum and the Unities. Milton meets the second group of objectors, not the first.

43–4. *Prologue*: Not to be confused with the *Prologos* (cf. Introduction, pp. 50, 51). By Prologue he meant a prefatory speech, outside the play itself, discussing its theme and plot, apologising for the actors etc. such as is found in Plautus, Ben Jonson and Shakespeare.

45. *Epistle*: a prefatory letter to the reader or patron, discussing or defending the work which follows. Martial had epistolary poems before Books I and II of his *Epigrams*. In the first he warned moral critics (like Cato) not to come to the theatre if they feared to be shocked; in the second he made his friend object to prefatory Epistles but admit 'I see why tragedies and comedies are allowed one, since they cannot speak for themselves'. Milton goes on to discuss the form of his poem.

49–50 *Chorus . . . Greek manner.* This means more than using the Chorus as in *Henry V*. It is on the stage all the time, converses with the hero and others, and comments on the action, expressing the doubts and hopes of the audience and answering them. The Chorus here is a participator in, not just an observer of, the action.

Commentary

53. *Italians.* Milton had praised the Italian critics Castelvetro, Tasso, Mazzoni and others for explaining 'what the laws are of a true *Epic* poem, what of a *Dramatic* . . . what Decorum is' etc. Here he refers chiefly to Italian writers of tragedy such as Trissino, Cinthio and Tasso, who worked over the Greek tragic themes and added new ones.

54. *measure.* Milton explains the system of versification in his Choruses.

55. *all sorts.* More than one kind of line is used.

56. *Monostrophic*: not divided into subsections (unlike the Pindaric Ode).

56. *Apolelymenon*: 'freed' (Gk.); without regular repetition of verse-form.

57. *Strophe, Antistrophe, or Epode.* Greek tragic Choruses were sung, and the stanza-forms of Strophe and Antistrophe were the same because sung to the same tune, as the Chorus moved either in unison or in two Semichoruses. The Epodes were sung standing still and to a different tune. Without music there was no point in keeping these divisions.

62. *Allæostropha*: in stanzas of varying form. The Choruses contain pauses and changes of rhythm corresponding to changes in mood or thought. Cf. Chorus 652–724, which has changes of rhythm and thought at 667, 687, 705, 710.

62. *Division into Act and Scene.* Greek tragedies were usually constructed of four or five sections and Milton follows the practice; but the classical manuscripts did not show the divisions as Acts or Scenes. Seneca the Roman used these, and from him they came into Renaissance drama.

67. *Plot.* Milton gives an admirable definition to this in the next lines. Aristotle had called Plot (the organisation of incidents) 'the soul of tragedy', to which character was subordinate. He had insisted that plot and character should fuse to make the end inevitable, however surprising some happenings might temporarily seem.

68. *whether intricate or explicit.* Aristotle divided plots into two kinds, 'complex', where there occur sudden reversals of the hero's fortunes from good to bad or *vice versa*, and 'simple', where there is no sudden reversal or *peripeteia*. Milton does not

say to which kind his tragedy belongs, but W. R. Parker (*Milton's Debt to Greek Tragedy in Samson Agonistes*, p. 91) shows that Milton is less 'simple' than Aeschylus, since the **action** ebbs and flows, with little surprises on the way; and finally there is abundant use of *peripeteia* when the hopes of Manoa and the Chorus are upset and Samson, turning the tables on his enemies, rises suddenly from uncertainty to recapture his old heroic splendour—so that, although Samson dies, his is a tragedy of reconciliation, with almost a happy ending.

75. *The circumscription of time*: There was no 'ancient rule'. The 'unity of time' was imposed by Castelvetro and other Renaissance theorists. Milton keeps well within the usual ancient practice—'a single revolution of the sun'.

THE ARGUMENT

Printed versions of plays often had a summary such as this prefixed to them. It reveals that almost all of Milton's plot is his own invention so that he may portray Samson's anguish and introduce visitors to recall the past and influence his mind towards recovery and triumph. *Gaza*, where the scene is set, was one of the chief Philistine cities. The *Chorus* of Danites are fellow-tribesmen of Samson and Manoa, who was 'of the family of the Danites' (Judges xiii. 2). The *Philistines* were a Semitic people like the Israelites but they seem to have reached the southern coast of Palestine by sea, perhaps driven out of Crete. The *Catastrophe* is used 'in the theatrical sense of the event which produces the climax of a play'. (Verity).

1–114. PROLOGOS. Samson's soliloquy has five parts which give Setting 1–11; Occasion 12–17; Exposition of cause and state of mind 18–66; Lyrical lament 67–109; Transition 110–14.

1–2. This situation is often compared with the opening scene of Sophocles' *Oedipus at Colonus* where Antigone leads on her blind father and with the scene in the *Phoenissae* (834–5) of Euripides where the blind Tiresias is guided by his daughter. Who guides Samson? Dalila's damsel-train (721) is also mute.

3. Cf. Antigone in *Oedipus at Colonus*:

> This place is sacred, by the laurel shade
> Olive and vine thick-planted . . . Here sit thee down . . .

Commentary

5. In Latin 'servilis labor', i.e. toil which slaves perform.

12–16. By mentioning the feast Samson lets us know that this is his last day on earth. The first speech prepares us for the Catastrophe.

13. *Dagon*: god of the Philistines, described in *P.L.* i. 462–3:

> Dagon his name, Sea monster, upward Man
> And downward Fish.

Luther had another idea: 'Dagon, which means "wheat", i.e. "Meats for the belly, the belly for meats" (1 Corinthians vi. 13). For whom do gluttons and luxurious men worship if not Dagon . . . Other peoples made him into Ceres and Bacchus.' (*On Psalm lix*). Milton seems to hint at this in describing the feast later.

16. *popular noise*: noise of the common people (populace). Latin sense. Cf. *P.L.* ii. 313–14.

19. Samson's anguish is more mental than physical (185, 458, 600).

22. Cf. the fallen Satan:

> Now conscience wakes despair
> That slumber'd, wakes the bitter memory
> Of what he was, what is . . .   (*P.L.* iv. 23–5).

23–9. Cf. Judges xiii. 3–5, 10–20. Samson is a true tragic hero in being greater than ordinary men; and in falling deeper.

27. Milton combines (1) the 'pillar of fire' of Exodus xiii. 21; (2) Elijah's translation to heaven in a chariot of fire (2 Kings ii. 11); (3) Josephus, *Antiquities*, v. viii, 'the angel ascended by means of smoke as by a vehicle'.

31. *separate.* Cf. Numbers vi. 2, where 'Nazarite' means 'set apart'. Samson is God's agent (243–4).

36. *Heav'n gifted strength.* So the tradition interpreted references to 'the spirit of the Lord' in Judges xiii. 5; xiv. 6, 19, etc.

38–9. The angel prophesied only that Samson should 'begin to deliver Israel out of the hand of the Philistines'. Cf. 1211–13.

41. *Gaza*: the Philistine capital.   *Mill*: for grinding corn, usually turned by a beam.

43–5. Here as in *P.L.* Milton insists that man has free will.

But there is dramatic irony also, for by the end of the day the prophecy in Judges has been fulfilled.

53–4. Ovid, *Metamorphoses*, xiii. 363, 'you have strength but no wisdom'.

53–6. Cf. Sophocles, *Ajax*, where Agamemnon says this.

58–9. Early commentators sited Samson's strength in his hair, as here. Later ones regarded his hair rather as a symbol of his Nazarite vow, as in 1140–4. Milton somehow accepts both views.

60–2. This is the text of the whole drama.

70. *prime work*. Creation began with God's words: 'Let there be light' (Genesis i).

75–7. Milton's life with his daughters was not happy, and they got on badly with his third wife. An old servant later asserted that he complained to her (before this marriage) that the girls defrauded him in housekeeping and even sold some of his books. Doubtless there were faults on both sides.

77–8. Imbeciles were often legally handed over to guardians who controlled their property and used them as jesters (L. Hotson, *Shakespeare's Motley*).

80. Samson's blindness is the more pathetic because 'Samson' means 'their Sun', or 'Strength of the Sun' (Rabanus).

87. 'luna silens' (L)—the moon when she does not shine. The phrase provides a striking mingling of the senses.

93. *She . . . part*. Here Milton's Platonism shows. Cf. Henry More, *Psychathanasia*, ii. 2. 32:

> th' humane Soul's essence
> Is indivisible, yet everywhere
> In this her body.

96. *feeling . . . diffus'd*. Cf. Sir John Davies, *Nosce Teipsum*:

> Lastly the feeling power, which is life's root
> Through every living part itself doth shed.

100. *a living death*. Remorseful Adam feared that his immortal soul might thus dwell in his dead body (*P.L.* x. 788).

115–75. PARODE: the first speech of the Chorus. In Milton, as in the earlier Greek tragedians, the choruses are not, as in

Commentary

Euripides, mere interludes, but enforce aspects of the action. Here the Chorus emphasises Samson's former heroism and present misery. Quarles's *History of Samson* contains a Meditation (xxii) in similar strain.

118. *diffus'd*. Cf. Ovid, *Epistles*, III. iii. 8, 'languid limbs were diffused ('fusa') over the entire bed'.

128. Judges xiv. 5–6.

132. *Cuirass*: a piece of body-armour reaching down to the waist, consisting of a breast-plate and a back-plate.

133. *Chalýbean*. Stress second syllable. The Chalybes in Asia Minor were famed metal workers.

134. *Adamantean*. Adamant, originally hard steel, came to include diamonds too. Satan's shield is of adamant (*P.L.* vi. 254).

138. *Ascalonite*: Samson 'went down to Askelon, and slew thirty men of them' to get clothing to pay his bet. Judges xiv. 19.

139–40. Milton is thinking of the deeds of knights like Artegall in *The Faerie Queene*, IV. iv. 41.

142. *what trivial weapon*. Cf. Judges xv. 16, 'With the jaw of an ass have I slain a thousand men.' Cf. Quarles:

> The jaw-bone of an Ass? How poor a thing
> God makes his powerful instrument to bring
> Some honour to his name . . .
>
> (*History of Sampson*, Meditation viii).

Commentators often allegorised it as the 'simplicity and patience of Christ's teaching' (Gregory the Great).

144. *Palestine*: Philistia.

145. Samson gave it the name. The margin of the Authorised Version (Judges xv. 17) translated the Hebrew as 'the casting away or the lifting up of the jawbone'.

147. *Azza*: Gaza. For this story see Judges xvi. 1–3.

148. *Hebron*: a hill-town over thirty miles east of Gaza and so no 'journey of a Sabbath day', which by Mosaic law was less than a mile (Exodus xvi. 29). *seat . . . old*: city of Arba, Anak and other giants (Joshua xv. 13, 14).

150. In Greek and Roman (Gentile) mythology the Titan,

Atlas, was condemned by Zeus to support the sky on his head and hands.

156. Cf. *Com.* 383–5 note. That the body is the prison of the soul was often asserted by Greek and Christian philosophers.

162–3. Sight was thought to be possible because the eyes emitted rays. In blindness these rays ceased. The 'inner light' of the soul cannot replace them.

165–9. This was the usual moral (tropological) interpretation of Samson's plight.

165. *Since . . . unparallel'd.* Cf. the Latin construction 'post urbem conditam' imitated in

> for never since created man
> Met such imbodied force . . .   (*P.L.* i. 573–4).

169. *pitch.* The word meant height, cast, musical 'pitch'. Milton adds the medieval idea of Fortune's wheel or sphere (172).

170–5. Samson is not just the medieval tragic hero cast down by Fortune, but the Aristotelian hero ruined by a moral flaw. Cf. *Oedipus Tyrannos*, 1211, 'From castled height Pride tumbles to the pit'.

175. A remarkable line usually scanned: $/x//x/x//x//x//x//x$, but it sounds even more trochaic: $/x//x \; x//x//x//x$.

176–292. THE FIRST EPISODE: dialogue between Samson and the Chorus.

181. *From Eshtaol and Zora's fruitful Vale*: towns lying in the valley west of Jerusalem (Joshua xv. 33). At Zora Samson was born, spent his boyhood and he was buried 'between Zorah and Eshtaol in the burying-place of Manoah' (Judges xvi. 31).

182–4. So Job's friends came 'to mourn with him and comfort him' (ii. 11). Job was afflicted by Satan with 'sore boils' (ii. 7).

184–6. Cf. Oceanus, visiting Aeschylus' Promethus:

> wise words
> are healers of the heart's distemperature   (379).

197. *heave the head.* Cf. *Com.* 885.

203. *sung.* This refers perhaps to the many ballads and broadsides about Samson current in the 16th and 17th centuries. *proverb'd.* Cf. Job xxx. 9, 'I am their song, yea I am their by-word.'

Commentary

210–11. In *Tetrachordon*, Milton wrote: 'The best and wisest men, amidst the sincere and most cordial designs of their hearts, do daily err in choosing their wives.'

215–17. Milton introduces this common objection against Samson in order to answer it according to the exegetical tradition. Jews were forbidden to marry foreign (heathen) women, yet Samson had dealings with three. Catholics and Protestants agreed that he 'followed the guidance of God' (Calvin). Cf. 318–21 and note.

219. *Timna*: Timnath, a Philistine city.

219–26. Cf. Judges xiv. 1–4 where the wish to marry her 'was of the Lord, that he sought an occasion against the Philistines'.

222. *motion'd*: moved, proposed. Cf. *P.L.* ix. 229–30.

227. *She . . . false*. She betrayed his riddle and then let herself be married to his groomsman (Judges xiv).

229. Judges xvi. 4, 'afterward he loved a woman in the valley of Sorek whose name was Delilah'.

231–3. The Bible does not say this.

234. Note Milton's insistence on this. After the first sin Adam blamed Eve more than himself (*P.L.* ix. 1160 ff.; x. 124 ff.) and was reproved by God.

> Was she thy God, that her thou didst obey
> Before his voice . . . ?

Samson fully realises his fault in trusting a woman. As Adam prophesied:

> Thus it shall befall
> Him who to worth in Woman overtrusting
> Lets her will rule. (*P.L.* ix. 1182 ff.)

235. Cf. Judges xvi. 16–17.

235–6. Cf. *S.A.* 404.

240. The tribes called after Israel's (Jacob's) sons are still in bondage. Samson's mission has failed. The Chorus, like Job's 'comforters', accuses him.

241–6. Milton has in mind his own countrymen who did not follow up the work of Cromwell. He returns to the subject again, 678–700.

248. The 'deeds' would be the burning of the corn and the subsequent slaughter (Judges xv. 1–8).

252–3. *Etham*: near Zora and Eshtaol within the borders of Judah. After smiting the Philistines 'hip and thigh' with a great slaughter . . . he went down and dwelt in the top of the rock Etam' (Judges xv. 8).

256–7. Instead of rebelling with him, the Jews want to give him up.

258. The conditions were that the men of Judah should not kill him but bind him and hand him over to the Philistines (Judges xv. 11–13).

263. Cf. 142 and note.

266. *Gath*: another important Philistine city.

268–76. Milton probably has the English in mind who had grown corrupt under the Stuarts and who, when the Puritan party won freedom in 1649, proved ungrateful to Cromwell, Lambert, Vane and their fellows and relapsed into Monarchy despite Milton's final plea to them not 'to fall back, or rather to creep back, to their once abjured and detested thraldom' (*Ready Way*, 1660).

271. The Hebrews toiling through the wilderness longed for 'the cucumbers and the melons and the leeks and the onions and the garlic' of Egypt (Numbers xi. 5).

274–5. *Deliverer*. Probably Cromwell is intended, whose rule had become unpopular before he died in 1658. Many Presbyterians turned Royalist, and General Monk brought back the King.

278. These places refused bread to Gideon's men when he was pursuing the Kings of Midian. Later he punished them. (Judges viii. 4–17.)

282–9. When the Ammonite sheikh raided the Israelites claiming land which the tribes had occupied, Jephthah the Gileadite leader appealed to him arguing (283) that his people had tried to avoid any clash (Judges xi. 4–28). The Ammonites persisted and Jephthah defeated them (xi. 29–33). He was then obliged to crush the Israelite tribe of Ephraim who resented being left out, and the Gileadites identified escaping survivors by their inability to say the word 'Shibboleth' correctly (289) (Judges xii. 1–6).

293–325. FIRST STASIMON. The Chorus develops the theme of 210 'Tax not divine disposal'; and in so doing touches on themes in Job, where doubts of God's justice are answered and his mystery and power are announced; then discusses God's part in actions of Samson which might seem sinful.

293–4. Cf. Elihu in Job: 'surely God will not do wickedly, neither will the Almighty pervert judgment' (xxxiv. 12). Also Revelation xv. 3, 'just and true are thy ways'. Milton's aim in *P.L.* was to 'justify the ways of God to man'.

295. 'Who think there is no God.'

297. *never . . . School*: no philosophical group or tradition (cf. the Stoics, Platonists).

298. 'The fool hath said in his heart, There is no God' (Psalm xiv. 1). Cf. the catalogue of God's works in Job xxxviii–xli.

300. Cf. Job's complaint in xvi. 11–21; and Bildad 'Doth God pervert judgment? or doth the Almighty pervert justice?' (viii. 3).

303. *his glory's diminution.* In Latin to 'diminish the glory of the Roman people' was to commit high treason; so here.

304–5. Doubters of God's justice become ever more confused, and tangle (ravel) themselves in difficulties they cannot resolve.

309. 'God's devices and therefore his actions, of what kind soever they be, are perfectly free' (*Christian Doctrine*, II. iii). The point here is that God can exempt men in particular circumstances from his general laws.

312. *National obstriction*: the Mosaic law which forbade the marriage of Jews and Gentiles (Deuteronomy vii. 3).

obstriction: (L. *obstrictus*, bound) obligation.

314. An important principle in discussing Samson's behaviour. As Luther declared, God's first commandment overrides all others (cf. Introduction, pp. 47, 48).

318. *Nazarite.* Luther wrote of this sect: 'Sacred and reserved to God. They did not drink anything intoxicating, and no scissors ever touched their hair . . . they were forbidden to

drink so that they could better serve God; for God demands chaste service.' (*On Judges*, xiii. 7). The Nazarite vow did not include celibacy (Numbers vi. 1–21), but Samson had married an 'unclean' foreigner.

320. The 'fallacious Bride' is probably the woman of Timnath.

321. *unclean*: 'because all other nations . . . were to [the Jews] unclean' (*Doctrine of Divorce*, i. 8).   *unchaste*. There is no mention in the Bible of Delilah's unchastity.

324. She ceased to be 'unclean' when she married him. 'Therefore', saith St. Paul, 'the unbelieving wife is sanctified by the husband, that is made pure and lawful to his use' (*Doctrine of Divorce*, I, viii). The quotation is from 1 Corinthians vii.

325. She became unchaste when she married Samson's groomsman after being married to him (Judges xiv. 20).

326–651. SECOND EPISODE: dialogue between Samson and Manoa.

338 *signal*: conspicuous (L. sense).

340. Manoa's role is rather like that of Oceanus in Aeschylus, *Prometheus Bound*.

342–4. Thus Milton explains Samson's ability to enter Gaza. He is the heroic adventurer. In his youth Job also was awesome: 'When I went out to the gate through the city, . . . the young men saw me and hid themselves; and the aged arose and stood up . . .' (Job xxix. 7–10).

348–9. Samson's sin was partly arrogance (*hubris*).

380. *Canaanite*. The Philistines invaded Canaan before the Hebrews.

382–7. Cf. Judges xiv. 11–18.

386. *my Spies*: Spies on me . . .

387. *Rivals*. She married one of them after Samson left her in anger.   *this other*: Dalila.

389. Cf. Judges xvi. 5.

392. *Thrice*. Cf. Introduction, p. 43, and Judges xvi. 6–14.

400. *contempt*. Milton believed that 'such a continual head-

Commentary

strong behaviour as tends to plain contempt of the husband' was in Scripture deserving of divorce (*Doctrine of Divorce*, II. xviii).

418. *blindness . . . this*. Commentators insisted on the 'caeca mens' (mental blindness) of Samson.

421–2. In the Bible Samson makes no such plea about his relations with Delilah.

434–9. Cf. Judges xvi. 23.

439. *who slews't . . . slain*: 'them' is a dative of reference as found in Greek and in French.

460–6. Samson means that his failure, by encouraging Dagon to boast, will cause God to work directly against the latter.

463. *lists*: enclosures where tournaments were fought. The imagery of medieval combat appears often in Milton.

473. *I . . . receive*. The reader knows better than Manoa that it *is* prophetic.

499–501. Milton refers to Tantalus, punished in Hades for revealing to men the secrets of the gods.

503–8. In *Christian Doctrine*, II. viii, Milton defines righteousness as justice to a man's self; 'opposed to this is, first, a perverse hatred of self. In this class are to be reckoned those who lay violent hands on themselves'. Some writers accused Samson of suicide.

522–32. Again Samson admits the sin of Pride.

528. *The Sons of Anak*. The Anakim, a race of giants, were supposed to dwell at Hebron.

534. Rabanus Maurus moralises: 'The rational sense in us is known as the man; but the flesh is regarded as the type of a woman. For if we yield to our flesh with alluring desire or other bad works, we despoil and cut off the graces of the spirit by which the hair of the Nazarite is signified . . .' (*On Judges*, II. xx).

536. *lascivious lap*: Judges xvi. 19.

541–6. The Nazarite must 'separate himself from wine and strong drink' (Numbers vi. 3) not, says Luther, because of any evil in it, but to preserve chastity and continence (*On Judges*,

Samson Agonistes

xiii. 7). Milton himself was 'temperate, rarely drank between meals' (Aubrey).

543. Proverbs xxiii. 31: 'Look not thou upon the wine when it is red . . . when it moveth itself aright.' *P.L.* v. 633 has 'rubied nectar'.

545. Judges ix. 13: ' . . . wine, which cheereth God and Man'.

548. Cf. Burton, *Anatomy of Melancholy*, ii. 2. i. i: 'Rain-water is purest . . . next to it fountain-water that riseth in the east, and runneth eastward, from a quick running spring.'

549. *Heav'n's fiery rod*: i.e. the Sun's 'Magnetic beam' (*P.L.* iii. 583–6).

550. *milky juice*. Cf. *P.L.* v. 306, 'nectarous draughts between from milky stream'.

553–7. In *P.L.* Michael shows Adam

> The rule of not too much, by temperance taught,
> In what thou eat'st and drink'st   (xi. 528–9).

564–72. Milton may sometimes have thought of himself thus, though he was 'of a very cheerfull humour' (Aubrey) and had many visitors.

582. *From . . . ground*. Cf. Judges xv. 17–19. Commentators differed about whether the water came from the jawbone itself or from the ground; Josephus thought from 'a certain rock, whence . . . Samson called the place The Jawbone' (*Antiquities*, v. iii. 9).

600. *humours black*: the physical constituent melancholy, or black bile, which caused mental 'black moods'. Cf. *Com.* 809.

628. *Vernal Air*: springtime breeze. Cf. *P.L.* iv. 264.

632. Chrysippus called grief 'a dissolution of the whole man'. Samson's grief is greater because it is a 'dark night of the Soul' —a sense of abandonment by God. In mystical practice this state often precedes regeneration, as here.

652–709. SECOND STASIMON

654. Patience was praised by the Stoics as a proof of indifference to passion. Cicero's essay *On Grief of Mind* describes how different philosophers sought to console sufferers (sect. 31–33).

657. *Consolatories*. Boethius's *De Consolatione Philosophiae* was one of the best known of such books.

Commentary

662. *mood*: double meaning (1) mood of the mind and (2) one of the four 'modes' or measures of Greek music (Dorian, Ionian, Phrygian and Lydian).

667–71. An echo of Job 'What is man, that thou shouldest magnify him? . . . and that thou shouldest . . . try him at every moment? . . . why hast thou set me as a mark against thee, so that I am a burden to myself?' (vii. 17–20), and of the Chorus in Seneca's *Hippolytus* where the early undeserved fate of the hero is lamented.

672. *Th' Angelic orders.* Early Christian philosophy divided the nine orders of angels into three hierarchies, and each hierarchy into three orders. Cf. *P.L.* i. 737, 'Each in his hierarchy, the Orders bright'.

678–89. Milton takes a commonplace medieval idea about Fortune and turns it to religious use. Stoic works on consolation gave many examples of great persons suddenly being cast down, but the words 'in part they effect' suggest that Milton was also thinking of what had happened since the Restoration to some of his own party which had only partly succeeded in its aims.

683. He himself after long and devoted service, had gone blind at the age of forty-four. Cf. the *Sonnet on his Blindness.*

688. He does not complain about his own obscure life.

689–91. This is the theme of many a tragedy—the punishment exceeding the error.

692–4. e.g. Crusaders, pilgrims, etc. The bodies of Cromwell, Ireton and Bradshaw were dug up in 1660 and exposed at Tyburn.

695–6. Probably a reference to men like Sir Henry Vane and General John Lambert whom the Parliament of 1661 sentenced to execution and life imprisonment respectively.

697–700. Milton was not given to self-pity and we should not exaggerate the autobiographical element here. He lost property at the Restoration and his house was burned in the Great Fire (1666). But 'only towards his latter end he was visited with the Gout, spring and fall: he would be cheerful in his Gout-fits, and sing' (Aubrey). His hands had become deformed.

703–5. All this recalls Job's lament. It is also summed up in the final Chorus of *Oedipus Tyrannos*, ending: 'Call no man happy till his last hour ends without his tasting woe.'

710–1009. THIRD EPISODE: Samson and Dalila.

714–15. The 'ships of Tarshish' are often mentioned in scripture. Milton thought they came from Tarsus in Cilicia.

716. *Javan*: Greece, said to have been peopled by Javan, son of Japhet. *Gadier:* Cadiz in Spain, a Phoenician city.

717–19. Milton probably remembered the description in Giles Fletcher's *Christ's Victory on Earth* (35), of Presumption, a vain painted lady, who comes to tempt Christ, moving fairly, though like a ship without a Pilot, 'And painted masts with silken sails embraves, . . . Her waving streamers loosely she lets play'.

724. Usually called Dalida (Δαλιδά) in Middle Ages, and by Luther. Rabanus has Dalila ('weak little woman' or 'declining').

thy wife. Judges xvi does not mention marriage, but Milton, to lift blame from Samson, follows Chrysostom and others against Josephus and St. Ambrose (who made Dalila his concubine). Milton speaks of her 'Harlot-lap' in *P.L.* ix. 1060.

726–8. The Chorus in Sophocles' *Antigone* describes Ismene thus (532).

727. *head declin'd.* Editors see here a reference to her name.

736–7. Cajetan, the only commentator to defend Dalila, uses this excuse. Cf. 800 and note.

739–42. So Mary Powell, after three year's absence, 'of her own accord came and submitted to him' (J. Phillips). As W. R. Parker shows, the scene which follows resembles Euripides' *Trojan Women* (914–1037) where Menelaus comes seeking revenge on his wife Helen. She comes out, 'not humble, not dressed in tattered rags, trembling with dread, and with (her) head shaven,' but having adorned herself. Like Dalila she excuses herself sentimentally and with lies.

748. *Hyaena.* Cf. 'a wilde beast that counterfaiteth the voyce of men, and so enticeth them out of their houses and devoureth them' (Geneva Gloss to Ecclesiasticus xiii. 18), and 'Hyaena, the most salacious of animals' (Clement of Alexandria).

Commentary

775. The weakness was curiosity, i.e. to be inquisitive and importunate.

778. She tries to turn the tables on Samson. He also was weak. What she says is all too true, but no excuse. Cf. Eve to Adam after her sinning:

> Hadst thou been firm and fixed in thy dissent,
> Neither had I transgress'd, nor thou with me.
>
> *(P.L.* ix. 1160–1).

793–5. Specious; but Samson left his first wife because she had betrayed his secret and her kinsmen had tricked him. He returned to her with a present and found her married to another man (Judges xiv. 19, and xv. 1–2).

800–2. Cajetan thought that the Lords pretended that they would not treat him cruelly (*Opera*, 1637, ii. 63). But cf. Judges xvi. 5.

807–8. Her idea that Samson might live with her in confinement may come from Luther's note (based on Jerome) for Judges xvi. 21 'grinding', in which he interprets the Hebrew as meaning that Samson was to be kept to breed strong children by a Philistine woman (who might be Dalila).

811. Dalila has the 'romantic' view of Love as justifying any treachery. Euripides' Helen blames Venus.

836–7. Samson answers her sophistry. Cf. Seneca, 'Love if you wish to be loved '(*Epistles*, ix).

857–61. The Bible mentions no priests, but Milton makes her the agent of the false god.

885–6. Cf. Genesis ii. 24: 'Therefore shall a man leave his father and his mother and shall cleave unto his wife.'

890. Milton has in mind such provisions as that a wife cannot be forced to bear witness against her husband.

891. *an impious crew.* That is how she should have regarded them.

901. Cf. 'painting his lewd and deceitful principles with a smooth and glossy varnish' (Milton, *Animadversions*).

920. Cf. 1250 and 1457.

934–5. Dalila is like Circe. Cf. *Com.* 50–3.

936. Cf. Psalm lviii. 4–5, 'the deaf adder that stoppeth her

ear; which will not hearken to the voice of the charmers, charming never so wisely'.

941. *now*: Samson was still only about forty.

Milton's own life with his third wife was happy. Christopher Milton declared that his brother had 'complained, but without passion, that his children had been very unkind to him, but that his wife had been very kind and careful of him'.

953. The blinded Polymestor in Euripides' *Hecuba* wishes to 'seize her in my hands, tear her piecemeal and mangle her body' (1126).

967. *evil omen*: referring to 954–59, Samson's ironical farewell.

971–4. Partly taken from Chaucer who in his *House of Fame*, bk. iii, describes Fame as having Aeolus, god of the winds, as trumpeter with two trumpets, one black (Slander) and the other gold (Noble Praise). Jonson's *Masque of Queens* has '*Fama bona* . . . with white wings'.

971. *double-fac'd*: like Janus.

976. *Dan*: Samson's own tribe. *Judah*: the nearest Jewish tribe east of Gaza.

981. Four of the five principal cities of the Philistines; Askelon was the fifth.

987. *with odours visited*. Cf. Jeremiah xxxiv. 5. 'But thou shalt die in peace; . . . so shall they burn odours for thee.'

988–90. Judges iv. 17–22, tells how Jael enticed the Canaanite leader, Sisera, to shelter with her and then killed him. Jael was celebrated in the Song of Deborah (who lived near Mt. Ephraim).

993. *piety*: from L. *pietas*, devotion to family or country.

1003–5. Adam forgave Eve (*P.L.*, x. 937–46), and Milton took back his own wife, but Samson's case is different.

1008. 'The quarrelling of lovers is the knitting up of love' (Terence, *Andria*).

1010–1060. THIRD STASIMON

1016–17. See note on 382–7.

1026–7. Some writers went further. In the Commentaries on St. Paul's Epistles ascribed to St. Ambrose 'there is a doubt made, whether the woman were created according to God's Image' (Donne in Sermon XXV, insisting that woman *is* 'in possession of a reasonable and an immortal soul').

1034–7. Euripides makes Hippolytus cry out

> Why should a place in the light of the Sun, O Zeus,
> Be granted to women, that specious curse upon men.
>
> (*Hippolytus*, 616–18).

1035. Milton had described the married unhappiness of 'the sober man honouring the appearance of modesty, and hoping well of every social virtue under the veil' (*Doctrine of Divorce*, I. iii).

1039. *A cleaving mischief*: combines the thorn image (1037) with that of a sword, and the idea of division in the home.

1044–5. Adam in *P.L.*, x. 896–8, foretold

> innumerable
> Disturbances on Earth through Female Snares,
> And straight conjunction with this Sex.

1046–8. Adam says

> nothing lovelier can be found
> In woman, than to study household good,
> And good works in her Husband to promote.
>
> (*P.L.*, ix. 232–4.)

The ideal marriage is that of Adam and Eve in *P.L.*, iv. Cf. Proverbs xii. 4.

1050. Milton's vigorous idea of virtue recurs here. It is even better to have to conquer temptation and trouble than to have a smooth and happy marriage.

1053–60. These commonly held ideas Milton expounded in his *Divorce Tractates* and in *P.L.* iv. 295–9, 635–8; ix. 1182–6; x. 145–56 and 888–95. He quoted St. Paul, 'Suffer not the woman to usurp authority over the man'. Cf. Luther: 'The woman is subject to her man'.

1061–1267. FOURTH EPISODE: Samson and Harapha.

1061–4. An approach to the stichomythia found in *Com.* 277–90.

1064. Cf. 382–7; 1017–33.

1068. *Harapha*: 'Ha Raphah' the Giant. Neither the name

nor the incident appears in Judges. In the Authorised Version gloss on 2 Samuel xxi. 16, 17, Philistine champions are called 'the sons of Rapha'. Harapha 'is the instrument of temptation by violence and fear' (Krouse, p. 130).

1080. *Og*: King of Bashan. In Deuteronomy iii. 2, he is one of the 'remnant of the giants'. The giant Anak was the father of the Anakim (528). *Emims*: 'also were accounted giants' (Deuteronomy ii. 10–11) and dwelt in 'the plain of Kiriathaim' (Genesis xiv. 5, gloss).

1082. Cf. *P.L.* iv. 830: 'Not to know me argues yourselves unknown'.

1091. Cf. *P.R.* ii. 131, where Satan, speaking of Christ, says that he has 'found him, view'd him, tasted him'.

1112. *chamber-ambushes*: referring to the four occasions when they hid in the room while Dalila tried to bind him.

1119–55. Milton mingles medieval with classical and Biblical ideas in this encounter.

1122. *A Weaver's beam*: the wooden roller on which yarn is rolled for weaving. *seven-times-folded shield*: like the shield 'seven ox-hides thick' of *Iliad*, vii. 220.

1132–4. Magic spells and talismens were used as protection in battle, cf. *Com.* 647. The Schoolman Rupert of St. Héribert, questioning Samson's saintliness, thought he worked 'by means of magic, that is, by alliance with Satan rather than by the Holy Spirit' (Krouse, p. 130). Harapha enables Milton to answer this aspersion.

1133. Cf. 1278 for another internal rhyme.

1134–5. Of course Harapha had not heard of the Greek Nisus whose success in battle depended on a yellow lock amongst his hair. His daughter Scylla (like Dalila) cut off the hair to help his enemy Minos.

1138. *ruffl'd Porcupines*. Cf. *Hamlet*, i. v. 19–20:

> And each particular hair to stand on end,
> Like quills upon the fretful porpentine.

1139. Todd gives the oath of a medieval champion: 'I do swear that I have not upon me, nor upon any of the arms I shall use, words, charms, or enchantments, to which I trust for help

Commentary

to conquer my enemy, but that I do only trust in God, in my right, and in the strength of my body and arms.'

1168. *indignities*: unjust taunts.

1171–7. Note the sudden renewal of hope in Samson's mind.

1175–6. It is to be a medieval 'trial by combat' to decide whose cause is right. Contrast Elijah with the prophets of Baal in 1 Kings xviii.

1180. 'Harapha's imputation . . . creates an occasion for the hero to reply to commentators who regarded him as an un-authorised privateer' (Krouse, p. 130).

1183–8. Judges xiv–xv. Some good Christians had doubts about the virtue of this act. Samson's next speech gives Milton's answer.

1185–8. Cf. Judges xiv. 19.

1195–7. Milton follows Josephus (*Antiquities*, v. viii. 6) who wrote that the youths were 'in pretence to be his companions, but in reality to be a guard upon him'. Quarles too wrote that they ordered

> that thirty men of arms,
> Under the mask of bridemen, should attend
> Until the nuptial ceremonies end.

1198. This follows Judges xiv. 15, 'lest we burn thee and thy father's house with fire'.

1211–13. This was the view of most commentators from Theodoret to Calvin and Paræus. Samson 'followed the guidance of God' (Calvin). Milton makes more of the patriotic motive.

1218. *known offence*: i.e. revealing his secret to Dalila.

1222. It was the 'custom and the law of arms, to give the challenge and to sound the trumpet thrice' (Newton). Cf. 1151 and 1174.

1224. The honour of single combat was refused to men guilty of treason, to freebooters '. . . and all other persons, not living as a gentleman or a soldier' (V. Saviolo, 1595).

1231. *Baal-zebub*. Baal (the Fly-god) was worshipped by the Philistines at Ekron.

1242. *Astaroth*. The moon-goddess of the Canaanites—the Greek Astarte and Ephesian Diana.

Samson Agonistes

1248–9. In 2 Samuel xxi. 22 we read of four sons 'born to the giant in Gath'. Milton makes the fifth son Goliath.

1268–96. FOURTH STASIMON

1268–96. In this section the Chorus, heartened by signs of moral revival in Samson, describes two kinds of Saints, the heroic, warlike 'Deliverers' (1268–86), and the 'Sufferers'. The question is still, to which sort will Samson belong?

1271. *invincible might*. Milton may well have thought of Cromwell and his victories as described in his letters, e.g. the letters about the Battle of Warrington (20 August 1648) where his men defeated nearly three times their number. 'Surely, Sir, this is nothing but the hand of God, and whenever anything in this world is exalted, or exalts itself, God will pull it down.'

1288. *Saints*: in the Puritan sense of 'Sanctified' or 'chosen', who may fall but rise again.

1289. *his own Deliverer*: in contrast with 1270 they free themselves in spirit.

1294. *sight bereav'd*: Latin construction, cf. 1433 'message told'.

1300–1426. FIFTH EPISODE: The officer comes to take Samson to the feast of Dagon.

1306. *A public Officer*. Greek tragedy had many such figures. W. R. Parker notes his efficiency and kindness, and some resemblance to the enemy herald Talthybius in *The Trojan Women*, and to Hephaestus in *Prometheus Bound*.

1308. *Ebrews:* from Middle English form 'Ebreu' (Old French *ebreu*). Hebrew came later from Vulgate Latin. Milton uses both forms.

1320. Cf. Exodus xx. 4–5, 'Thou shalt not bow down thyself to them, nor serve them'.

1323–5. Milton gives a list of entertainers at holiday-sports in his own time. He had attacked Sunday games in *Church Discipline*.

1334. Samson thinks not of his own safety but of his duty and hope of 'the sweet peace that goodness bosoms ever' (*Com.* 368).

1347. The hint of action in 1266–7 recurs as the officer goes off.

1348–9. 'The metaphor is from a taut rope' (Chambers).

Commentary

The Chorus seems to counsel prudence like the Chorus in *Prometheus Bound* (1040) after Hermes' threats.

1355. 'Howbeit the hair of his head began to grow again after he was shaven' (Judges xvi. 22). Cf. 586–7. His reviving will begins to be strengthened by the means to execute it.

1365–7. It was normal for prisoners to work for their keep.

1368. An idea well known since Aristotle. Good or evil consists not in the act but in the will or intention.

1369. *outward force*: physical force against the will of the person constrained.

1372–6. Milton insists that Samson's going to the feast is an act of free will. This is important, showing that Samson is master of himself, no longer passive. If he sins it will not be blindly.

1377–9. In *Christian Doctrine*, ii. v, Milton points out that Naaman the Syrian was allowed to attend idol-worship (2 Kings v. 17–19). But here the idea is Luther's, that God may dispense with all other commandments but the first 'for some important cause'. See 314 note.

1381–3. He feels excitement but has no definite plan.

1388–9. Irony; it is both.

1399–1407. This is not said in pride or fear but to hide his new desire to go where God leads him.

1418. Luther and others take 'Philistines' to mean 'falling in drink', i.e. 'those who by gluttony &c. rush into luxury' (*On Psalm lix*).

1418–22. There may be a reference in 1418–19 to Restoration lords and priests; the 'holy-days' seem to be contemporary like the entertainers in 1323–5. In *Church Government* Milton had compared the clergy to the 'hireling priest Balaam, seeking to draw the Israelites from the sanctuary of God to the luxurious and ribald feasts of Baalpeor' (Todd). The Restoration brought a revival of wakes, sports, and Sabbath-breaking.

1426. Samson goes and this is the last we see of him, since Greek practice did not allow bloodshed on the stage.

1427–40. FIFTH STASIMON

1431. *Angel of thy Birth*: see 24, 361 and 635.

1435–6. Judges xiii. 25: 'And the spirit of the Lord began to move him at times in the camp of Dan.'

1441–758. EXODE: Chorus and Manoa. 'The methods of this final scene are thoroughly Greek, in their presentation of the matter with most effect' (Prince). There are three parts: in 1441–540 Manoa comes full of hope for Samson's liberation and the dialogue is interrupted by cries outside; in 1541–659 a messenger tells of Samson's death and how he died; 1660–758 form the Kommos.

1461–71. The various attitudes to Samson could be paralleled after the Restoration when friends of Milton and others in danger appealed for their pardon.

1463. These were like the High Church party.

1481. Ironical, as is soon proved.

1485. Prince notes the 'gnomic concision' of the Chorus's comments in this scene.

1494. Todd compares the description in Ovid, *Metamorphoses*, viii. 10: 'In whose hair was fastened the assurance of a great kingdom.'

1496–8. Is there some trace here of the allegorical interpretation of Samson's hair as 'the peoples of the Church' (Gregory the Great), or as 'the virtuous deeds which a man does by gift of the Holy Spirit; whence in *Judges* we read that as long as Samson kept the seven locks of his hair whole, he was invincible' (Rabanus, *De Universo*)?

1508. The noise of catastrophe comes just when hopes run high, and the Chorus which follows is very different from that which precedes.

1515. *ruin*. Cf. *P.L.* vi. 868, 'Heav'n ruining from Heav'n'.

1521–30. The Greek Chorus has an ordinary man's fears; but it must not leave the stage! Note the mingling of hope with which we sympathise, though it is unfounded.

1529. *dealing dole*: a favourite phrase about heroes in romances.

1541. The Messenger is important in Greek tragedy because the Catastrophe, if it involves bloodshed, must occur offstage and be described at length by an eye-witness. So at the climax narrative must do the work of representation. Hence the elaboration of scenes such as this, the teasing suspense, the broad general outline (1558–70) with details filled in at leisure.

1570. Such forceful brevity after long preparation is very effective. Cf. Sophocles, *Electra*, 673, 'Orestes is dead; I say it, putting the whole in brief.'

1574. *conceiv'd*. Cf. 390–1, for a similar, but less fully developed, play on the word.

1605–10. 'Conceive the building as follows: There is a large semi-circular *covered* space or amphitheatre, filled up with tiers of seats—the roof of which semi-circular building is supported by two great pillars rising from the ground about midpoint of the diameter of the semi-circle. There is no *wall* at this diameter, but only these two pillars; standing near which Samson would look *inside* upon the congregated Philistine lords and others of rank, occupying the tiers of seats under the roof. *Behind* Samson was then an uncovered space where the poorer spectators could stand on any kind of benches under the open sky, seeing Samson's back and, save where the pillars might interrupt the view, all that went on inside' (Masson). Milton describes not a temple but a theatre or circus, with the 'groundlings' in the open air so that only the lords will be killed. Krouse (pp. 68–9) illustrates with a floorplan of the Temple of Gaza from B. A. Montanus, *De Varia Republica*, published at Antwerp in 1592.

1623. *patient*: suffering, enduring.

1626. There are six strong stresses in this line.

1627. *stupendious*. This, the common spelling, was used in *P.L.* x. 351.

1634. The poet George Sandys described Gaza, with its remains of 'goodly pillars of Parian marble' and 'the ruins of huge arches sunk low in the earth, and other foundations of a stately building. . . . The Jews do fable this place to have been the theatre of Samson . . .' Sandys thought it 'perhaps some palace there built by Ptolemy, or Pompey who re-edified the city' (*Travells*, 1670 edn., p. 116). Milton may have got the arch here, or from Quarles:

Samson Agonistes

> her arched roof was all
> Builded with massie stone   (*History of Sampson.*)

1637–8. Milton departs from Judges xvi. 28 in not making Samson cry out for revenge, but reflect gravely (1638) before coming to his decision.

1645. *strike all who behold.* There is deadly irony in 'strike'.

1647–8. Cf. *P.L.* i. 230–7; vi. 195–8. Earthquakes were thought to be caused by underground winds and water bursting out.

1661–707. The Chorus speaks first in unison, then in two Semichoruses, coming together again after Manoa's final speech for the valedictory ode.

1664–5. *self-kill'd; Not willingly.* Milton's Samson does not say (with Judges xvi. 30) 'Let me die with the Philistines', for Milton wishes to oppose the accusation of suicide which Donne (in *Biathanatos*) and others based on those words. His death is not a willed act in itself but the inevitable result of his will to slay God's enemies. Milton does not think that God would set aside 'his canon 'gainst self-slaughter'.

1667–8. Cf. Judges xvi. 30.

1674. *Silo*: or Shiloh, 65 miles N.E. of Gaza. *bright Sanctuary*: because at times 'the glory of the Lord filled the Tabernacle' (Exodus xl. 34).

1675. *frenzy.* Luther distinguished physical drunkenness (1670) from spiritual drunkenness, which is more dangerous (*On Judges*, xiii. 7).

1675–8. In accordance with the proverb 'Whom God wishes to destroy he first makes mad'.

1680–1. Milton brings out the irony of it.

1682–6. Is there a hint here of Gregory the Great's interpretation of the Philistines as types of the Fallen Angels, 'who are humiliated like the Philistines when the demons are sent into the eternal fires prepared for them from the beginning of the world'?

1686. *blindness internal.* Samson had complained of this in himself (418). The position has been reversed.

1689. *inward eyes*: a phrase beloved of the Cambridge Platonists, cf. Henry More, *Psychozoia*: 'But corporal life doth so

Commentary

obscubilate [overcloud] our inward eyes that they be nothing bright'. Cf. 162.

1699. *that self-begotten bird*: The phoenix of Arabia which, after living for 500 years was fabled to be burned in its nest by the sun's heat, and a new phoenix to rise from the ashes. It became a type of immortality for Christian poets. Cf. Henry Vaughan's *Resurrection and Immortality* where the intrinsic virtue in all created things, 'Phoenix-like renew'th Both life and youth'.

1700. *Arabian woods*. Cf. Lyly in *Euphues*, 'there is but one tree in Arabia wherein she buildeth', and Shakespeare in *The Phoenix and Turtle*, 'sole Arabian tree'.

1713. *Sons of Caphtor*. See Amos ix. 7: 'Have not I brought up . . . the Philistines from Caphtor?' Some scholars think Caphtor is Crete, others the Nile Delta.

1721–4. In this superb epitaph Manoa achieves great nobility.

1730–3. See Judges xvi. 31.

1735–7. Laurel wreaths and palm branches were symbols or triumph. Here Samson is both the chivalric knight with his 'trophies' and the Saint whose Acts and Legend must be written down.

1745–54. The Chorus sums up the course and meaning of the drama and concludes with a reference to the effect on itself and the audience. M. Y. Hughes compares the Chorus which Euripides used to end four of his plays.

> In many forms the gods appear,
> And many things unhoped they do;
> Forecasts of men they bring not to pass
> What is unforecast they bestow.

Milton ends on a deeper note than Euripides, for his tragedy, like *P.L.*, has justified God's ways to man.

1749. Cf. Psalm xxvii. 9.

1758. *all passion spent*. Compare Milton's preface: 'Tragedy . . . is of power by raising pity and fear, . . . to purge the mind of those and such like passions—that is, to temper and reduce them to just measure.'

APPENDIX

MILTON'S LIFE

(important events occurring during his lifetime are shown in square brackets)

1608 Born on December 9 in London, the third child of John Milton, a scrivener (lawyer and law-stationer).

1610 [Giles Fletcher's *Christ's Victory and Triumph*; Phineas Fletcher's *The Purple Island*.]

1611 [The 'Authorised Version' of the Bible published.]

1616 [Death of Shakespeare. Ben Jonson Folio published.]

1620 Entered St. Paul's School. [Pilgrim Fathers landed in New England.]

1623 [Shakespeare First Folio published.]

1625 Entered Christ's College, Cambridge, in the Easter term. [Charles I became King.]

1626 Rusticated for a term.

1627 [Phineas Fletcher's *The Locusts*.]

1629 Took B.A. degree. *At a Solemn Music* and *On the Morning of Christ's Nativity* were already written.

1632 Took M.A. degree. Left Cambridge and lived at his father's house at Horton in Buckinghamshire for six years. *L'Allegro*, *Il Penseroso*, *Arcades*, *Comus* and *Lycidas* probably all written at Horton. [Shakespeare Second Folio published. Giles Fletcher's *Christ's Victory and Triumph* republished.]

1633 [Laud became Archbishop of Canterbury.]

1634 *Comus* performed at Ludlow Castle, September 29. [*Comus* of Puteanus published in Oxford.]

1637 *Lycidas*.

1638–9 Continental tour to Paris and Italy.

1639 Settled in London and became interested in Church-reform, education, marriage and politics. [Treaty of Berwick ended First Bishops' War.]

1640 [Short Parliament. Second Bishops' War. Long Parliament met, Strafford and Laud impeached.]

1641 [Execution of Strafford. Irish Rebellion.]

Milton's Life

1641–2 Wrote five pamphlets on Church-reform: *Of Reformation touching Church-Discipline in England*; *Of Prelatical Episcopacy*; *Animadversions upon the Remonstrants' Defence*; *The Reason of Church Government*; *Apology for Smectymnuus.*

1642 Married Mary Powell in May or June. She returned to her family in July. [Civil War. Battle of Edgehill. Closing of the theatres.]

1643 [First Battle of Newbury.]

1643–5 Published the pamphlets on divorce: *The Doctrine and Discipline of Divorce*; *The Judgement of Martin Bucer concerning Divorce*; *Tetrachordon*; *Colasterion.*

1644 Published *Of Education*; *Areopagitica*. [Battles of Marston Moor and second Newbury.]

1645 Reconciliation with his wife. [Execution of Laud.]

1645–6 *Miscellaneous Poems* published.

1646 [End of first Civil War.]

1648 [Opening of second Civil War.]

1649 *The Tenure of Kings and Magistrates*. Appointed Latin Secretary to the Council of State. *Eikonoklastes*. [Execution of Charles I. England a Commonwealth.]

1651 Published *Pro Populo Anglicano Defensio.*

1652 Death of his wife. Milton went blind.

1653 [Cromwell made Lord Protector.]

1654 *Defensio Secunda.*

1655 *Pro Se Defensio.*

1656 Married Katherine Woodcock who died in 1658.

1658 [Death of Cromwell.]

1659 *A Treatise of Civil Power in Ecclesiastical Causes*; *Considerations touching the Likeliest Means to remove Hirelings out of the Church*. [Abdication of Richard Cromwell.]

1660 *The Ready and Easy Way to establish a Free Commonwealth*, March. Dismissed from office. [Restoration of Charles II, May.]

1663 Married Elizabeth Minshull.

1667 *Paradise Lost* published.

1671 *Paradise Regained* and *Samson Agonistes.*

1673 *Of True Religion, Heresy, Schism*. Second edition of the Minor Poems.

1674 Second edition of *Paradise Lost*. Milton died on November 8.